THE CULTURAL CONTEXT
IN BUSINESS COMMUNICATION

THE CULTURAL
CONTEXT IN BUSINESS
COMMUNICATION

SUSANNE NIEMEIER

University of Bremen Germany

CHARLES P. CAMPBELL

New Mexico Institute of Mining and Technology, USA

RENE DIRVEN

Gerhard Mercator University, Duisburg, Germany

JOHN BENJAMINS PUBLISHING COMPANY
AMSTERDAM/PHILADELPHIA

^{TM} The paper used in this publication meets the minimum requirements of American National Standard for Information Sciences — Permanence of Paper for Printed Library Materials, ANSI Z39.48-1984.

Library of Congress Cataloging-in-Publication Data

Niemeier, Susanne. 1960-
The cultural context in business communication / Susanne Niemeier, Charles P. Campbell, Rene Dirven.
   p.   cm.
Includes bibliographical references and index.
   1. Business communication--Cross-cultural studies. 2. Business writing--Cross-cultural studies. I. Campbell, Charles P. II. Dirven, René. III. Title.
HF5718.N53   1998
651.7--dc21   97-52990
ISBN 90 272 2176 6 (Eur.) / 1 55619 530 3 (US) (Hb; alk. paper)   CIP

John Benjamins Publishing Co. • P.O.Box 75577 • 1070 AN Amsterdam • The Netherlands
John Benjamins North America • P.O.Box 27519 • Philadelphia PA 19118-0519 • USA

Contents

Introduction

Susanne Niemeier

University of Bremen, Germany

1. The cultural context in international business communication

The present volume is mainly based on contributions to the 24th LAUD symposium, which was held in Duisburg, Germany, 25-31 March 1996. This symposium was organized in a twofold way: its overall topic being "The Cultural Context in Communication across Languages", it comprised two sub-symposia, namely "The Cultural Context in International Business Communication" and "The Cultural Context in Foreign Language Learning". The proceedings of this second part have been edited by Martin Pütz, 1997.

The two subtopics have more in common than might first appear. In schools, the keyword of "communicative competence" describes the aim to be reached by institutionalized language teaching in most of the Western world. Competence of course is not possible without teaching the foreign culture as well, language and culture being inseparably interwoven. Our language is shaped by our cultural environment and those fragments of our environment that we wish to discuss or draw attention to have received names in our culture.

Therefore, we tend not to talk about things and events that lack any relation or importance to our culture, but everything we say is related to our culture's view of them. Thus, while talking we subconsciously assume values and norms to be common ones that are in fact peculiar to our own culture.

Such assumptiorns can become especially important in intercultural business encounters. The role that cultural differences play in any given international business negotiation may be crucial. Here, members of two or more different nations — and thus usually two or more different languages and cultures — meet to discuss business topics. All over the world, but in the

Western world especially, they tend to use English as the *lingua franca* for business negotiations, even if it is not the mother-tongue of any of the negotiators. In that case, the English used is commonly a variety in which the mother tongue interferes not only phonetically or phonologically, but also in the cultural norms and attitudes expressed by the speakers. Their nonverbal behavior, for example, does not automatically switch to an "Englishized" nonverbal behavior but normally stays rooted in their home culture. Thus, even when they think the negotiation partner should have understood the (verbal and nonverbal) signs they are using, misunderstandings still occur because some signs may be differently encoded — and decoded — in the other's culture or may not be noticed to be signs at all.

There are many other ways in which an intercultural business negotiator may face problems which have less to do with the hard facts of the business deal than with the way those are presented and understood. The different contributions to this volume will help to shed light on several of these aspects and thus enable business negotiators or future business negotiators, or their trainers, to become aware of the different kinds of intercultural traps they may encounter when dealing with representatives of foreign cultures.

2.   Structure of the volume

Though the overall topic of culture's rule in business communication is highlighted differently in each of the articles, they seem to the editors to fall into five groups:

    I.   Theoretical issues
    II. Interculturality
    III. The cultural context
    IV. Linguistic perspectives
    V.   Training

I.   Theoretical issues

The first part presents two theoretical approaches underlying business communication research. These approaches can also be considered to be the foundations of related fields of study. Thus, before talking about culture and interculturality in connection with business communication, it is advisable to get a firmly established picture of what "culture" means in this context. There are about as many definitions of culture as there are people asked for a definition; therefore, we have to find a definition that is not too general but may nevertheless serve as a common denominator for the contributions in this volume.

One glance at this book's table of contents will reveal that the word *culture* usually refers to national cultures. Such reference is of course common and legitimate for analysis' sake. Differences in communication styles occur at all levels, also within national boundaries and even within companies, and national borders do not automatically coincide with cultural borders. However, this book aims not at providing recipes for business negotiators on how to ameliorate their corporate cultures but rather at introducing various analytical and practical approaches to the topic of international business communication.

Edward T. Hall (formerly with Northwestern University, USA) looks for a very basic definition in going back to different phases of human evolution. Culture is not a definite entity, but a conceptualization in our brains, and therefore it makes sense to resort to recent research concerning the structure of our brains. Hall relies on the studies by MacLean, who postulates a three-level brain structure and who claims that those three levels — which Hall names as the *reptilian brain*, the *early mammalian or limbic system,* and the *neocortex* — reflect different periods of evolution from the lowest form (reptiles) via a higher form (mammals) to the present form (neo-mammals), and that accordingly each brain level has very distinct functions. The three kinds of brain are closely interconnected but still operate independently to a certain extent.

Hall links these three kinds of brain to the three kinds of culture he introduced in *The Silent Language*. He relates the reptilian brain to the formal/hierarchical bureaucratic culture, the limbic system to the informal/intuitive emotional culture, and the neocortex to the technical/intellectual culture. These different types of culture are present to differing degrees in national cultures; thus Hall describes Germans, Swedes, Danes, and Norwegians as placing special emphasis on a technical/neocortex-orientation, whereas Italians and Japanese are a mixture of limbic and neocortical orientation. These insights have important repercussions on international business communication.

Charles P. Campbell (New Mexico Institute of Mining and Technology, USA) bases his work on another of Hall's well-known distinctions, i.e. the distinction between high-context cultures like the French or the Japanese and low-context cultures like the Germans or the North-Americans, a distinction which has far-reaching consequences for every cross-cultural business encounter. Campbell suggests bridging the gap between these two types of cultures by resorting to what he calls "rhetorical ethos". In his argument, he uses written business texts in English and in Chinese and suggests using Western rhetorical principles to accomodate other cultural patterns. In business correspondence, people from these two cultures tend to indavertently offend or at least bewilder their business partners because they tacitly assume them to share their cultural values. By using a rhetorical framework in order to approach their addressee's conditions and in order to designate their own place and rank vis-à-vis their addressees, they may achieve better results. Although this may be difficult for communicators from low-context countries, Campbell suggests that business correspondence standards may be changing due to the extensive use of English as a *lingua franca* for business.

II. Interculturality

The second part of the volume approaches the topic from a more practical side. Businesspersons who actively participate in international negotiation are often faced with problems and misunderstandings that are not immediately connected with the topic they are discussing but which have their roots in the different cultural backgrounds of the negotiation partners. It is not enough to memorize a list with do's and don'ts of the culture/s in question, nor is it sufficient to rely on one' s common sense or on the knowledge of "culturemes" learned in some crash course on international business and management.

Stephen E. Weiss (York University, Canada) has kindly agreed to the editors' suggestion to have his fundamentally important paper reprinted after more than ten years. This also explains the paper's idiosyncracy. Weiss analyses the effects of culture on intercultural business communication under twelve different variables which he defines as culturally sensitive, namely the basic concept of the negotiation process, the most significant type of issue, the selection of negotiators, the individuals' aspirations, the decision-making in groups, the orientation towards time, the risk-taking propensity, the bases of trust, the concern with protocol, the communication complexity, the nature of persuasion, and the form of agreement. All of these factors should contribute to enhancing the negotiators' familiarity with their respective business partners' culture and may allow them to coordinate their negotiation strategies.

Weiss aims at making business negotiators aware of possible culturally-based differences concerning negotiation attitudes, behaviors, and contexts, to make them reflect on these topics and by giving them explicit advice to help them in their own research, future preparation of business negotiations as well as for further investigations. The six cultures chosen for these purposes are the Chinese (PRC), French, Japanese, Mexican, Nigerian, and Saudi cultures. These cultures were chosen on the one hand for their diversity, and on the other hand for their significance to North Americans in business.

III. The cultural context

Whereas the second part concentrates mainly on global strategies, which nevertheless have to be exemplified with actual cultures, the third part presents case studies from different cultures and from different perspectives which very convincingly show the importance of the cultural context. Without any information on this cultural context, business negotiators would not be able to perform optimally, and what is worse, they might seriously endanger their or their enterprise's business connections. Hilkka Yli-Jokipii analyzes some differences between the Finnish, the English, and the American cultures, and Fred Scharf and Séamus Mac Mathúna discuss the clash of two cultures in Ireland and its consequences for international business.

Hilkka Yli-Jokipii (University of Turku, Finland) looks into some basic questions concerning the realization of requests in current corporate writing in Finnish and in English. She discusses important issues such as how the situational conditions affect the realization of requests, or what bearing the level of acquaintance between the writer and the receiver has on the realization of the requests. Furthermore she is interested in the aspect of the power bestowed on the participants and in how far it influences the outcome of a request, and to which degree cultural aspects play a role in the realization of requests.

These issues are analyzed in a contrastive study of an extensive corpus of authentic business letters and telefax messages in Britain, America, and Finland, supplemented by texts from education materials. The aspects under scrutiny are the different concepts of power and distance that are prevalent in those different cultures and languages. These concepts very clearly show in the use of linguistic devices, for example Finnish business writers are much more distant and less creative than British business writers and seem to be more conscious of the balance of power between the interactants. British business writers, on the other hand, run into face-threatening problems when they know their addressee well but are not supposed to use an informal style due to the constraints of the context of business writing.

Fred Scharf and Séamus Mac Mathúna (University of Ulster, Northern Ireland) take a different approach to point out the interconnection between the cultural context and economic performance. With their background experience of living and working in the heated climate of Northern Ireland, they are in a position to show the importance of politics for economic growth.

The authors start their argument from the assumption that in the Republic of Ireland there has been a readjustment in the emphasis attaching to those cultural values which appear to contribute to the creation of a favorable environment for economic expansion; whereas in Northern Ireland the development has been such as to place emphasis on cultural characteristics such as conservatism and introversion which detract from the creation and development of conditions favorable to economic growth. The present contribution aims at testing the validity of these assumptions by first discussing the recent and present economic trends in both parts of Ireland and then by discussing factors such as some of Hofstede's cultural dimensions (individualism vs. collectivism and uncertainty avoidance) and Hall's differentiation between high-context vs. low-context cultures in order to point out and to discuss the significant differences between the two Irish cultures, which are geographically close together but politically and economically far apart. On the basis of their analysis, the authors present the economic situation in both parts of the island and make predictions as to Ireland's economic future.

IV. Linguistic perspectives

Whereas the previous parts highlight the *business* aspect of business communication, the fourth part combines the business aspect with the *communication* aspect. Thus, in all three contributions, researchers use linguistic tools for the analysis of business texts. The concept of *text* is used in a very general sense here, because the first paper in this section (Grundy) analyzes written texts, namely business letters, and the other two papers (Li & Koole, Pörings) deal with simulated business negotiations, i.e. oral (transcribed) texts. They all look at the construction of meaning by linguistic and extra-linguistic factors and the context-dependence — and with that the culture-dependence — of these texts and suggest various ways of analysis.

Peter Grundy (University of Durham, UK) discusses parallel texts in diverging cultures, i.e. cross-linguistically variable data occurring in an identical social situation. He argues that any text, even bilingual texts that purport to be parallel in every respect to each other, invariably invoke the cultural contexts in which they are read, and that texts that fail to provide their readers with expected cultural presuppositions will not reach their readers in an adequate way.

The data used consist of a small representative sample of parallel Cantonese/English texts originating in Hong Kong, written for a Hong Kong readership. The parallel texts are intended to convey the same information to both Cantonese and English speaking residents of Hong Kong. However, the analysis highlights the fact that "parallel texts" may not exist at all.

The author shows that the texts differ in locational context, in linguistic context, and also in the use of structural and stylistic devices. Furthermore, the texts' metalinguistic and face-address features tend to reveal differing styles of audience address. The author tries to link these results to the cultural contexts in which the texts were produced and which are linguistically invoked.

Xiangling Li (University of Eindhoven, Netherlands) and Tom Koole (University of Utrecht, Netherlands) analyze business interactions between Chinese and Dutch negotiators. These cultures being very distant from each other, negotiations between them can present serious difficulties and negotiators can easily run into misunderstandings. The authors therefore discuss the relevance of understanding some of the most important keywords, i.e. words specific to cultural conventions and regularly brought up by negotiators in the negotiation process, of both cultures in question. For this purpose, they are using four simulated Chinese-Dutch and Chinese-Chinese business negotiations. The Chinese keywords that came up in their analysis were what can be called typically high-context-oriented values such as *support, understanding, friendship*, and *trust*, whereas the Dutch keywords crystallized into typically low-context-oriented terms such as *risk, fairness, long-term relationship,* and *rule.*

The authors suggest that the use of these keywords is not haphazard and that they are connected to deep-rooted cultural values, expectations, and conventions. Using these keywords during a negotiation, negotiators aim at certain argumentative or affective effects. Furthermore, general principles regarding business and business relationships seem to be coded by these keywords. However, negotiators are often not aware of the complex meaning load of these keywords, and a lack of understanding and appreciation may result in frustration, despair, or even hostility among the negotiators, causing the business negotiation to come to an abrupt end.

The contribution by Ralf Pörings (University of Gießen, Germany) contrasts the English and the German cultures. In the line of recent negotiation research, the author conceives of negotiation participants as interdependent partners looking for a mutual gain rather than competitors fighting for their positions. Thus, what negotiators should aim at is a harmoniously smooth way of interaction, i.e. a negotiation without conflict on the interpersonal level despite the conflicting interests on the topical level of the interaction. However, it is absolutely unclear what a *harmonious* relationship might entail, and the issue becomes even more problematic in an intercultural setting.

The author argues that harmony is an important concept not only in collectivist high-context cultures but also in individualist low-context ones, such as the English or the German culture, but is of course subject to cultural variability. The paper analyzes a simulated business negotiation in order to find out the differences in the English and German concepts of *harmony* as, for example, reflected in the use of turn-taking strategies, mitigators, and conflict styles. These linguistic findings are interpreted with regard to three underlying dimensions of the concept of harmony, namely the social distance between interactants, orientation toward self or others, and directness. The outcomes of this interpretation are stated in terms of Wierzbicka's NSM (natural semantic metalanguage) approach, which means a universal set of concepts which are culture-free and allow formulating culturally-specific concepts in a non-culturally-specific way.

V. Training

The final part raises the very important question of what to do with the results of analyses as those presented in the foregoing sections. Is it possible to teach business communication skills? Is it possible to train intercultural or even "global" managers or negotiators? Although these aims seem a bit farfetched, it is certainly not too ambitious to integrate elements from business communication research into training courses for future business negotiators.

Business communication trainees have to be made aware of potentially problematic issues and they have to develop their own strategies of how to deal with them. There are no step-by-step guidelines or programs because every negotiation starts from slightly different preconditions, depending on aspects such as the national cultures, the corporate cultures, prior experience with the negotiation partner, the importance of the business deal, the political situation involved, and many more. Therefore, what can be taught are, for example, strategies of flexibility, of adaptability, of respect for the other's culture, but the central, overall issue is still a question of awareness-raising. Furthermore, the very important notion of awareness-raising is one of the central issues in today's language teaching. Thus, also negotiators have to become aware of the overriding role that intercultural differences can play in business negotiations.

Lut Baten and Mia Ingels (University of Leuven, Belgium) report on a newly developed learner-centered course for Business English for commercial engineers that has been organized at their university as part of a three-year curriculum for the foreign languages program offered by the faculty of economics. This course was intended to provide for general negotiating skills as well as for the relevant skills in the English language. In Belgium, it is quite common for managers to negotiate in English, and job applicants are expected to speak at least two foreign languages.

The authors' teaching method does not make use of the more traditional functional approach, but the teaching materials developed focus on advanced interaction patterns used in negotiations, which the students often did not even know in their mothertongue. The students were quite inexperienced regarding real business negotiations, but given their general communication skills and their motivation, they needed more than a functional approach. The overall framework had to be an autonomous learning environment so that students could work in a self-controlled and confidence-building way.

The authors discuss the development of their ESP (English for Special Purposes) teaching materials and their teaching methodology, especially focussing on discourse analysis of unprepared spoken conversations by the students in the course, modeling of decision making, and metalanguage. Furthermore, the students have to understand the generic features of meetings and of effective conversations, and the role of cultural influences. The authors' aim is to supply their students with a pragmatic and custom-tailored input and thus to guide them towards a stepwise attainment of perfection, which should enable them to function autonomously in actual business situations.

The fifth part — and the volume — closes with a contribution by J. Piet Verckens (Handelshogeschool Antwerp, Belgium), Kenneth Davis (Indiana University and Purdue University at Indianapolis, USA), and Teun de Rycker (Handelshogeschool Antwerp, Belgium). They report on a course in international business writing for advanced students of economics and business which they developed in collaboration with U. Connor and M. Phillips. This course was based on three pillars: first, a theoretical study of a textbook on cross-cultural communication; second, a practical field-research during which the students interviewed managers; and third, an experiential interactive business game with American, Belgian, and Finnish participants. The main objective of the course is to give students the opportunity of getting acquainted with "sameness in differences", i.e. they should experience what it means to communicate and do business with different people who obviously are alike in several basic ways.

The course was designed with different aims in mind: the first two pillars of this course, i.e. the theoretical part and the practical part, were aiming at influencing and shaping the way in which participants actually communicate with each other. The third pillar, i.e. the experiential part, offered the students the possibility of participating in actual written communication with people from different cultures, of competing in a cross-cultural environment and thereby experiencing real anxiety and uncertainty, and of exercising a foreign language in a natural functional context. In this integrated course, students are comprehensively prepared for their future professional lives.

In the name of all the editors of this volume, I would like to thank the organizing staff of the symposium, in particular Jörg Behrndt, who also assisted me to prepare this book for publication, the anonymous reviewers, as well as all the participants of this symposium who helped making it a success.

Susanne Niemeier
Bremen, April 1998

I. Theoretical Issues

Three domains of culture
and the triune brain

Edward T. Hall

0. Introduction

Human nature, according to Paul McLean, is not one thing but a combination of three quite disparate neurological bases governing how each of us organizes and experiences the world. Unlike the conventional view, it may come as a surprise that instead of a single brain, we all are endowed with three quite different brains rooted in three different evolutionary stages: reptilian (called the R complex), the early mammalian or limbic system, and the neocortex, each representing different periods of our human past. The brains can either work together in harmony or fight it out with each other. The battles — and the harmonious adjustments — can be observed in their behavioral extensions, i.e., in cultural systems. In *The Silent Language*, I described these extensions as the formal, the informal, and the technical domains, and there is one domain for each brain, which will be described below.

1. How the culture, the brain, and the self came together

Following the basic definition of the cultural system later described in *The Silent Language* (Hall 1959), my friend David Rioch — Chief of Psychiatric Research for the army at Walter Reed General Hospital — suggested that I "...might be interested in what Paul McLean is doing out in Rockville [Maryland]." As luck would have it, John Calhoun, who was studying the effects of crowding on rats, thinking that there might be a connection between MacLean's work and mine, arranged for me to talk to him and his staff.

When we met, in 1955, I sensed a certain enigmatic quality about MacLean and no suitable niches into which he could be fit. It was obvious from the beginning that he was in charge. He had sharp eyes with a penetrating look that was difficult to get beyond; he was quick-witted and coherent. This was no ordinary man by any means, not necessarily aloof in the De Gaulle mode, but still not easy to know well, either. I arrived early at his laboratory, which left time for him to show me around and explain the work. He had already published *Man and His Animal Brains* as well as numerous articles. His book *The Triune Brain in Evolution* was yet to come. I couldn't avoid being deeply impressed by the power of MacLean's research.

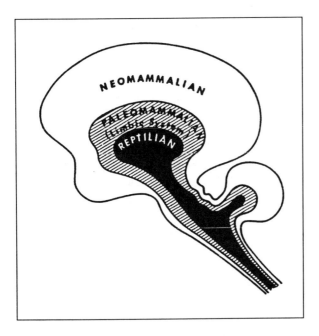

Figure 1. Diagram of triune development of primate brain. Forebrain itself evolves and expands along lines of three basic formations (labeled) that anatomically and biochemically reflect ancestral commonalities with reptiles, early mammals and late mammals (after MacLean 1973:9).

In the process of acquainting myself with his work I could see that there was much to be learned. (The following sketchy description can only serve as preliminary orienting statement, awaiting a more complete description later.)

His premise was that human beings had three brains: the first descended from the reptiles, the *R-complex*, with a 250,00,00 year past; the second, the *limbic system*, rooted in the mammalian stage of evolution (180,00,00 years ago); and the third and what we think of as the most characteristically human — the symbol-oriented *neo-cortex* (40,000 years). Actually, it takes all three to make a human being anywhere in the world.

When I discovered that Paul MacLean was describing and demonstrating a new, physically different aspect of human nature and putting it in a 250,000,000 year frame, I realized that this would mean rethinking psychology, anthropology, social relationships, institutional relationships, and psycho-therapy; it would also call for the identification of great overriding patterns (mega-patterns) sufficiently inclusive to conform to the demands of entire cultures. I was able to put into context my observations that, while quite different, Italy and Japan are feeling-thinking peoples (*limbic-neocortical*), stressing emotions. The Germans, Swedes, Danes, and Norwegians have exiled the feelings and are very particular about how things are done (*technical and neocortical*). The Tewa Indians are deeply religious, including nature's com-plex patterns (*limbic*) in every aspect of their lives.

2. The triune brain according to Paul MacLean

2.1. *The reptilian brain*

Also called the *R-complex*, *primal mind*, or *protoreptilian*, this 250,000,000 year old brain is the oldest and can be aptly studied in modern reptiles, descendants of mammal-like reptiles of the Triassic period. It is primarily formed of clumped nerve cells — ganglia — and is located in the base of the forebrain in all animals. This brain is commonly associated with motor functions, but it also houses the following twenty-five behavioral characteris-tics which are found in reptiles, mammals, and humans. Those behaviors are necessary for self- and species preservation, and are what McLean calls protomentation, that is driven by instincts, obsessions, impulses, and the like:

1. Homesite selection & preparation
2. Use of home range
3. Trail making
4. Territory establishment
5. Territory making
6. Place-preference showing
7. Territory patrolling
8. Territory defense displays (color & adornment)
9. Formal intraspecific fighting in defense and territory
10. Triumphal display of successful defense
11. Postures & coloration to signal surrender
12. Foraging
13. Hunting
14. Homing
15. Hoarding
16. Use of defecation postures
17. Formation of social groups
18. Formation of social hierarchy
19. Greeting
20. Grooming
21. Courtship w/ displays
22. Mating
23. Breeding, rare attending offspring
24. Flocking and
25. Migration
    (MacLean 1982:291-316)

The above non-verbal behaviors are either signals-displays for social communication or routines/subroutines. MacLean breaks them down further into five
interoperative behaviors: isopraxis, preservative, tropistic, reenactment, or
deceptive (McLean 1977:306-328). A similar kind of behavior (isopraxis) is
how members of a species identify each other (McLean 1977:316). The
displays themselves are broken down into four types of signals — signature,
challenge, courtship, and submissive — and are the means by which reptiles
communicate socially. Displays are acts of self-assertion (McLean 1982).

The above behaviors are not learned and are not just motor functions;
they are hard-wired, but can adapt to environmental changes via conditioning.
This brain gets information from the external world only, and is space-

oriented (as in territory preference). In humans, routine is seen in obeisance to precedent in law or to our leaders, as well as religious and other ceremonies.

Most reptiles are deaf, mute, and often cannibalistic. Parents usually leave eggs to hatch on their own. Any kind of call coming from the young would bring too much attention to themselves. Genital display in Bushman children and inner-city vandalism are excellent examples of display and territory marking in humans (MacLean 1983:359-374).

2.2. *The limbic system*

Otherwise known as the paleomammalian or feeling brain, like the R-complex it can't communicate verbally, but has an extensive communication system. About 180,000,000 years old (Gayer & Stein 1979:595-597), this mammalian brain has, in addition to the above reptilian characteristics, evolved with three key behavioral changes that came about with warm-bloodedness. The limbic system is the common denominator to all mammals. To the reptilian behavioral characteristics we can add:

26. Nursing and parental care
27. Audiovocal communication (separation call) and
28. Play.

Secondary behavior characteristics include long-term maternal attention, family groups, and feelings of separation/isolation or emotional intensity. As mammals evolved, the time and care given to the young increased progressively.

The mammal's brain gets information from emotions to guide behavior, in addition to the instinctal, reptilian information. Studies of epileptic parents have shown that the limbic part of the brain is responsible for feelings of what is real, true, and important, i.e. feelings of conviction. This brain gets information from the internal, subjective world and is present-time oriented. Through the process of acquisition, it compares current experience with past, and develops memory.

The three main subdivisions of the limbic system are:

1. amygdala (oral, self-preservation, feeding, fighting, protection)
2. septal (genital, sociability, and procreative) and
3. anterior thalamic (autonomic and somatovisceral functions as well as familial relations).

The amygdala and septal divisions of the limbic system are close to the olfactory apparatus, but with the anterior thalamic nuclei (or rostromedial thalamus) there is a shift to the visceral, bypassing the olfactory. The anterior thalamic is also connected to the prefrontal cortex. Reptiles do not have this third division, and it is most developed in humans.

According to MacLean, "case histories of limbic epilepsy also indicate (1) that the limbic system is basic for affective feelings of reality of the self and of the environment and (2) that ictal disruptions of its functions may result in changes of mood, distortions of perception, feelings of depersonalization, hallucinations, and paranoid delusions. In other words, "...information from the outside and inside worlds is essential for a feeling of individuality and personal identity" (MacLean 1985:35). MacLean also proposes that the development of family and play promotes harmony in the "nest" and strengthens group affiliation.

2.3. *The neocortex*

Approximately 40,000 years ago, this neo-mammalian brain consisting of layers of nerve cells began looking to the future with objective intelligence. It is material-oriented and concerned primarily with events from the outside world.

With this brain comes a physiological shift to sensation and perception in addition to feeling and instinct of the first two brains. Adding to the list of behaviors are:

29. Production of symbolic language (writing, reading, math)
30. Abstract thought (invention)
31. Planning/foresight and
32. Use of conscience.

Symbolic language is the means by which the neo-cortex communicates, but it by no means replaces the "prosematic", non-verbal aspect of social communication since the reptilian and the limbic systems do not have the capacity for language. Although there is an extensive communication between the three brains, the neo-cortex and the information represented therein does not replace that of the first two.

This brain, combined with the limbic system, uses what we now call "conscience", or the ability to combine inner and outer world information not only for the self but others as well. With a focus on the procreation and preservation of ideas (instead of self or species), it learns by processing information from the outside world with a focus on detail, comparable to a "cold" computer. However, the pre-frontal cortex's intimate connection with the third division of the limbic system is the "heart" for the computer, where empathy and altruism take place. It is that which gives insight into others' feelings and needs and is strongly associated with play and nurturing.

2.4. *The human brain*

The human brain is composed of all three: the reptilian, the limbic, and the neo-cortex. Because each brain has its own reality, what we think of as "fact" cannot be either true or false: they become things which are publicly (within a group, or culturally) agreed upon. Each brain "...has its own special kind of intelligence, its own special memory, its own sense of time and space, and its own motor and other functions...although the three brains are extensively interconnected and functionally dependent, there is evidence that each is capable of operating somewhat independently" (MacLean 1977:313). Moreover, they are all different in structure and chemistry. The histoflourescence technique, for example, showed that the highest concentration of dopamine and serotonin (both neurotransmitters) as well as iron were found in the R-complex, although they are also found in other parts of the central nervous system including the limbic system and frontal cortex.

The limbic system is vital because without it (ref. study of mammals with limbic system removed) we become wild, non-maternal, and cannot play.

Nietzsche's view of human nature, that "all that proceeds from power is good, all that springs from weakness is bad," or his "will to power," can be tied to the reptilian brain's defense of territory, where power is used to gain and defend territory. This "superman" view of human nature is also cortical in the sense that it uses computer-like analytical capacities to destroy one's own kind; the neo-cortex, without the limbic system's empathetic feelings, cannot feel for other living beings.

What the neo-cortex (human) does that the others can't do is to not only learn, but *unlearn*. Whereas higher animals can be "reprogrammed"/"reconditioned" to change behavior, humans can actively "... unlearn an old, ingrained response before learning something new" and "...unlearn what's been learned over millions of years" (MacLean 1985:369).

Contrary to Montagu and others who believe that all human behavior is learned, MacLean asks "...why it is that in spite of all our intelligence and culturally determined behavior, we continue to do all the ordinary things that animals do?" (MacLean 1982:302).

Whereas reptiles shed their skin and birds preen, mammals "groom"; grooming is done alone, actively, socially, in culturally different ways, continuously, and to such a degree in humans that our extensions get groomed as well. Unhealthy animals don't groom properly; a "healthy integument" is a reflection of the animal's inner condition, as is so for humans. Neglect of any of the three brains can lead to illness of body and mind, as when information obtained from one of the brains is not on par with information from another brain. Succinctly, mental illness can and does occur when "what we feel" is different than, for example, "what we know". McLean relates the three brains to three drivers all vying for control. Human potential is achieved when there is healthy utilization and understanding of all three brains, including one's drivers, feelings and thoughts, as well as those of others.

Even with this short description it should be evident that I have added some new dimensions to the usual concepts of culture. First there is the division of culture into what amounts to at least ten bio-basic fields, each of which can be, and almost inevitably is, treated in three different ways: the *formal, informal,* and the *technical.* Another is the out-of-awareness nature of the informal which makes up somewhere between 80% and 90% of culture. The informal will be found to be rooted in the *limbic system* of the brain, the formal in the R-complex, and the technical in the neocortex.

My previous work was rooted in, and dependent upon, observation and analysis of patterns of everyday life. What has been added in the intervening years between my earlier works and the present ones are two important dimensions: first, the examination of our various selves in the process of a Jungian analysis with a special emphasis on the importance of identifying the true self, the core or center in which a non-judgemental synthesis occurs between the inherited components; second, the environmental components which have been overlaid by the rationalizations of life which we call culture. It is at this point between the "self-environment complex" and the agents of culture — parents and society — where the three brains (the R-complex, the limbic system, and the cortex) either fight it out or work out various degrees of harmony with each other. These battles and these adjustments can be seen at work by observing their behavioral extensions in the formal, the informal, and the technical domains, one for each brain.

For example, the R-complex favors hierarchies, has no emotions, is highly ceremonial, territorial, and exceedingly narrow; and does not distinguish between individuals. The profiles of the R-complex and those of bureaucracies, large organizations including the military, are at times virtually indistinguishable.

The **limbic system**, on the other hand, is an environmental brain, pattern sensitive, feeling- or emotion-oriented. It bonds with others and is fast acting. Responses to environmental changes are rapid and virtually unconscious. It is the seat of Freud's unconscious; acquisition is its method "learning".

The cortex is the thinking brain and learning is its mode of behavior modification. As is readily apparent, these three brains provide us and other mammals with a wide variety of options with which to meet the exigencies of life. Working together they can do practically anything, meet any challenge, meet all needs.

Unfortunately, it seldom works that way. That old R-complex likes to run things and also has been known to eat its young, which is why they are born mobile.

The limbic system can produce not only love but hate, and unless mediated by the cortex, it can get us into terrible trouble. None of these brains by itself (or their cultural extensions — formal, informal, or technical) is capable of solving life's problems.

3. The three modes of culture

3.1. *The transition from animals to humans*

The model promulgated in *The Silent Language* linked animal behavior to its cultural descendants. Examples are territoriality in animals and my proxemic studies, as well as phonetic notation, and the vocal apparatus. But going still deeper is the identification of three different brains rooted in a past beginning 250,000,000 years ago, leading to even more insights into human behavior.

Briefly: one brain rooted in a reptilian past was hierarchical, without emotions; another was mammalian in nature, loaded with feelings but with no words; while the third was symbolically oriented, with words but no feelings! One can explain a lot with that combination and all that goes with it: intercultural conflicts and misunderstandings, Freud und Jung and their quest for self, why some individuals and some cultures demonstrate such great differences in talents, conflict between the true self and the culture, and why organizations behave the way they do (most are definitely reptilian).

On the surface, the Japanese appear to be even more bureaucratic than Europeans (that is, the R-complex with its highly structured ceremonies is invoked). Yet in reality — informally — they move up a notch to the limbic system, bringing feelings into the picture, which must be on the table before a decision can be made. Feedback is a built-in responsibility of the CEO. This can be justified by the Japanese system of logic which is, as one would expect, entirely different from ours; ours is a cortical function. In other words, when it works according to the basic designs, the Japanese organizations use all three brains in an integrated way so that they don't interfere with each other. Even the great Einstein felt he could not really examine a subject until he had reduced it to the experiental. I return, therefore, to the man who works in a field that would ultimately provide a biological foundation for the triune character of my own work. Articulating the connection between MacLean's studies and my own did not happen overnight. Not only was a long period of gestation required, but it was essential for me to do three things: accustom myself to MacLean's thinking, immerse myself in his research, and conduct further research in my own field. In strictly operational terms, the relationship between MacLean's work and my work was relevant and compatible in the way that properly matched couples can work together effectively to complete a series of disparate tasks.

There is nothing in the world that comes close to the complexity of the interaction among the three brains, or among the formal, informal, and technical levels of the environmental culture. In fact, it is difficult to fully assess all the implications of this extraordinary process. Human beings have a particular kind of central nervous system and we grow, mature, and adapt to a wide variety of environments. Furthermore, there is the matter of what we call enculturation — the process of adjusting to and reaching rapprochement with the environment which, because of our three brains, we master in three very different ways (see Chapter 4 in *The Silent Language - The Major Triad*).

3.2. *Combining the systems*

The time required for me to work out the multiple relationships between the three brains and the triune nature of culture was more than forty years. Given the revolution in my own thinking to accomplish this task, plus the field work to test and support it, forty years is actually about right for a synthesis of this sort. Ultimately, the two systems — MacLean's and mine — complement each other like hand and glove, one being the agent of the other. MacLean's work also provides a phylogenetic base for the formal, informal, and technical modes of culture. This base also allows for things to be put together in three different slots: sets, what one first observes, made up of parts called *isolates*, and *patterns of sets* that produce meaning. An example, developed in detail in my book *The Dance of Life*, is the difference between polychronic time — doing many things at once — and monochronic time — doing one thing at a time in sequence, the system preferred in Northern Europe and in most of the U.S. The two types of time affect everything else, almost as though they were a language. How appointments, schedules, priorities, human relationships, and commitments in time are handled, and the ranking of relationships — all are signalled differently in the two different time systems. Given the mono-chronic "M" time base experienced in the U.S. and Northern Europe, we find that institutions and practices by their very nature fall in line; attitudes towards time, schedules, routines, social organization, and personal relation-ships are linear. But where monochronic is linear and compartmentalizing, polychronic favors networks and personal relationships.

3.3. *Spinoffs*

There are other important conclusions to be drawn from this new synthesis of triune brain and triune culture. For example: while I was working with Kunio Shimizu, a Japanese friend, on the tacit dimensions of our two cultures, his face lit up as he said: "Now I can see that culture is rooted in something real [referring to the triune brain]... In a case of this sort a concept like culture has been much too abstract for us Japanese. As you know we have a basic distrust of anything that depends solely on words. For us, words cannot be pinned down. They depend too much on what you have so ably defined as 'context' which we take for granted and know how to handle. We need something basic in nature to link to a concept like culture. You Europeans have never been able to provide us with the proper natural roots for human nature, the problem being that you could never pin human nature down. It was simply that one person defines human nature one way while someone else would say some-thing different. Your answer to this was that culture had such an overwhelming influence on human nature that it was impossible to define."

The triune brain perspective raises the question of whether large organizations are inherently reptilian — or can they be made more responsive?

3.4. *Which brain am I talking to?*

Using the "which brain am I talking to" approach, Shimizu explained that the Japanese could not place trust in the European concept of culture. In fact, he knew from studying us that "human nature" as we saw it was a concept framed almost entirely in words, that in our American studies we had failed to look for what was behind the words. Thus, Europeans, including Americans, talked and wrote about culture as though there were no such thing as human nature — bypassing the subject entirely. The New Mexico Tewa, however, speak from the pattern-oriented limbic system and see the world as alive and integrated.

3.5. *Human nature*

By treating human nature as a precursor of or a foundation to culture, there is a culture-free base from which we can define human nature. There are also explanations of, as well as answers to, many of the problems plaguing our species. Moreover, there is now the added advantage of this new perspective for the rest of the world who view their culture in ways which are difficult, if not virtually impossible, for those of us of North European extraction to understand.

That is, we lacked adequate bridges — precultural bases — to which to refer. It was at this point that my friend Shimizu could accept the link between authentic human nature and culture, human nature being the programmed base that is shared with all cultures but deeply modified as when people grow up and become enculturated. Culture was described in a new way, tying all cultures definitely and irrevocably to their phylogenetic past. In other words instead of saying that human beings and the societies they live in are hierarchical, a quality they share with other animals, we can think of hierarchy as reptilian and associated with other traits in the "R" mode.

3.6. *Why we are different*

In addition, it is now possible to say more about who we really are, who we might be, and how to use the various parts of ourselves in appropriate ways. It is possible to explain why we as human beings have had so much trouble not only with ourselves but with each other. One explanation is that on the cultural side, the *formal, informal,* and *technical* modes don't mix. There is also the tendency to use each brain in its own way. Our schools, for example, are organized and administered bureaucratically (reptilian) whereas the instruction that takes place in the classroom is a combination of cortical and reptilian. Except for sports, the limbic, feeling, pattern part of the brain is left out entirely in the typical school. Which makes little sense, since it is now known that the limbic system — and not only its feelings, but the ability to sort out patterns — drives the cortex.

White Americans, when compared with the rest of the world, use words in excess (a function of the cortex) whereas the limbically-oriented New Mexico Tewa Indians use words sparingly as though they were sacred — which they are. The entire Tewa way of life conforms to nature, while our compartmentalized, "every person for him/herself," white world pays attention to nature's laws only when forced to — laws which the Tewa, Hopi, and Navajo already take for granted.

3.7. *The formal, the informal, and the technical (hierarchical, intuitive, and intellectual)*

The knowledge that these three domains were rooted in three different brains made the distinctions among them even clearer for me than they had originally been. Different cultures emphasize and use the three brains — as do different individuals — each in their own way. Behavior can be said to have *conditioned, acquired,* and *learned* inventories of responses. The syntax for these three systems on the level of individual behavior has yet to be worked out systematically. Examples would be that in the U.S., management is as a rule highly centralized, top down, which, as has been suggested earlier in regard to organizations in general, is a reptilian mode. Remember what we are referring to: no feelings, and highly territorial behavior with centralized command. The cortex is a learning, thinking "rational" instrument adept at manipulating symbols and for whatever reason is the preferred mode for the French, while the pattern-oriented Japanese distrust words and psych things out before they move.

Since each brain has its own way of adapting to changing conditions, indiscriminate use of the term "learning", which is solely a cortical function, should be avoided. The R-complex is modified primarily by Skinnerian reinforcement and conditioning, while the limbic system is influenced under the heading of "acquisition or imprinting". Language is "acquired" by infants and cannot be taught until most of the basic forms are mastered. It seems that even for those who know, it is necessary to remind ourselves that "acquisition" is fundamentally different from "learning". We are hard-wired to accomplish the process of acquiring the language in which we are enveloped when young; we humans literally incorporate patterns of the medium in which we are spawned. Learning takes over later in life once the acquired base has been established.

3.8. *The limbic system as the central system*

Most people know that just because we evolved we did not leave anything behind. We only incorporated the old into the new. This incorporation of the old reptilian brain formed two hundred and fifty million years ago into the limbic system, or old mammalian brain, a hundred and eighty million years ago into yet a third neocortical brain only about forty thousand years ago, has provided us with three entirely different ways of living, experiencing, acting, responding, perceiving, feeling, and thinking, to mention only a few of the ways in which our lives are affected by our past. The anthropologists are going to have a fit over this one and they won't be the only ones either. Compartments are difficult to shake. But the most important aspect of our triune brain is the one in the middle, the limbic system. The limbic system is the source of miracles of a sort, it is the brain that one psychologist had in mind when he said: "there is a part of us that knows more than we do". Well, as luck would have it, it is the limbic system that controls the tacit side of culture, the pattern side. It is also the neurological base for the unconscious which Freud and his followers could not find because it had no words. It is the behaviors that are captured, analyzed, and passed on by the limbic system which I have been studying and writing about for all these years. It is the environmental brain, the pattern brain in fact; though, originally and possibly even now, while it has no words, it still enables us to do some extraordinarily complex tasks in seconds and fractions of seconds. All normal humans participate in the acquisition of language. For language is not learned, it is acquired; and if it is not acquired, there is no way to teach it. I am not going any further down this road except to say that we all have a genius inside and we don´t know it and don´t know how to use it. Explanations of such abstruse concerns such as consciousness or awareness are relatively easy to explain once you crank in the limbic system and the R-complex (the reptilian brain).

It now appears quite evident, on the basis of my earlier studies, that some cultures are more limbic in emphasis than others. Our own emphasis on hierarchies, controls, and ceremonies shows a preference for the reptilian model, whereas our educational system is almost entirely cerebral in nature.

It is impossible for me to consider the self divorced from either the culture or the central nervous system. In fact the culture, the self, and the third part which is a product of the interaction between them, enable us to internalize others or, stated differently, to see others as a projection of the self, a complex and wonderful process around which much of life for human revolves.

The evidence for the relationship between the central nervous system and culture and what it does to and for us, once you feed in the triune brain concept, is overwhelming. A lot that didn't make sense now does make sense. To understand it, however, one needs at least the rudiments of how the three systems — the self-systems, the culture systems, and the nervous system that produces both — works.

3.9. *Learning and our three brains*

The earliest (reptilian brain) change was either genetic (very slow) or Pavlovian, emphasizing conditioning. The second — early mammalian brain — emphasized *acquisition*, which is tacit in nature and out of awareness. The third (the cortex) depends on verbalized *learning*. Each brain, like specialized organs elsewhere in the body, has its own characteristic strengths and abilities, with very little overlap. The earliest brain is quite good at building hierarchies and linear organizations, but very poor at seeing patterns and dealing with people. The mid-brain (I term it an environmental brain) is pattern-oriented, extremely fast, and highly adaptable. But it has no words. The cortex, dealing with symbols and their manipulation, apparently depends chiefly on learning. It is highly imaginative with a capacity to manipulate and rearrange symbols.

1. Formal=R-Complex=Conditioned response (including Pavlovian & Skinnerian principles)
2. Informal=Limbic=Acquisition - intra-organismic
3. Technical=Neocortex=Learning - extra-organismic (a transaction between teacher and learner and extensions of each)

One should not be ranked above another, while relevance is a matter of pragmatics.

4. Conclusions

Each of our brains has its own permutations of behavior, its own way of doing things, its own type of self, its own way of adapting to change, its own social system, its own emotional base (or lack of it in reptiles), its own ways of modifying behavior (learning in humans), and its own perceptual systems. We are in effect at least three organisms in one.

Culture and its institutions grow out of these earlier precultural bases. And while the three precultural bases (reptilian, early mammalian, and cortical) appear to be in harmony for most species, with the evolution of culture *and language*, which went with it, our forebears started to travel, ultimately populating the earth and its many diverse environments, literally filling every available niche. Each niche, of course, placed its own demands on our ancestors, leading literally to a flattened-out tower of cultural Babel. No two cultures were alike because over the years and the millennia each had adapted to unique and frequently demanding, inevitably different environments.

Instead of maintaining a balance or synchrony among the three brains, we humans out of necessity intervened in our own evolution. We really did make ourselves, and in the process left Eden behind. In each case, one and at times two of our brains proved most useful. Three species in one, reinforced by the tools we invented, we became the most adaptable and the toughest species on earth, predators who, reinforced by our extensions, could track down and kill all of the others.

Europeans, particularly in the north, managed to link the hierarchical, ceremonial reptilian system brain with the more linear word and numbers-oriented neocortex and in the process managed to play down the feeling, nurturing system.

Asiatics in the meantime (including those that migrated into the "new world"), distrusting words, placed their bets on the ability to read and use patterns. While the North Europeans emphasized the hierarchies and control at the expense of feelings, the Japanese emphasized the feelings at the expense of words. Neglecting the feeling part, which incidentally drives the cortex, we managed to deprive ourselves literally of the root systems for thinking, which forced us to evolve systems for thinking outside the body - "introjects" such as logic for example.

Mind you, all over the world we find all three. It is just that the emphasis is different. That is, we have been developing one aspect of human nature, which endowed us with a greater edge on survival. Since our extensions evolved many times faster than our bodies (nervous system included) we have managed not only to create environments that are far removed from nature but literally grown out of sync with ourselves, and that is where the roots of many of our evils lie.

Nevertheless the goal of life has always been to make the best of the dish (evolution) served up to us — in our case, in this instance, to conquer alienation with harmony while reconciling the conflicting roles imposed by three fundamentally different selves, each identified with a particular phase of our past. The trick is and will continue to be using each set of talents appropriately through the proper application as the formal, the informal, and technical rules for living as described in *The Silent Language*.

References

Gaiher, Neal S. and Barry E. Stein, 1979. "Reptiles and mammals use similar sensory organizations in the midbrain". In: *Science*, Vol. 205, 595-597.

Hall, Edward T. 1947. "Race prejudice and Negro-White relations in the army." *American Journal of Sociology* 3.

Hall, Edward T. 1959. *The Silent Language*. Garden City, New York: Doubleday.

Hall, Edward T. 1966. *The Hidden Dimension*. Garden City, New York: Doubleday.

Hall, Edward T. 1977. *Beyond Culture*. Garden City, New York: Doubleday.

Hall, Edward T. 1983a. *The Dance of Life: The Other Dimension of Time*. Garden City, New York: Anchor.

Hall, Edward T. 1983b. *Hidden Differences: Studies in International Communication*. Hamburg: Gruner und Jahr.

Hall, Edward T. 1987. *Hidden Differences: Doing Business with the Japanese*. Garden City, New York: Anchor Books/Doubleday.
Hall, Edward T. 1994. *West of the Thirties. Discoveries among the Navaho and Hopi*. Garden City, New York: Anchor Books/Doubleday.
Hall, Edward T. and Mildred Reed Hall. 1990. *Understanding Cultural Differences*. Yarmouth, Maine: Intercultural Press.
MacLean, Paul D. 1964. "Man and his animal brains". *Modern Medicine* 32: 95-106.
MacLean, Paul D. 1973. "A tribune of the brain and behavior". The Clarence M. Hencks Lectures, 1969. In: T.J. Boag and D. Campbell (eds.), *A Tribune Concept of the Brain and Behavior*. Toronto: University of Toronto Press, pp. 4-66.
MacLean, Paul D. 1977. "On the evolution of the three mentalities". In: Silvane Arieti and Gerald Chrizanowski (eds.), *New Dimensions in Psychiatry: A World View*, Vol. 2. New York: John Wiley, pp. 306-328.
MacLean, Paul D. 1978. "A mind of three minds: Educating the triune brain". *77th Yearbook of the National Society for the Study of Education*. Chicago, Illinois, 308-342.
MacLean, Paul D. 1982a. "On the origin and progressive evolution of the triune brain". In: Esre Amstrong and Dean Falk (eds.), *Primate Brain Evolution: Methods and Concepts*. New York: Plenum Publishing, 291-316.
MacLean, Paul D. 1982b. "A triangular brief on the evolution of brain and law". *Journal of Social Biol. Struct.*, Vol. 5, 369-379.
MacLean, Paul D. 1982c. "Evolution of the psychencephalon". *Zygion*, Vol. 17, No. 2, 187-211.
MacLean, Paul D. 1983. "Brain roots of the will-to-power". *Zygion*, Vol. 18, No. 4, 359-374.
MacLean, Paul D. 1984. "Commentary by Paul D. MacLean, M.D.". *Integrative Psychiatry*, Vol. 2, 102-103.
MacLean, Paul D. 1985. "Brain evolution relating to family, play, and the separation call", *Archives of General Psychiatry*, Vol. 42, 405-412. Adapted from the Adolf Meyer Lecture, 135th annual meeting of the American Psychiatric Association, Toronto, 1982.
MacLean, Paul D. 1986. "Neurobehavioral significance of the mammal-like reptiles (therapsids)". In: Nicholas Hotton (ed.), *The Ecology and Biology of Mammal-like Reptiles*. Washington D.C.: Smithsonian, pp. 1-21.
MacLean, Paul D. 1990. *The Triune Brain in Evolution: Role in Paleocerebral Functions*. New York: Plenum.
McLuhan, Marshall. 1964. *Understanding Media*. New York: McGraw-Hill.
Murphy, Michael R., Paul D. MacLean and Sue C. Hamilton. 1981. "Species-typical behavior of hamsters deprived from birth of the neocortex". *Science*, Vol. 213, 459-461.
Trager, George L. 1958. "Paralanguage: a first approximation". *Studies in Linguistics* 13: 1-12.

Rhetorical ethos

A bridge between high-context
and low-context cultures?

Charles P. Campbell
New Mexico Institute of Mining & Technology (USA)

0. Introduction

Working with people of other nations and cultures is rewarding, but also full of traps for the unwary. This paper explores how differences in cultural background may affect business' correspondence. Business people from Northern Europe and North America sometimes fail to communicate effectively because they incorrectly assume that their correspondents share their values. Letters might be more effective if writers used a rhetorical framework to conceptualize in their letters a sense of their addressees' conditions and of their own roles in relation to their addressees. Using the example of rhetorical patterns in English and Chinese business letters, I suggest a way to use Western rhetorical principles to accommodate other cultural patterns.

1. Cultural influences on rhetorical patterns

1.1. Definitions: rhetoric, culture

The terms *rhetoric* and *culture* have several meanings apiece, so definition seems in order. The word *rhetoric* is used in the several senses shown in

What is rhetoric?	**What is culture?**
__A. Inflated, vague, abstract, and/or evasive language used by business-persons, bureaucrats and politicians to try to fool the public.	__A. What your neighbor, who plays dreadful music at high volume and lets her dog ruin your garden, doesn't have.
—B. A body of amoral techniques, developed by sophists and used by pitchmen, con artists, and advertisers, to convince people to act against their own best interests.	—B. The totality of socially transmitted behavior patterns, arts, beliefs, institutions, and all other products of human work and thought characteristic of a community or population.
__C. A common process whereby people, with or without formal training, place themselves in relation to a topic and an audience to determine the facts of events in the past, to deliberate the needful actions to be taken in future, or to acknowledge important public matters in the present.	__C. The collective programming of the mind which distinguishe the members of one category of people from another.

Figure 1. Definitions of rhetoric   *Figure 2. Definitions of culture*

Figure 1. "A" is the vulgar sense — the way the term is most often used. "B" is a slant developed by Plato[1], who wished to dissociate the "true" from the merely expedient. "C" is the technical sense of the word, traceable to Aristotle[2], which I will be using here.

For *culture* (Figure 2), sense "A" is common; it is a way of distinguishing ourselves from others less enlightened. It is close to sense "C" in recognizing culture not only as creating commonalities but as making distinctions. Sense "B," from the *American Heritage Dictionary*, is too abstract to be useful. Sense "C" quotes Hofstede, who adds:

> National culture is that component of our mental programming which we share with most of our compatriots as opposed to most other world citizens. Besides our national component, our cultural programs contain components associated with our profession, regional background, sex, age group, and the organizations to which we belong. National cultural programming leads to patterns of thinking, feeling, and acting.
>
> (quoted in Ulijn & Strother 1995:186)

Quoting Hofstede's definition, Ulijn notes that it is "rather cognition-based," and adds, "Of course this national cultural programming is reflected not only in international negotiation behavior, but also writing in a foreign language" (1995:186).

Thus, culturally influenced assumptions and patterns of organization appear in the English writing of nonnative speakers. What is less obvious to native speakers of English is that such patterns and assumptions appear in our own writing, and that they may cause us problems in negotiating with or writing to people with different cultural backgrounds.

1.2. *Where culture and rhetoric meet: contrastive rhetoric*

This cultural component of communication has become the subject of study in a hybrid field called contrastive rhetoric. Kaplan's diagram (Figure 3) is often used to describe international negotiations in business. Perhaps it is useful because paragraphing strategies reflect cultural styles. In countries whose languages derive from old German — including German, Dutch, and English — negotiation styles tend to be linear and direct.

But these countries also tend to have what Hall calls "low-context cultures." Hall sees meaning as comprising both context — i.e., stored or shared information — and transmitted or explicit information (Figure 4). The more shared context there is, the less information must be transmitted, and the less shared context there is, the more information must be transmitted. Low-context cultures tend to value goals and procedures and short-term, purposive behavior; high-context cultures tend to value long-term relationships. Low-context cultures also tend to be individualist, while high-context ones tend to be more collectivist.

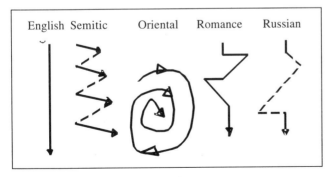

Figure 3. Styles of paragraph development (after Kaplan 1966)

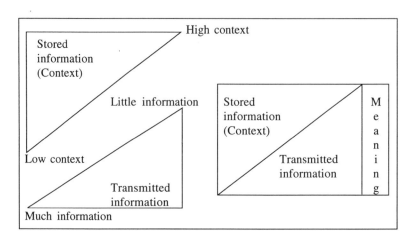

Figure 4. The relation of context to explicit information (after Hall 1983:61)

1.3. *A culture of individuals*

Two decades ago, the American sociologist Slater asserted that the American's "most characteristic trait is that he imagines himself to be alone on the continent" (1976:145). This somewhat hyperbolic statement is partly borne out by the work of Hofstede in the IBM studies reported in *Culture's Consequences* (1980) and reformulated in *Cultures and Organizations: Software of the Mind* (1991). On an index ranking the countries in the study from individualist (100) to collectivist (0), only the United States and Australia ranked in the 90s (1991:53).

Because it is such a large country, Americans may never meet people who speak different languages and have different values. I live in New Mexico, a state where English is the newest language and where the aboriginal languages, along with Spanish, are still spoken, but even New Mexico has become more homogeneous within my lifetime. It's a far cry from the land described in Hall's *An Anthropology of Everyday Life* (1992) and *West of the Thirties* (1994). When Hall first went to the Navajo and Hopi reservations in 1933, the reservations were still so isolated that a Navajo might stop him on the road to find out the location of a sing (though they lived in isolated hogans, Navajos had a powerful sense of community and participation.) When I lived in New Mexico as a child in the 1940s, I could feel certain that anyone with a Spanish surname could speak Spanish. That is no longer true, as I was surprised to discover when I returned to live in New Mexico in 1979.

As in New Mexico, the influence of commerce and electronic media seems all over the world to be speeding up and spreading wide the normal processes of cultural accommodation. Cultural leveling tends to follow the export of television programs, so cultural differences may be fading. But "culture" is perhaps like a glacier — fluid and fast-moving where it contacts the air, but frozen and slow-moving at bottom, that is at the level Hall calls core culture or primary-level (PL) culture. "One of the principal characteristics of PL culture," Hall reminds us (1983:7), "is that it is particularly resistant to manipulative attempts to change it from the outside."

My aims are more modest. I suggest a strategy for the point at which glaciers meet, so to speak — to suggest how some knowledge of cultural characteristics might be combined with some concepts from Western classical rhetoric to smooth business correspondence at the interface.

2.   The business letter as arena of misunderstanding

2.1. *All very nice, but who are you?*

Figure 5 reproduces a letter to a delegation of Chinese who had visited the United States. They had expressed some interest in the products of Mr. Jones's company, so he wrote them a letter, hoping to make some sales.

Dear Sir:

Your name and address were referred to me by the Illinois Department of Agriculture — Far East Office. They stated that you had expressed an interest in our products and requested further information.

I am therefore enclosing a brochure which itemizes our products and services. Please let me know your exact requirements. I will be happy to provide you with further details.

Thank you for your participation at the Illinois Slide and Catalog Show. I look forward to your reply.

Sincerely,
Pete Jones
Director of Sales
Agri-Equipment Division

Enclosure

Figure 5. Ineffective cross-cultural letter (Source: Boiarsky 1995)

However, as Boiarsky (1995) informs us, his letter drew no response.

The letter follows the cultural conventions of English letters. It is highly purposive and does not waste the reader's time, since time, to an American, is money, and money is an abstract value to which Americans are devoted.

To illustrate how greatly rhetorical patterns can vary across cultures, let me contrast a letter written in English by a Chinese scientist.

2.2. Can Chinese rhetoric survive translation?

Several years ago, a visiting scientist from China was connected with a research lab where a student of mine was working as an editor intern. The scientist had drafted a letter (Figure 6), in English, to a Japanese organization and had asked the intern simply "to put the letter into good English." However, the rhetorical form of the letter was so strange to him that the intern asked me for advice.

My early readings of the letter (Campbell & Bernick, 1993) were influenced by Kaplan's characterization of cultural styles in learning (1966). It is easy to see here "an approach by indirection," with "things [being] developed in terms of what they are not, rather than in terms of what they are." This kind of development is also characteristic of Japanese, as in the Japanese proverb quoted by Dennett (1988:116): "Not to say is better than to say." At first, to American eyes, the letter seems hopelessly indirect — it gets to the point only at the very end. But the letter does have a definite if unfamiliar rhetorical strategy, and a rather subtle one at that. The Japanese concept *kishotenketsu* seems to explain the descriptive but lengthy introductory remarks as well as the structure. *Kishotenketsu* is explained this way by a Japanese linguist quoted by Dennett (1988:116): "First you have the subject, *ki*, then you raise it, *sho*, next roll it, *ten*, and then . . . you end it beautifully, *ketsu*." The four paragraphs resemble that structure: the first paragraph names a subject (explosives), the second "raises" it by mentioning the professional exchanges, the third "rolls" it by acknowledging Japanese achievements, and the fourth "ends it beautifully" by offering congratulations.

The scientist's letter can be interpreted through its parallels to *kishotenketsu*, but its subtlety and effectiveness can also be appreciated through the framework of Western rhetoric, in particular the Aristotelian concept of artistic proofs.

[Name], Director
The Industrial Explosives Society, Japan
[Address]
[City], Japan

Dear Dr. [Director's name]:

The development of gunpowder was certainly one of the greatest achievements of
the medieval world. European historians have recognized in the first salvoes of
the fourteenth century bombards the death-knell of the castle, and hence of
Western military aristocratic feudalism. The development of modern powder and
high explosive technology pushes the society ahead further, but at the mean time,
it helped several strong countries to invade the weak countries and hence caused
enormous sad result between the peoples.

Evidences show that there was exchange of knowledge of gunpowder and blasting
bombs between Japan and China not later than the thirteenth century. The
relationship between scientists in the field of explosives of these two countries is
improved and becoming better and better since the beginning of this decade.
Professor [A], Professor [B] and many other Japanese scholars visited China: and
at the same time many Chinese colleagues visited Japan. I enjoyed very much the
kind invitation of Professor [A] to give a guest lecture on the Academic Conference of The Industrial Explosives Society, Japan in the May of 1987. Very kind
arrangement by Professor [B] made it possible for me to visit the University of
Tokyo, the University of Kyoto, and many other institutions. I am very much
indebted to the generosity of my hosts for their warm reception.

In these years of close relationship with Japanese colleagues, I am deeply
impressed on two points. The first point is that they always put the safety problem
on the first place. According to the statistics, the frequency rate of injury (FRI) of
industries is keeping going down from almost 40 in the early fifties to as low as
2.22 in 1987. In 1985, the FRI of the U. S. A. is 9.90 in compared with 2.52 of
Japan. The second point is that the four main islands, Hokkaido, Honshu,
Shikoku, and Kyushu, have been linked by bridges and tunnels completely in
1988 and reliable transportation routes inter-connecting these islands have been
provided. The explosive scientists and engineers played a big role in the underwater blasting and construction work.

On the occasion of the fifty years anniversary of the Industrial Explosives
Society, Japan, I would like to send my sincere congratulations for your past
achievements and my best wishes for your future success. I am also looking
forward to a more intimate cooperation between scientists and engineers in the
field of explosive science and technology for our two great neighboring countries.

Yours very sincerely,

[Chinese scientist's signature]

Figure 6. An example of Chinese rhetoric

2.3. *Aristotle's insight*

Aristotle noted that there are two kinds of persuasion, one stemming from
sources external to the persuader (inartistic or atechnic proofs — witnesses,
contracts, tortures, oaths)[3] and those the speaker has to invent — entechnic
proofs. "One must *use* the former and *invent* the latter" (Aristotle 1991:37).
These entechnic proofs he divided into three parts, as shown in Figure 7.
Aristotle did not use a triangular graphic, but his differentiation of atechnic
and entechnic proofs and his division of the entechnic into three parts suggests that he saw *ethos*, *logos*, and *pathos* as inseparable. I regard the entechnic proof complex as unitary, in much the same way Saussure (1959) gave the
two indivisible parts of the unitary sign two different names. In other words,
I'd argue that any written document always has all three elements, even
though they are not equally well developed. That is, the *logos* represents
arguments and evidence in the matter under discussion, *pathos* (emotion) the
reader's stake in that matter, and *ethos* (character) the claims of the author. As
I have argued elsewhere (Campbell 1995), professional writing in this century
has been antirhetorical and has mistrusted appeals to *ethos* and particularly
to *pathos*. Others (e.g. Bock 1995, Brockmann 1989) have noted similar
tendencies.[4]

Thus, in contrasting the Pete Jones letter (Figure 5) with the Chinese
scientist's letter, what we see within the Asiatic indirect approach is a difference in how character and emotion are handled. The Jones letter gives almost

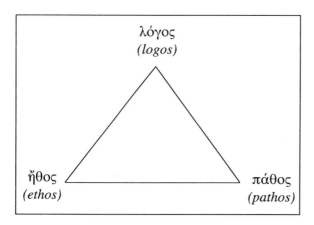

Figure 7. Aristotle's "Communication Triangle"

no sense of Jones's character as a human; the "I" is reduced to a function. Similarly, "you" has no distinguishing characteristics either. Lacking any appeal to either *ethos* or *pathos*, the letter is sterile.

2.4. *The Chinese scientist's letter and the artistic proofs*

In the scientist's letter (Figure 6), the allusion to the long, often troubled history of relations between China and Japan forms a dark backdrop. A Japanese, most likely, already knows that the gunpowder that ended European feudalism was invented in China. Nor is that reader likely to misinterpret the remark about stronger countries invading weaker ones, causing "enormous sad result". This somber background will contrast with the more hopeful message that is to follow.

The second paragraph moves us immediately from the thirteenth to the twentieth century, and is perhaps doing several things at once: establishing the writer's credentials as a scientist (*ethos*), acknowledging the present enlightened attitude of the Japanese (*pathos*), and encouraging continuance of scientific exchanges (*logos*).

The third paragraph seems puzzling — why do Japanese readers need to be told the names of their four main islands, to be reminded of their interisland connectors, and to have cited back to them figures that likely came from the Explosives Society of Japan in the first place? Again, in the terms of Aristotelian rhetoric, the writer, a non-Japanese, establishes credibility (*ethos*) by demonstrating his knowledge (*logos*) and by acknowledging the accomplishments of the readers (*pathos*). Or, in terms of Asian rhetoric, he creates face for himself and gives face to his readers.

So when in the last paragraph the writer finally delivers the message of congratulations, he has already built a relationship with his reader and the message carries some weight. The ostensible subject of the letter is congratulations on achievements in explosives technology, but the psychological aim is relation-building.

2.5. *The scientist's letter and the Chinese tradition in writing*

Additional evidence that the letter represents "good writing" in the Chinese sense comes from Li Xiao-ming's *"Good Writing" in Cross-cultural Context*. Li's interest is in seeing what is valued in the teaching of composition in the

USA as compared to China. He quotes a Chinese teacher of writing:

> Basically we think a piece of writing should have four components: intro-
> duction, development, transition, and closure *[qi3 cheng2 zhuan3 he2]*. I
> think this basic format is still valid because they are in accord with the way
> we think . . . . We have three thousand years of writing history . . . Teachers
> have the responsibility to teach a student the successful writing experiences
> of our forefathers. (1996:73-74)

Another Chinese teacher adds:

> It is very unlikely that one would start a piece from a form; we all start from
> ideas or from experience in life. . . . Especially in a country like China that
> has a literary history of thousands of years, it is arrogant to think that one
> can surpass his predecessors without first learning from them. (1996:74)

Two characteristics that contribute to good writing are the qualities *qing* and
li. As the second teacher describes them:

> *Qing* has great persuasive powers. *Li* (reason) is inseparable from *qing*: *qing*
> is couched in *li*, and *li* is couched in *qing*. *Li* (reason) is different from *lizhi*
> (rational). Being rational, one is emotionally controlled, somber, com-
> posed, exercising only intellectual and reasoning faculties. Reason, how-
> ever, deals with truths. Truths, though existing in objectivity, are
> approached and learned only through subjectivity. Truths should be learned
> with passion and conviction. (1966:55)

I wish that Li Xiao-ming had said more about the differences the writing
systems make in the way writers conceive and express the world. It is
exceedingly difficult to know which of the many Chinese characters that
correspond roughly to the sound *qing* might be meant, and in Chinese, the
character is less ambiguous than the spoken word. A Chinese-American
friend pointed out to me that *li* has the sense of both "reasoning" and
"decorum"; it seems similar to the ancient Greek *nomos*, often translated
"law" but not meaning written or codified law — closer to "the right way of
being or behaving that everybody knows," or perhaps to "common sense."

The conception of reason couched in emotion marks a difference between Chinese and Western rhetorics. While *li* appears roughly analogous to
logos, *qing* seems to represent the axis of relationship between *ethos* and
pathos. That is, Chinese rhetoric does not appear to make Aristotle's distinction between speaker and audience. Emotions are not yours or mine, but ours.

Emotion, though, is not usually expressed overtly. The indirect quality
comes from *jing*. Quoting again the first teacher:

> Traditionally, there are two ways to express one's *qing*: either directly express it, or indirectly through a description of nature. And because Chinese are mostly reserved and introverted in temperament, we prefer to "couch *qing* in *jing*," suggest what one feels through the description of nature. (1996:87).

I think we can find some *qing* couched in *jing* in the first paragraph, though most of the letter is more direct. But in any event, whether we look at the letter from an Aristotelian or a Chinese perspective, we can see that there is a subtle strategy at work.

The qualities of the scientist's letter that make it seem like "good writing" also make it less effective, possibly because it was written in English and not Chinese, but also because the kind of writing Li studied was the personal essay. The letter to the Explosives Society does seem more like an essay than like the usual Western business letter.

3. Good writing? For whom?

3.1. *An Eastern vote for a Western structure*

A few years ago, when my colleague Philip Bernick was working in Japan, we had a chance to get reactions to the Chinese scientist's letter from a number of Asians who had strong English skills and were writing and editing documents in English for a large electronics company. The surprise for Bernick and me in our 1993 survey was that our Asian respondents didn't like the letter. Our Asian editors (six women and five men) also made a number of guesses about the author of the letter (Figure 8): he was well educated, much

---

- Writer's goals were unclear.
- Doesn't really read like a letter.
- Three unnecessary paragraphs.
- Needs to be shorter.
- Inappropriate way for authors to develop *ethos*.
- Style would be more appropriate in Japanese, or even Chinese, but for English it is clearly inappropriate.
- Length detracts from letter, and makes it ineffective and confusing.

Figure 8. Asian editors' reaction to letter written in English with Chinese structure

older (probably at least in his 70's) and was from an upper-middle- or upper-class home. These comments were motivated by the excessive politeness. Our editors also felt that if the letter had been translated directly into Japanese that it would have been more acceptable than it was in English, but that translation wouldn't make it more effective or less confusing.

3.2. *A not-unexpected agreement from Northern Europeans*

The structure of the scientist's letter seems strange to Northern European technical communicators as well, judging by the preferences expressed at Forum 95 (Campbell & Bernick, 1996). People there were asked to react to three versions — the original, a version edited for idiom but not structure, and a radically revised version. The "radical" version (Figure 9) was preferred by most respondents (native speakers of English, German, Norwegian, Dutch, and Danish): it gets to what Westerners believe to be the point of the letter at once.

Figure 9's version of the letter, by putting the (apparent) point first, makes it harder to build the relationship as the writer did so carefully in the original — who is this "I" in the first paragraph? Putting the hope for future cooperation into the first paragraph still allows the second paragraph to do useful work, but leaves the third paragraph an orphan: it supports the reasons for congratulation, now a paragraph and a half away. And since the conclusion has become the beginning, it has to repeat the congratulation to gain some kind of closure.

3.3. *"Letter writing and text should be different than literature"*

There may be another issue behind the Western and Asian responses to the letter: the difference between "good" writing and effective writing. As one of the respondents at Forum 95 observed, "Letter writing and text should be different than literature." At least in China and the United States, there seems to be a tradition of teaching writing *as* writing, without reference to the actual needs of readers. The kind of writing done by the Chinese students in Li's study is part of a millennia-old tradition.

On the fiftieth anniversary of the Industrial Explosives Society, Japan, I send my sincere congratulations for your past achievements and my best wishes for your future success. I am also looking forward to even more intimate cooperation in explosive science and technology between scientists and engineers of our two great neighboring countries.

In the field of explosives, the relationship between Japanese and Chinese scientists has improved steadily since the beginning of this decade. Professor [A], Professor [B], and many other Japanese scholars visited China; many of my Chinese colleagues have visited Japan. I enjoyed very much the kind invitation of Professor [A] to give a guest lecture at the Academic Conference of The Industrial Explosives Society, Japan, in May 1987. Very kind arrangements by Professor [B] made it possible for me to visit the University of Tokyo, the University of Kyoto, and many other institutions. I am very much indebted to the generosity of my hosts for their warm reception.

In these years of close relationship with Japanese colleagues, I am deeply impressed on two points. First, they always give high priority to the problem of safety. The frequency rate of injury (FRI) of industries has continued to decrease, from almost 40 in the early 1950s to as low as 2.22 in 1987. In 1985, the FRI of the United States of America was 9.90, compared with Japan's 2.52. Second, explosive scientists and engineers played a big role in the underwater blasting and construction work in linking the four main islands by bridges and tunnels. Completed in 1988, this work has provided reliable transportation routes connecting these islands.

Again, congratulations on these achievements to the Industrial Explosives Society, Japan, with best wishes for continuing future success.

Figure 9. Westernized letter of congratulation

The kind of writing done by the American students in his study, on the other hand, comes from a much shorter tradition. It is the tradition of the departments of English in American universities, which around 1900 lost interest in teaching rhetoric and focused instead on literature (see Stewart 1982, Berlin 1987), but still got stuck with teaching writing to several generations of bemused first-year students. This literary turn is described by Winterowd (1996:27) as "the death of *pathos*," responsibility for which he lays at the feet of Ralph Waldo Emerson, "the essentialized Romantic Idealist whose solipsism . . . [results in] a rhetoric (or antirhetoric) that is self-expressive rather than communicative."

Self-expression is what has been chiefly taught in composition classes. Winterowd (1996:34) notes that "of the three sorts of rhetoric named by

Aristotle, only epideictic is not aimed at action." Epideictic is also called ceremonial rhetoric. Its province is the present, whereas forensic rhetoric tries to establish what happened in the past and deliberative rhetoric tries to set a course for the future. In rhetorical terms, business letters are not often ceremonial; they usually try to explain why something happened or exhort someone to do something.

The "Explosives Society" letter seems ceremonial, and therefore unusual for a business context. So perhaps it should not be so surprising the Asian readers of English tended to agree with the Northern Europeans. This agreement indicates that where documents in English are concerned, they should follow the cultural conventions of English letters.

However, since business letters that *do* follow the conventions of being direct, blunt, and objective seem not to be always effective, perhaps consciously employing the artistic proofs could improve business letters.

4.   What can people from low-context cultures do?

It does seem possible to adapt Western rhetoric's conceptual framework of entechnic proofs so as to include *ethos* and *pathos*, thereby achieving something like *qing*. The Jones letter in Figure 5, as a Chinese writing teacher might explain, has managed to separate *li* and *qing* and to provide none of the latter. It does not acknowledge its recipients as humans with whom one might build a relationship, and relationship-building is important almost everywhere except in the low-context Western cultures. True, it does use the personal pronouns *I* and *you*, but a reader gets no sense of that *I* as a person. Even in the terms of Western rhetoric, it's a cold letter — there is little *ethos*, personal or corporate, to establish credibility or identification, nor is there much *pathos*, awareness of the reader's condition or needs.

One way to deal with the problem of corresponding across cultures, one also recommended by Ulijn & Strother (1995:234), is to use people of the appropriate cultural background within your own company to do the writing, as did the company in Boiarsky's example. The second letter (Figure 10) did receive a number of responses.

Dear Mr. Yen Zen-jiu:

I hope that you have had a safe journey home and that you have found your family in good health. The midwestern part of our country which you graciously visited continues to have wet weather, but I am thankful for the rain after our two years of drought.

Ag-World wishes to thank you for your participation at the state Agricultural Convention and for stopping by our booth.

Our firm is situated in Bloomington, Illinois, the heart of grain and cattle country. It has a history of 10 years' experience in selling livestock and livestock equipment. It has trade relations with more than 45 countries in the world. Our firm is well known for its excellent service and good quality products.

In 1987 we sold 168 hogs to China. We wish to establish relations with China on a regular basis. We would like to know whether our breeding livestock and livestock equipment, such as Pork-Preg, Pork-alert, and Beef-o-meter, could benefit you in any way. I will be very happy to provide you with further information.

I am also enclosing two price lists of our equipment; one is the regular price, the other one is the pricing for demonstrators.

May your seasons be fruitful and plentiful.

Sincerely,

Tan Wen-lan

Figure 10: More effective cross-cultural letter (Source: Boiarsky 1995)

Though formulaic, the first paragraph of Tan's letter establishes the basis of relationship. The second paragraph gives face to the reader, and the third establishes the writer's face. Since the mode of identification is different in Chinese than in Western languages, it couches *qing* in *jing* through the imagery of weather, which, to people in agribusiness, is a subject of constant concern. Translating this opening strategy into the terms of Western rhetoric, the opening works along the *ethos-pathos* axis of Aristotle's triangle (Figure 7) by establishing a "commons", or meeting ground. *Pathos*, acknowledging the condition of the reader, is followed by *ethos*, establishing the writer's organizational credibility. Only then comes the matter or *logos* of the letter: the offer to provide product information.

For business-letter writers in low-context cultures writing in English to readers in high-context cultures (Latin or Asian), this advice may be as simple as remembering that their cultures predispose readers to be more interested in long-term relations with reliable people than in products or profits for their own sake. Hence, letters begin with paragraphs that establish common ground and show understanding of the readers. This strategy, in my own experience, works pretty well even for readers in low-context cultures.

Notes

1.   See the dialog *Gorgias*, in which Plato has Socrates compare rhetoric to cookery and classify both as branches of the art of pandering, which "pays no regard to the welfare of its object, but catches fools with the bait of ephemeral pleasure and tricks them into holding it in the highest esteem" (Plato 1971:46).

2.   This definition combines the ideas of "see[ing] the available means of persuasion in each case" (Aristotle 1991:35); the artistic proofs of character, emotion, and content of argument (37-39); and the three species of rhetoric: judicial or forensic (past), legislative or deliberative (future), and epideictic or demonstrative (47-48).

3.   Physical evidence, the sort of facts that to Westerners speak for themselves, seem to have played little role in Athenian justice.

4.   There is some evidence that the balance of *logos*, *pathos*, and *ethos* has shifted within this century. Brockmann (1989) notes that ethical exhortation in manuals around 1900 was fairly usual and served to remind readers of shared civic values, whereas manuals today shy away from ethical exhortation. Bock thinks management-dictated use of simplified language to facilitate translation and eliminate cultural reference has led to "Technical communication acts involving writer and product instead of writer and reader" (1995). Coney (1992) has shown how texts can theorize roles for their readers — a function that we might characterize as providing a "you" within the text so that the reader can find a role by which to make meaning of the text. I've noticed myself that computer manuals seldom theorize a role for me. That is, they seldom tell me why certain features might be helpful or why I might want to use them.

References

Aristotle. 1991. *Aristotle on Rhetoric: A Theory of Civic Discourse.* Tr. George A. Kennedy. New York: Oxford.

Berlin, James A. 1987. *Rhetoric and Reality: Writing Instruction in American Colleges, 1900-1985.* Carbondale, IL: Southern Illinois University Press.

Bock, Gabriele. 1995. "The Disappearing of Communication Culture in Technical Documents". *Forum 95 Preseedings*. In: M. F. Steehouder (ed.). INTECOM, the International Council for Technical Communication, n.p.

Boiarsky, Carolyn. 1995. "The relationship between cultural and rhetorical conventions: Engaging in international communication". *Technical Communication Quarterly* 4: 245-259.

Brockmann, R. John. 1989. "A historical consideration of ethics and the technical writer: From the 1880's to the 1980's". In: R. John Brockmann and Fern Rook (eds.), *Technical Communication and Ethics*. Arlington, VA: Society for Technical Communication, pp. 107-112.

Campbell, Charles P. and Philip Bernick. 1993. "Editors, "good English," and international readers". *IPCC 93 Proceedings*. Piscataway, NJ: IEEE, 38-43.

Campbell, Charles P. 1995. "Ethos: Character and ethics in technical writing". *IEEE Transactions on Professional Communication* 38, 3: 132-138.

Campbell, Charles P. and Philip Bernick. 1996. "What counts as "Good English" in an international business letter?" In: M. F. Steehouder (ed.), *Forum 95 Postharvest*. INTECOM, the International Council for Technical Communication, n.p.

Coney, Mary B. 1992. Technical readers and their rhetorical roles. *IEEE Transactions on Professional Communication* 35 (June):58-63.

Dennett, Joann Temple. 1988. ""Not to say is better than to say": How rhetorical structure reflects cultural context in Japanese-English technical writing". *IEEE Transactions on Professional Communication* 31: 116-9.

Hall, Edward T. 1983. *The Dance of Life: The Other Dimension of Time*. New York: Doubleday.

Hall, Edward T. 1992. *An Anthropology of Everyday Life*. New York: Doubleday.

Hall, Edward T. 1994. *West of the Thirties*. New York: Doubleday.

Hofstede, Geert H. 1991. *Cultures and Organizations: Software of the Mind*. New York : McGraw-Hill.

Hofstede, Geert H. 1980. *Culture's Consequences: International Differences in Work-related Values*. Beverly Hills, Calif.: Sage Publications.

Kaplan, Robert B. 1966. "Cultural thought patterns in inter-cultural education". *Language Learning* 16: 1-20.

Li, Xiao-ming. 1996. *"Good Writing" in cross-cultural context*. Albany: State University of New York Press.

Plato. 1971. *Gorgios*. Tr. Walter Hamilton. Harmondsworth: Penguin.

Saussure, Ferdinand de. 1959. *Course in General Linguistics* (~1891). New York: McGraw-Hill.

Slater, Philip. 1976. *The Pursuit of Loneliness: American Culture at the Breaking Point*. Rev. ed. Boston: Beacon.

Stewart, Donald C. 1982. "Two model teachers and the harvardization of English departments". In: James J. Murphy (ed.), *The Rhetorical Tradition and Modern Writing*. New York: Modern Language Association, pp. 118-129.

Ulijn, Jan M. and Judith B. Strother. 1995. *Communicating in Business and Technology: From Psycholinguistic Theory to International Practice*. Frankfurt am Main: Peter Lang.

Winterowd, W. Ross. 1996. "Emerson and the death of *pathos. JAC: A Journal of Composition Theory* 16: 27-40.

II. Interculturality

Negotiating with foreign business persons

An introduction for Americans with propositions on six cultures

Stephen E. Weiss with William Stripp*
York University, Canada

Ten years after "Negotiating with foreign business persons": A 1995 preface

In December, 1984, I completed the first draft of this manuscript on cross-cultural negotiation. I had worked eagerly, for this subject was a longstanding interest whose pursuit I had postponed in order to concentrate on other research concerning negotiators' communications. What emerged was too long for a journal article, too short for a book.

Even as a university working paper, the manuscript quickly circulated internationally. Its analytic framework, in particular, attracted attention. It appeared in books such as Harris & Moran's *Managing Cultural Differences* (Houston: Gulf, 1987) and Gauthey et al.'s *Leaders sans frontières* (Paris: McGraw-Hill, 1988). Though never published in its entirety, the paper influenced thinking, particularly in North America, about cultural dimensions of negotiation.

* This manuscript was originally written while the first author served on the faculty of New York University's Stern School of Business. It was indexed there as NYU Working Paper #85-6. For this printing of the manuscript, the original text remains largely unchanged. The only modifications were relabelling some elements of the framework and reordering text to correspond to the framework.
Additional research assistance was provided by Gaik Eng Lim and Betty J. Punnett.

The editors' offer to insert my earlier paper in this volume, some 10 years later, indicates its continuing appeal and usefulness. Indeed, I hope — and believe — that it occupies more than an historical spot in the development of knowledge about international and, specifically, cross-cultural negotiation. This preface provides an opportunity to recall the original context and purposes for the paper, but also to highlight subsequent development of the field, a modification of the original framework, and contemporary uses for it.

In the early 1980s, US-based management research and practitioner literature on the cultural dimensions of negotiation was very limited. One of the most insightful books at the time was *International Negotiation: A Cross-Cultural Perspective* (Chicago: Intercultural Press, 1980), written by former US diplomat Glen Fisher. Management researchers were just getting started on the subject. In sum, there existed little systematic, comparative research on business negotiations.

Thus I set out to develop, for American researchers and practitioners, a preliminary yet encompassing framework by which to consider cultural aspects of negotiation. I was interested in mapping out as much as I could of the territory as a whole, first by identifying a variety of possible variables (which I technically called "focal points for cultural impact") and second, by "pushing the envelope" to uncover their full range of variation. That was the impetus for selecting 6 diverse national cultures to explore. Alternatively put, this work was essentially a pre-empirical effort intended to sensitize readers to possible culturally-based differences in negotiation attitudes, behaviors, and contexts; organize thinking about the subject; and by stating explicit propositions, stimulate discussion and further investigation.

Since those days, the field of international business negotiation has grown steadily, aided greatly by the booming development of the two fields it intersects: international business, and negotiation. Now there is a substantial body of research on the subject (for details, see the 1996 reference below). In the tradition of this manuscript, one can find an entire stream of comparative research on business negotiations in different cultures. Experimental studies spearheaded by one American researcher, John Graham, have been conducted in some 20 countries. There is also a sizeable amount, albeit of varying quality, of practitioner-oriented literature on cross-cultural negotiation.

Given these developments, how can the ideas in this manuscript be used today? The 12-point framework continues to be adopted or adapted, as seen in Moran & Stripp's *Dynamics of Successful International Business Negotia-*

tions (Houston: Gulf, 1991), Salacuse's *Making Global Deals* (Boston: Houghton Mifflin, 1991), and Foster's *Bargaining Across Borders* (New York: McGraw-Hill, 1992). These and other authors have used the framework to show how culture affects negotiation and to describe negotiation practices in different countries.

In my own work now, I use a modified form of the original framework. For ease of use, it consists of 4 "blocks" of the 12 points — not the undifferentiated list. These 4 areas of negotiation had prompted identification of the focal points in the first place (see Figure 1 of the manuscript), but they had not been made explicit in the text. The 4 blocks are: the general model of negotiation, the role of the individual, negotiator interaction, and negotiation outcome.

In either form, this framework has a contemporary usefulness beyond what was first foreseen. It provides a "profile" of the negotiation attitudes and practices of any counterpart. Inspired by cultural considerations, it is not, however, inherently limited in use to "foreign" counterparts. The framework applies to compatriots and colleagues, and to individuals as well as representatives of groups. Indeed, an individual negotiator may use it for personal reflection, to gain self-awareness of predispositions and expectations. Profiles may be developed in different ways. Early in the process, one can employ the framework as a guide for information-gathering that points out particular information needs. It can also organize information that has already been obtained. Lastly, each such profile represents a negotiation approach that a negotiator might actually follow in a negotiation.

What this framework, like most comparative studies, does not suggest is how to conduct intercultural negotiations effectively. As the conclusion of the manuscript notes, "...we have simply assumed 'When in Rome, do as the Romans do.'" In two recent articles, which are in many ways sequels to this manuscript (see references), I have proposed and illustrated a set of "culturally responsive strategies."

The manuscript before you is the original, unrevised work (text was reordered only to fall in line with the modified form of the framework). It has been an eventful decade for the 6 countries: "Tiananmen Square" in China, the bursting of Japan's bubble economy and fall of the Liberal Democratic Party, political and economic upheaval in Mexico, and the Gulf Crisis for Saudi Arabia, to name just a few events. Thus the introductory section for each culture in the manuscript, which contains such political and economic facts, is clearly dated. And some observations and comments in the manuscript strike me today as somewhat naive or misguided.

Yet, I have kept the original manuscript intact. It shows "from whence" the field of cross-cultural negotiation in the US has come. The information on the cultures has staying power not measurable in terms of political events and economic conditions. Moreover, it is certainly my hope that you will find even today, the original manuscript is thoughtful and thought-provoking.

Stephen E. Weiss
Toronto, December, 1995

In 1982, Americans made over 2 million business trips overseas, trips bound to have entailed negotiation. Sales, coordination of activities within corporations, and development of joint or mixed ventures all involve, in one way or another, the process of working toward mutual agreement. In international business, this process often has major consequences, and if number of trips is a good indicator, Americans' use and reliance upon it are growing very rapidly. In one year (1983), the figure doubled.[1] It is this picture that makes all the more significant a basic observation: international negotiation tends to be marked by numerous hurdles.

Many of these hurdles — more than most people realize — arise from fundamental cultural differences. There are the readily apparent ones: to Americans, robes and turbans, meals of eel and seaweed, and bewildering symbols and sounds. But differences are often subtle and more pervasive, for culture denotes "the categories, plans, and rules people employ to interpret their world and to act purposefully within it" (Spradley & McCurdy 1971:2).[2] Culture influences the very core of an individual's actions toward others and his expectations concerning their actions toward him.

Indeed, as a process of interaction, negotiation is bound to be affected by culture. The anthropologists Nader & Todd (1978:29), writing on the general subject of dispute processing, have observed that:

> ... every disputing action has its ideological or cultural component. Discovery of the cultural dimension ... opens a door to reveal how informants [the individuals studied] perceive the world, including the way in which they see and evaluate the machinery for processing disputes and decide on their course of action.

This point also draws support from U.S. news reports of failed or agonizing international negotiations: the year long ordeal with the Iranians over the hostages, trade negotiations with the Japanese, and new joint venture arrangements with the Chinese, to name only a few. And yet, we seem to understand so little about the effects of culture on interactions between negotiators, not to mention the appropriateness of possible responses.[3]

As compelling as the need may be, this is not an easy area to investigate. How, for example, does one separate national or ethnic culture from political, institutional, and bureaucratic practices, or separate it, for that matter, from an organizational culture or the "subculture" created by veteran negotiators? Has the extension of Western business practices across the globe overshadowed the impact of the "native" cultures of the elites overseas who often control business with foreigners? In describing a culture, how does one balance the simplifications sought by anxious outsiders with the actual richness of the culture; the awareness of overt manifestations with the gestalt "feeling" for subtleties; and the stability of traditional, core features of the culture with the dynamism of change and adaptation? To what extent do business persons from different cultures slip out of negotiating behavior typical in their own cultures to act in ways specific or unique to their jointly shaped situation? And how can an analyst distinguish between influences of personality and disposition, and influences of culture in trying to understand an individual's actions as a negotiator? Such questions point to some real difficulties for conceptual and empirical approaches.[4]

Guided by an awareness of these problems, this paper takes an introductory look at cultural factors likely to affect the success of American business persons negotiating with corporate and government officials from other cultures by: a) proposing twelve variables of negotiation as foci for cross-cultural comparisons, and b) presenting corresponding propositions for these variables in each of six cultural groups — Chinese (PRC), French, Japanese, Mexicans, Nigerians, and Saudis. These groups were chosen primarily for their diversity, but also for their significance to North Americans in business. An orientation toward Americans anchors the first section and should facilitate pairwise comparisons later. Generally, these propositions are intended to apply to situations in which cultural differences are likely to matter, not to any and all situations involving representatives (e.g., very cosmopolitan ones) of these groups.[5]

Defining the phenomenon

For starters, consider the very concept of negotiation. What Americans label "negotiation" may differ markedly from what the French mean by the term. In studying dispute processing in Germany, Lebanon, Mexico and other countries, Nader & Todd (1978:27) sometimes found that they had to redefine the very domain of their work.

With negotiation specifically, the extent of cultural bias in understanding and use of the term seems to depend on the explicitness of one's conception of the process. In his pioneering work on international (political) negotiation, Ikle (1964:3) has defined negotiation as: "a process in which explicit proposals are put forward ostensibly for the purpose of reaching an agreement on an exchange or the realization of a common interest where conflicting interests are present." Compare that to this definition (also American): "the science of accurate observation, realistic assumptions, correct factual analysis, logical inferences, planned behavior, and optimal presentation for each moment of a changing bargaining situation" (Sperber 1979:69). So behavioral a view probably encompasses very few encounters within, say, the Mexican and Saudi cultures. Ikle's definition highlights some essential, seemingly cross-cultural aspects: a process of interaction, the parties' common and conflicting interests, and the ostensible goal of reaching agreement. But the emphasis on explicit proposals may be culturally bound.

With Ikle's general points in mind, one might best adopt the following as a working definition of negotiation: "the deliberate interaction of two or more complex social units which are attempting to *define or redefine terms of their interdependence* (Walton & McKersie 1965:3) [emphasis added]. For the purposes of this paper, one can substitute "parties" or "actors" for "complex social units"; the concepts most useful here are the ones italicized. This definition avoids the pitfalls of the two before it and, if more general, it still directs attention to the essence of negotiation.[6]

Variables for cross-cultural comparison

Even within one culture, negotiators' successfulness hinges potentially on many variables, singly and in combination (see Figure 1). In cross-cultural settings, their variety broadens and values disperse. An observer can look into

INDIVIDUALS
personality and style
motivational orientation
personal agenda
background: education, culture

ORGANIZATIONS
role obligations and boundaries
relations within negotiating team
resources of organization
structure, objectives, procedures

ENVIRONMENT
legislation and customs
political and social climate and
events
economic conditions

NEGOTIATOR INTERACTION

| ISSUES |
number
formulation

| GOALS |
needs *vs.* goals
preferences
specificity
commonality

| PROCESS |
approaches:
joint problem-solving (search, evaluation, choice)
bargaining (offer-counteroffer)
phases of interaction
factors:
communication
information-gathering, evaluation, use
power: its forms and effects

| OUTCOMES |
clarity
evaluation
attainment of agreement
comprehensiveness
anticipated duration
fairness
efficacy and enforcement
effect on relationship
satisfaction of individual parties
continuity

| CONDITIONS |
shared norms
nature of prior
relationship
number of parties
audience
negotiator subculture

threefold choice: settle, leave, continue
potential changes in:
number and prominence of issues
power
information and expectations
preferences and goals

Figure 1. Selected elements in the analysis of negotiation

general attitudes toward conflict and its management; basics of negotiation itself, such as the purpose of negotiation; issues, such as the relative importance of the relationship, substance, and intangibles (e.g., self-esteem, reputation); parties' attributes, such as degree of internal unity; conditions, such as concern with protocol; dynamic process elements, such as amount and types of information exchanged; and outcomes, such as what constitutes an enforceable or satisfactory agreement. And that is merely the beginning of a list.

For this paper, twelve variables were selected, and each of them represents a focal point for cultural impact. This tack should be more useful to negotiators and researchers in the field than say, a general description of a culture from which various effects must be inferred. Furthermore, this paper is an effort not in describing six cultures extensively but in discerning and beginning to consider cultural points of impact on negotiation.

1. *Basic concept of the negotiation process*

In American business, negotiation has traditionally been, and in many places continues to be, construed as a competitive process of offers and counter-offers in which one party's gains are the other's losses. Formally, this has been called "distributive bargaining" (Walton & McKersie 1965). An alternative general model is joint problem-solving ("integrative bargaining"). Another possibility is a contingency view which admits the use of either problem-solving or distributive bargaining, depending on the issue at hand. And one could see negotiation as primarily a debate. All four treat problems or issues explicitly. In some cultures, however, negotiation may be a wide-ranging discussion in which changes in attitudes and goals take place subtly and without verbal announcements.

As a general variable, a basic concept of (business) negotiation seems to rest on four related, cultural factors: a) attitude toward conflict (functional vs. dysfunctional, zero-sum vs. nonzero-sum); b) prevailing response (direct vs. indirect; confrontational vs. avoidant); c) predominant view of business relationships (competitive vs. collaborative); and d) purpose of negotiation (maximization of individual vs. joint benefit, attending to relationships vs. "performing," carrying out a rite).

2. *Most significant type of issue*

At least four types of issues (read concerns) may call for negotiation or arise during it: substantive, relationship-based, procedural, and personal/internal. The first covers such matters as price and number of units to be sold; the second, compatibility of styles and mutual trust; the third, although related to the second, the type of structure — format — of discussions concerning substantive and relationship-based issues (e.g., preconditions, agenda-setting); and the fourth, respect, reputation, and dissent within one's own negotiating team. The appropriateness of acknowledging and openly addressing these issues may vary by culture. So, too, may the importance attached to their resolution. That importance, which is emphasized in this paper, can obviously affect the course of discussions, their content, and the very likelihood of agreement.[7]

The popularity of the expressions "getting the job done" and "getting results" reflects the predominance for Americans of substantive types of issues (see Beliaev, Mullen, & Punnett 1984).

3. *Selection of negotiators*

These criteria include negotiating experience, status (seniority, political affiliation, sex, ethnic ties, or kinship), knowledge of the subject, and personal attributes (e.g., affability, loyalty, and trustworthiness in the eyes of the principal).[8] Negotiating skill *per se*, as indicated by record of success, reputation, or particular skills now being recognized, could also be used as a criterion. Some of these qualities overlap or coincide, but each carries a different emphasis.

In some cases, all of the criteria may be represented by a party to negotiation. A negotiating team is a clear example. When teams tend to be appointed, one can still ask how composition of a team of a given size varies from culture to culture. The number of negotiators considered appropriate itself probably varies by culture.

Americans seem to invoke the ability criterion (substantive knowledge, negotiating skill *per se*) most, although negotiating experience probably runs a close second. Several specific skills identified by senior officers at a large U.S. bank were reported by Raiffa (1982:120).

4. *Individuals' aspirations*

The emphasis negotiators place on their individual goals and needs for recognition may also vary. Some take the attitude "to thine own self be true," while others "know their station in life" and closely align their own needs with the community good. This community could be a negotiator's team, company, relatives, tribe, or even compatriots. Thus the weight carried by individual aspirations affects intra-team dynamics generally and more specifically, helps to explain the bases of individual negotiators' own positions and their perceptions of their counterparts' incentives and rewards.

Both historically and in contemporary practice, Americans tend to encourage individual aspirations and applaud individual achievements. The force of this position is usually tempered, of course, when a negotiator is representing his company. Still, when compared with negotiators from other cultures in similar situations, Americans emerge as relatively individualistic.

5. *Decision-making in groups*

This variable refers to the system by which negotiators reach decisions within their teams, and between their teams and the organization they represent. Consensus decision-making can be contrasted with majority voting and authoritative decisions.

The latter are clearly more common options in the U.S., recent moves toward "participative management" notwithstanding.

6. *Orientation toward time*

For most Americans, "time is money". This monochronic, compartmentalized attitude toward time is evinced in the importance attached to setting specific appointments in advance, the punctuality expected and observed in keeping appointments, and the urgency imputed to meeting deadlines. These expectations surely affect negotiators' conduct. The practice of "stopping the clock" is just one example.

Expectations can be based on the opposite attitude (polychronic): namely, time is plentiful, detailed plans cannot affect the course of nature, human affairs should not be subject to attempts at rigid control, and a long run perspective is desirable. These negotiators see little urgency in efforts to conclude an agreement and appear far less preoccupied with time. They put issues off in order to get to know the other party and neglect tight schedules.

7. *Risk-taking propensity*

After an extensive study of one multinational's employees in forty countries, Hofstede (1984) concluded that avoidance of uncertainty was a primary cultural variable. Americans showed up well below the mean for avoiding risk. Some cultural groups were much higher (e.g., Greece, Japan), others much lower (e.g., Singapore).

In negotiations, such differences show up in willingness to divulge critical information when counterparts' trustworthiness is questionable; openness to novel approaches to outstanding issues; willingness to go beyond superiors' directives and authorizations; responses to proposals with unknowns or contingencies; and the desired form of a final agreement.

8. *Bases of trust*

Concern about trustworthiness pervades negotiation, for it enters into considerations about disclosure and retention of information during discussions as well as desirability of a comprehensive argument. Negotiators can go with past record of trustworthiness (documented evidence, direct experience, professional reputation), intuition (status/visibility, knowledge/expertise), or the existence of external sanctions by which to regulate conduct (e.g., "bargaining in good faith"), or enforce an agreement. Only one or all may be feasible in a particular negotiation. The nature of past experiences between the negotiators themselves is probably a major determinant.[9]

American practices are difficult to call. Past experience seems very important. Where it is absent, however, it seems accurate to say that Americans probably feel much better about the availability of legal enforcement and recourse in their culture than they would about extensive use of intuition and "social" or moral sanctions.

9. *Concern with protocol*

Concern with protocol has to do with the importance placed on the existence of and adherence to rules for acceptable self-presentation and social behavior.

In short, this is a matter of formality. It may entail dress codes, extent of use of titles (from none to several in sequence), location of negotiations, and seating arrangements. These rules are worth distinguishing from procedural aspects of negotiation because the latter center on negotiating conduct in a particular case, whereas rules of protocol tend to apply from one negotiation to the next.

On a bipolar, formal-informal dimension, even the American representatives of tightly run U.S. corporations are considered informal by their counterparts in other cultures.

10. *Communication complexity*

Complexity refers to the degree of reliance on nonverbal cues to convey and to interpret intentions and information in dialogue. These cues include distance (space), gaze, gestures, and silence, to name just a few. They are especially valuable when a counterpart's verbal expressions appear irrelevant, evasive, ambiguous, vague, or simply muted (or nonexistent).

Linguists in the U.S. continue to debate the relative contributions of various communication channels to meanings in American conversations.[10] Some writers contend that nonverbal cues predominate, that they always override the verbal. Instead of entering this debate over the components of "true" meaning, it seems more important in this paper to attend to the deliberateness of negotiators' use of nonverbal cues. The common characterization in cross-cultural research of American communication patterns as "low complexity" then seems more telling (Ting Toomey 1983).

11. *Nature of persuasion*

One way or another, negotiation involves attempts to influence the other party, to be persuasive both in presenting one's own goals and in responding to others'. Verbal attempts, here labeled "arguments" in the broad sense of the term, may vary markedly in style. Behind style, supporting and motivating it, there are fundamental touchstones to which one appeals: empirically-based reason (facts, assumptions, inference), intuition, experience (tradition), dogma (ideology), and emotion.[11]

In the U.S., rational presentation with detailed information is generally considered desirable and effective.

12. *Form of agreement*

The desired form of a negotiated agreement is based on many concerns and practices: trust, communication, credibility, salience of certain types of issues, commitment, enforceability, and more. They seem to cluster around two categories: explicit and implicit forms. Explicit forms are detailed, written contracts that cover most contingencies and bind parties legally, whereas implicit forms consist of broad, general principles often agreed to orally. Their implementation tends to be negotiated *ad hoc*.

Apart from some special situations (e.g., trading floors), Americans commonly favor and expect written, legally binding contracts.

SUMMARY OF TWELVE VARIABLES

GENERAL MODEL

 I   Basic Concept of the Negotiation Process
        distributive bargaining / joint problem-solving / debate / contingency bargaining / nondirective discussion

 2   Most Significant Type of Issue
        substantive / relationship-based / procedural / personal-internal

ROLE OF THE INDIVIDUAL

 3   Selection of Negotiators
        knowledge / negotiating experience / personal attributes / status

 4   Individuals' Aspirations
        individual <– –> *community*

 5   Decision-Making in Groups
        authoritative <– –> *consensual*

INTERACTION: Dispositions

 6   Orientation toward Time
        monochronic <– –> *polychronic*

 7   Risk-Taking Propensity
        high <– –> *low*

 8   Bases of Trust
        external sanctions / other's reputation / intuition / shared experiences

INTERACTION: Process

 9   Concern with Protocol
        informal <– –> *formal*

10   Communication Complexity
     low <— —> *high*

11   Nature of Persuasion
     direct experience / logic / tradition / dogma / emotion / intuition

OUTCOME
12   Form of Agreement
     contractual <— —> *implicit*

Among the twelve variables above, there are some tie-ins and overlaps. For instance, communication complexity relates to nature of persuasion and form of agreement, and individual's aspirations affects the impact of selection of negotiators. Understanding these kinds of relationships enhances a negotiator's effectiveness abroad, but space requirements limit this paper to individual considerations of the variables.

In summary, North Americans lie on or near the left side of each list or range for the twelve variables. Now let us look at the six other cultures.[12]

Negotiating with the Chinese (PRC)

The Chinese have witnessed tremendous political and social change in this century. Rule by divine emperor, which had endured thousands of years, ended in 1911 with Sun Yat-Sen's overthrow of the Manchu Dynasty and his advocacy of nationalism, democracy, and Western industrial and agricultural ways (this, after 70 years of hostile confrontations with the West and Japan). That was followed years later by civil war between the new republicans and local warlords, war with the Japanese from 1937-1945, and a renewed civil war (1945-49), this time between Chiang Kai-Shek's Nationalists and Mao Zedong's Communists. When it ended, Mao controlled all but Taiwan, Mongolia, Hong Kong and Macao, and proclaimed the People's Republic of China. In 1958, he undertook the Great Leap Forward to push development of rural communes and village industrialization. From 1966 on, the Cultural Revolution attempted to root out old ideas and customs. Mao, Zhou Enlai, his long time premier, and Zhu De, another long time comrade and chairman of the People's Congress, all died in 1976, and their deaths sparked new political struggles. Deng Xiaoping emerged at the helm of this country of one billion people.

Deng has pushed for "pragmatic communism," particularly with respect to the economy (an effort formally endorsed by the Central Committee in October, 1984). His government has allowed both individual citizens and industrial managers some capitalist freedoms in hopes of stimulating initiative and improving efficiency. Plans have been made for modernization of farming, energy, transportation, communication, textiles, pharmaceuticals, and manufacture of construction machinery, and some $1 billion is to be spent on Western technology in 1984. At the same time, foreigners are being encouraged to invest: special economic zones have been set up (e.g., Xiamen, Shenzhen). China is also investing abroad.

With respect to American business people, relations have multiplied manyfold since President Nixon's trip to China in 1972. U.S.-China trade for 1984 is expected to increase 25% over 1983's $4.7 billion total.[13] According to the U.S. embassy in Beijing, U.S. investments in China now total $500 million and involve such companies as American Motors, Coca-Cola, Occidental Petroleum, Squibb, Minnesota Mining and Manufacturing, RJ Reynolds, Gillette Company, and Eastman Kodak. Meanwhile, the Chinese have invested in U.S. companies in Iowa, New Hampshire, and Pennsylvania.

How much have these contacts affected the Chinese bureaucracy? More critically, how has the communist system altered traditional Chinese culture? To many Americans, mainland Chinese still seem "stoic" or "inscrutable" — impressions that at least suggest the continuing relevance of a Confucian heritage. It centers on filial piety and emphasizes the importance to an individual of group identities (especially the family), influence by example, and obedience. But the overall picture is considerably more complicated.

Basic concept of the negotiation process

Distributive bargaining mixed with integrative aspects. Dysfunctional, zero-sum. Indirect, avoidant. Competitive.

The Chinese view of negotiation is influenced by a longstanding cultural aversion to openly confronting conflict, a tendency complemented if not caused by hierarchy in social relationships and Confucian norms. In this light, negotiation *per se* appears even foreign. But it is used: mediation committees helped to resolve some 7 million cases in 1983, a figure attributed partly to the undesirability of courts and other public fora.

That does not, however, preclude the occurrence of emotionally overt, intense conflicts. In the same vein, keep in mind that communist ideology espouses dialectics.

With foreigners, Chinese negotiating behavior seems to draw from all of the models mentioned earlier. The Chinese underscore mutual interests and friendship, discuss general principles, and shun proposal-counterproposal procedures at the table. To Americans, dialogue often seems to roam. At some point, details are bargained out, often discreetly, away from the table. But Chinese negotiators have also become known for use of distributive bargaining tactics: taking extreme positions, making concessions very slowly, and so forth.

This mixture of models that Americans generally separate is explained partly by an observation that the Chinese simultaneously negotiate on a manifest level involving concrete details and on a latent level concerning emotional bargains. There is a concept of *guanxi*: the use of "connections"— commitments between individuals to help each other (help now for help later) — in order to get things done. To Americans, this relationship appears demanding, but it is subtle. Pragmatics also play a central role: the Chinese bargained much less for highly desired computer equipment from Control Data in 1973-78 than they did for Boeing's planes in 1972.[14]

Most significant type of issue
The nature of the parties' relationship is the primary issue, albeit, with foreigners, not to the exclusion of substantive issues.

Chinese negotiators attempt to create emotional ties with their counterparts and value friendship, favorable extracontractual actions, tolerance, and trust, all of which seem to be understandable extensions of their cultural tradition.

With foreigners, relationship-based issues are especially important. They arose early on, during the Sino-French controversy over Annam (Vietnam), for example. China's historical relationship with Annam was framed by a "tributary system" in which Annam was simultaneously under China's control and independent. In the 1870's, when the French interfered in this to them incomprehensible system, the Chinese did not query them because that would "hurt the feelings of a friendly country." The "Unequal Treaties" that followed set the stage for distrust that continues, particularly when it comes to outdated technology. So becoming a "foreign friend" often takes a long time.

In negotiations, the Chinese see no need to take command of discussions nor do they seem very concerned about procedural issues. (This is due partly to their setting an agenda beforehand, but it also remains consistent with the relationship emphasis.) Nonetheless, they can push hard for favorable prices and especially for detailed, technical information. They expect favorable terms from good friends (*guanxi*). The Chinese see it as give and take, though, and do offer good friends future business.[15]

Selection of negotiators
Large teams of varied composition tend to be used.

When Americans send 1-3 negotiators, the Chinese send 1-40. According to one diplomat, Mao deliberately exploited the power of numbers at international political conferences, but many cadres needed international experience then. Today, one can probably point more meaningfully to such reasons as internal *guanxi*, the long established tradition of group effort, and the political purpose of restraining individual discretion.

The individuals on teams met in China may be government officials or cadres (national, provincial, or city), managers of individual enterprises, technical personnel, or political appointees there to watch others. Lawyers are rare; they are low in status and limited in number (15,000 full and part-time). Whatever their position, however, Chinese negotiators tend to be exceptional in their endurance and meticulousness.

The leaders of these groups are usually the individuals who speak first, but their authority can be difficult to determine. It does not come with rank alone. Members come and go and the groups look large, but they are well-coordinated units.[16]

Individuals' aspirations
Individual aspirations play a minor but changing role.

Traditional norms encourage the Chinese "to perfect oneself, family, country, world" (Confucius), to depend on each other for support and protection, and to preserve the extant social order. The communist government has advocated "serving the people" (the Party) as a national ethic. The emphasis on the group, then, is strong, and Chinese negotiators' superiors reinforce it with queries about what has been accomplished for China.

With Deng's policy changes, individual aspirations and accomplishments are gaining much more attention. Peasants are working for their own gains, to buy appliances and trucks; city dwellers are setting their sights as well. But group ties (cf. Japanese collectivism) are likely to remain strong for some time to come.

Decision-making in groups
Decisions tend to be made authoritatively.

Status and hierarchy define social as well as political relationships in China. One author has called the Chinese society second to none in this regard. Thus decision-making seems to be by authoritative rather than consensual processes.

> But there is a twist to this: ... the Chinese system, while undeniably authoritarian, is in its essence a bureaucratic process in which the critical art is to avoid responsibilities, diffuse decisions, and blunt all commands that might later leave one vulnerable to criticisms . . . In Chinese political culture, there is no assumption that power must be tied to responsibility; on the contrary, in the ranks of the powerful, proof of importance lies precisely in being shielded from accountability.

Calling this a "system" may be fitting a round peg into a square hole.

Sometimes individuals who can make a final decision, i.e. who do not need to consult superiors, do sit on teams negotiating with foreign business persons.[17]

Orientation toward time
For the foreigner, patience is the watchword.

The Chinese culture, if one looks at it singularly, has existed for thousands of years, much longer than the American, and the Chinese seem to take a much longer view of time.

Still, their attitude does not appear to be quite as simple as that. One observer notes that once fears concerning superiors and threats to others have dissipated, the Chinese are "compulsive" in moving toward action. For years, one American executive corresponded with a Chinese official about initiating a business venture, then one day, the official notified him in Hong Kong that he should visit "immediately."

With respect to negotiation specifically, the long lead and discussion times may have several causes. As a negotiating tactic, they allow the Chinese to learn as much as possible from a counterpart, particularly when technology is involved. Delays may also come from bureaucratic tangles and the need to consult superiors. Writers on the subject seem unwilling to say that it is strictly one or the other.[18]

Risk-taking propensity
Generally, risk is avoided.

Governmental politics have been so volatile in this century that individuals involved in international negotiations probably attempt to minimize risk. It is not a matter of just going by the book, however, since the book itself keeps changing. Consider the examples of the Gang of Four and even of Deng himself. Behind this condition lie two factors of import: 1) a culture conservative and slow changing by nature; 2) the threat of "shaming" individuals (refer also to earlier section on decision-making in groups).

On the other hand, the government has insisted upon assuming risk in some business ventures. It did so in the late 1970's in negotiations with Exxon, Mobil, and other companies seeking rights to offshore oil fields.

Business negotiations in China are also expected to be kept secret.[19]

Bases of trust
A critical element in negotiation with the Chinese, trustworthiness is assessed on the basis of past record.

Trust is important and must be earned. It is not accorded at the outset then tested. Thus trust is grounded in direct experience. It fits with the overall emphasis on relationship.

These points are illustrated in an article on Overseas Chinese, who, having left the Mainland, cannot enforce contracts but do seem to have some similar traits. They contend, "If you need a contract to hold a man to his obligations you ought not to be doing business with him at all." They will place a small order with a new company and often deliberately leave opportunity for cheating. If this and subsequent "tests of reliability and integrity" are passed, trust and the size of orders will build, albeit gradually.

Foreigners, then, face a difficult problem. They are working against the Chinese longstanding memories of the bad experiences with foreigners and with only limited, often very new contacts. Trustworthy intermediaries seem to play an important role.[20]

Concern with protocol
Formalities are observed assiduously.

Some basic social rules derive from *keqi*. Although it has no exact equivalent in English, it prescribes polite, courteous, and humble behavior — the attentiveness so apparent to American guests.

More generally, the Chinese have traditionally been taught early exactly how to behave in the relationships and circumstances that people in their status are likely to encounter. Status was clear-cut: families within clans were "graded"; so were clans within communities. And to discern the appropriate status of foreigners, the Chinese talked about family background, education, and company (but not religion or status) right at the outset of conversations, so superior status could be determined quickly and structure ensuing discourse. This concern over status and the clarity of status lines may be diminishing for the younger generation today. Still, prescribed, behavioral patterns are all reinforced by the social conviction that adherence makes a person good and reputable. (These are behavioral patterns, not Western-style principles.)

At the negotiating table, the Chinese refrain from small talk, even as a means of breaking tension, unless it is structured. Away from the table, they entertain only their closest Chinese friends in their homes. (There is a saying, "There should be a difference between insiders and outsiders.") Negotiation is a time to concentrate, in a dignified manner, on the business at hand.[21]

Communication complexity.
More complex than in the U.S., the Chinese context still involves heavy use of verbal cues.

The prevalence of indirection and reading between the lines makes the communicative context particularly difficult for those accustomed to direct and open dialogue. The two tendencies are, in one writer's words, "an expression of a cultural preference for harmonious and positive intercourse among people." With it comes concern for symbols and symbolic matters, no discomfort with long silences, and an aversion to emotional messages.

Agreement to a proposal may be stated as "the problems are not great" (*wenti buda*). "Perhaps it's not convenient" serves as a denial. General principles that have been agreed upon may be extended in meaning to exact concessions. The "spirit of an agreement" is important. And silence does not have invariant meaning: it can indicate "yes" or "no."

There is also the expression "We'll study it" (*yanjiu*). It may indicate that a) no feasible solution exists for this issue, b) the team is still trying to reach a consensus, c) not enough information is available, or d) the negotiator agrees but has insufficient authority to say so. In any case, it would usually be inappropriate to push for more action.

As a result of politicization perhaps, extreme or exaggerated language has also come into use. Twenty years ago, a diplomat remarked: "We must not expect to find fixed and verifiable meanings even in seemingly rigid statements... This faculty Peking has developed of using the same words to cover a spectrum of meanings ... adds to ... the difficulty of negotiation with China." This usage continues, and yet, "just a slight change can produce a completely different vocabulary."[22]

Nature of persuasion
Experience and dogma serve as primary bases of appeals.

"The Chinese tendency," one observer notes, "is to operate either at a very high level of generalities (and moral abstractions) or at the concrete level, thereby avoiding the middle level of generalization so important in science-oriented cultures." Indeed, generalities characterize traditional, cultural ways (e.g., Confucius) and communist ideology, from Mao's Red Book to Deng's pronouncements. Among the Chinese, a particularly persuasive basis for a position is the upholding of national interests and honor.

In form, the Chinese tend to state a position, give a few examples and justifications, and then rest their case. If they encounter opposition from foreign negotiators, they restate their original position rather than embellish it. Hence the impression by one observer of their making "dogmatic assertions of the righteousness of their own positions."

There are several factors to consider here. The Chinese language may limit possible forms: some researchers have argued that it does not allow for hypothetical (contrary-to-fact) reasoning. On the other hand, Chinese do exploit logical contradictions they find in foreigners' positions. Broad cultural factors denigrate other possible bases of persuasion: passion (e.g. anger), for example, signals a loss of self-confidence. Limitations on the Chinese negotiator's authority also affect his arguments.[23]

Form of agreement
Together with a concern for the spirit of agreements, the Chinese prefer written agreements that appear very general to Americans.

Within China, "contracts" set forth the parties' basic wishes and intents and leave much to trust and common sense. In other words, they are frameworks of general principles that allow details to be worked out as agreements are implemented. There is much less concern about rescission (the right to abrogate a contract) than there is about the continuing obligation to repair a bad situation.

This approach applies with foreigners, too, to some extent. Many considered the Joint Venture Law of 1979, for example, extremely general. Others have also contended that nothing is ever final in China. Occidental's Hammer has signed three agreements in four years on the Pingshuo coal development, each time expecting to close the deal.

The Chinese have an historical distrust of legalism. There was no judiciary system *per se* in traditional China, and the system now in place is influenced politically. Furthermore, the Chinese suspect Western concepts of law, have no real commercial law, and have been reluctant to agree to such practices as international arbitration. Keep in mind also that practices within China notwithstanding, the Chinese have unilaterally canceled some contracts with foreigners. One writer asserts that these moves have always been allowable by certain clauses in the contracts. Still, the investments were huge: in 1981, for example, billions of dollars involving a petrochemical industrial park in Nanjing, a copper mine in Giangxi, and more.[24]

Negotiating with the French

A people with a long history in Europe, the French were deeply shaken by World War II but rallied around Charles de Gaulle as a resistance hero then as head of the first postwar government. Years later, when the country struggled with decolonization, he returned as president and went on to overshadow social and political arenas with his ideas about "France not being France without greatness." Nine years into his ten-year long presidency, in May 1968, students and workers took to the streets with their dissatisfaction over his "paternalism," an ossified political left, social immobility, and static educational methods. The leftist parties made the next major, historical mark in May, 1981 by winning the presidential seat so strong in the French republican system (a 7 year term). The incumbent, Giscard d'Estaing, was defeated by Socialist leader Francois Mitterand.

Government and business have long had close ties in France, but Mitterand augmented them by immediately nationalizing major industrial companies (Compagnie Générale d'Electricité, Péchiney Ugine Kuhlman, Rhône-Poulenc, Saint-Gobain, Thomson) and 30 banks. (The nationalized sector now represents about one fourth of the country's industrial output.) In 1982, however, the newly nationalized companies lost $1.4 billion. 1983 did not relieve the problems: declining exports and industrial output, unemployment, relatively high social benefit packages. So Mitterand began a two-year austerity program, loosened control of some companies, and committed $2.5 billion in new capital (in 1983) to nationalized companies competing in the private sector. Industry continues to be restructured — decentralized and pushed in certain directions (The Ninth Plan, 1984-89). The state plans to invest $20 billion in high tech in the next five years.

The French and Americans have had the hot-and-cold relationships in business that they have had in governmental relations. De Gaulle decried U.S. hegemony for years; Mitterand has faulted U.S. monetary policies; and business and political groups in the two countries argued over the U.S. boycott on Dresser Industry's supplies to the Soviet pipeline. But trade seems relatively stable. In 1983, total volume was $12.3 billion with the U.S. exporting machinery and electrical equipment, soybeans, chemicals, aircraft and aerospace equipment, and France exporting iron and steel, beverages, and chemicals. Americans invested $9.1 billion in France in 1981. Ford recently added to its plant in Bordeaux, and IBM continues to be the largest foreign company.

Moreover, there are new opportunities in selected areas: computers and some other high technology (but not military equipment or telecommunications). In the U.S., Renault has taken over American Motors and Mack Trucks, Elf Aquitaine acquired Texas Gulf, and high tech joint ventures with the Compagnie Générale d'Electricité are on the drawing board.

The French are very proud of their culture, whether it is their language, art, literature, fashion, or cuisine. More than one American has come back from Paris complaining, however, that the people are cold, irritating, and aloof. Mark Twain is said to have once commented: "God made man a little lower than the angels and a little above the French." No matter how common that kind of attitude, there is much for an American businessperson to consider.

Basic concept of the negotiation process
Debate. Functional, zero-sum. Direct, confrontational. Competitive.

The French enjoy exchanges of ideas — controversy and argument. This penchant shows in the conversational attention given to intellectuals and the political writings of an Aron, Malraux, or Sartre, and shapes their approach to negotiation. To an American eye, the French seem to consider negotiation a debate requiring very careful preparation and a logical presentation of one's position. Negotiation is treated as a search for well-reasoned solutions.

One French academic clearly influenced by American research on negotiation has identified a confusion of negotiation with debate as an error commonly made by negotiators. But he also identifies skillful use of argumentation and communication techniques as one of ten best ways to negotiate successfully. His view on French negotiators as debaters, then, is somewhat confusing.

It is clear, however, that the French tend to respect dissent and recognize that some opinions cannot be reconciled. Often invigorated by conflict, they obviously accept it. Life is "combat," a "struggle." So one reads in a French diplomat's writings as well as in Sartre.[25]

Most significant type of issue
*The most significant issue is the "heart of the matter," but that does not mean
the "substantives" of price and quantity. Relationship-based, procedural, and
personal issues in a certain combination also draw attention.*

"The French always place a school of thought, a formula, convention, *a priori*
arguments, abstraction, and artificiality above reality; they prefer clarity to
truth, words to things, rhetoric to science." That, in the words of one outsider.
At least in emphasis, the statement is telling and corresponds with the penchant for debate. Specific "substantive" issues may become obscured. The
central issue in negotiations with the French may be, very literally, a "meeting
of the minds."

Such exchange has relationship-based dimensions. French people apparently like to engage others, especially those who disagree with them. But the
scope of the interaction is limited: family and personal matters, for example,
are kept separate from business. Affinity is not offered lightly, and as one Brit
put it, the French refuse "to suffer fools gladly." They also expect counterparts to respect their basic views and to play by the rules of the game. The
French will do so with a certain dignity. Once a good client-customer or other
relationship develops, it tends to endure.[26]

Selection of negotiators
Status is the major criterion, although ability is gaining in use.

The significance of status can be seen throughout society; it easily extends to
business affairs. Social class, degree obtained (and school, if it is one of the
nationally acclaimed ones), family ties, and age, in that order, all affect a
French person's status. Work accomplishments and performance alone were
not enough in the past and to some extent are not enough today for one to gain
respect from members of other social classes. The well-connected often enter
the highly regarded universities like the Ecole nationale d'administration. It
has graduated former President Giscard d'Estaing, Thomson Group chief
Alain Gomez, and numerous others in government and business.

With this kind of background, it is not surprising that U.S. diplomats are
impressed with the prestige of their French counterparts and the extent to
which their system backs them up. Such effects probably hold also for
negotiators for the many family-run corporations. These patterns, which have

been reinforced by the conservatism prevalent in social traditions in France, are changing according to one British observer. He argues that promotion by merit is becoming more common.[27]

Individuals' aspirations
Individualism is valued greatly by the French.

Individual opinion — independence of mind — is respected highly, perhaps more so than in the U.S. Acquisition of power (cf. attainment of goals) is also valued. Overall, however, when other factors such as individual initiative and achievement, responsibility only for self and immediate family, and aspiring to leadership and variety (rather than conformity and orderliness) were considered in one extensive, cross-cultural study, the French ranked below the Americans in individualism. The French responses ranked 11th highest out of 39 cultures.[28]

Decision-making in groups
Decision making is highly centralized both in the government (of old as well as of today) and in businesses.

Within organizations, decisions tend to be made authoritatively. In one writer's words, "the French concept of authority [is] something absolute, monarchic, and autonomous ... almost any firm [has] clearly defined areas of responsibility ... the links between them are strictly formal." In addition to this hierarchy, however, a complex consensus-building process exists in some organizations. They have "enterprise committees," groups made up of union and management representatives that meet once a month to consider economic issues.

The tie between business and government is also worth noting. In the words of Jean-Pierre Brunet, head of Compagnie Générale d'Electricité, "The state has always been powerful in France. When you've got a big decision to take it's hard to make it without consulting." That may hold especially for nationalized companies like Brunet's, but Minister of the Industry Laurent Fabius has at least advocated the expansion of these executives' independence.

It is also worth noting that the big industrial groups like CGE did not exist in France until the late 1960's. In many ways, it was and still is a country of small businesses whose decision-making apparatuses differ markedly from the industrials' practices.[29]

Orientation toward time
With timetables and appointments, punctuality is expected, but the general attitude toward time differs markedly from Americans'.

Organizations tend to have long-range goals and correspondingly long time horizons. Decisions are made slowly.

This view is apparent in other areas of French life as well. Consider the hour and a half to two hours taken for lunch or dinner. Outside of central Paris, shops often close for 2-3 hours between noon and 4 p.m. then open up again until 7 or so. Annual vacations are a month long; in fact, one is hard pressed to conduct business between July 14 and September 1. (For evidence, one need only look at the *autoroutes* leading out of Paris in early and late August.) In short, basic concerns about quality of life shape the French attitude toward time.

Risk-taking propensity
Traditionally, the French have been very conservative, but this orientation seems to be shifting.

Paraphrasing the French sociologist Crozier, one writer has stated:

> ... French society throughout its history has shown a tendency to resist change until the last possible moment, to allow an intolerable situation to build up and then, when the strain and inconvenience are too great, to change together in a vast reshuffle, usually under the impulse of a few pioneering individuals. This is happening today, probably on a grander scale than ever before, or at least since 1789 [French Revolution].

This historical tendency is reflected in the reputation of French business for conservative, safe management and "perfect blueprints" and ideal solutions rather than immediate responses to unsolved problems. The French prefer discrete rather than gradual change, and it is worth noting that once they have undertaken change, they rarely return to the *status quo ante*.

In the cross-cultural study by Hofstede, French employees appeared very high in their avoidance of uncertainty: the 6th highest out of 39 countries. A shift is evident, however. When the responses were controlled for age, that ranking dropped to 12th.[30]

Bases of trust
Trust emerges slowly, usually as a result of one's deeds.

Many writers cite a social mistrust, a cynicism among the French that suggests a wary orientation toward counterparts in negotiation. With new counterparts, the French base initial, limited trust on an intuitive evaluation of personality, particularly with regard to perceived status and intellect. Additional trust comes as proof (a good record) justifies it. Note, however, that some observers find the French difficult to impress and impatient with those who try to impress.[31]

Concern with protocol
Proper demeanor and formality generally are considered important aspects of interaction.

This orientation follows from status-consciousness and conservatism in interpersonal relationships, especially with strangers. But it also stems from a basic concern about and sensitivity to comportment.

Consider these examples of rules for self-presentation and social behavior. Greetings and partings are deliberate elements of an encounter. Students arriving at a *lycée* (high school) in the morning will greet each of their friends with handshakes or two, three, or four kisses on the cheek and do so again as they leave in the afternoon. The French language has two forms for "you," *tu* and *vous*. The former is used with relatives and friends, while the latter is used with strangers and those whom one respects. In negotiations, an American businessperson will probably hear — and need not be insulted by — *vous*. Meals are elaborate presentations of different courses in a standard order each complemented by an appropriate type of wine.

Formality is readily evident in the standard closing for a business letter: *"Veuillez accueillir, Monsieur, l'expression de mes sentiments les plus distingués."* Rather than a simple "Sincerely," it is more on the order of "I ask you to accept, Sir, the expression of my most sincere sentiments." Subordinates and superiors do not mix informally at work. One French sociologist has dubbed their fear of doing so the most characteristic of French traits. Work routines and chains of command are codified. One more quick note: the price of something a person owns, income, and family affairs are among the conversational topics considered taboo.[32]

Communication complexity
The French seem more involved than Americans in verbal and in nonverbal communication, which makes their context not simply low or high.

The animation noticeable in conversations reflects the significance of nonverbal aspects of communication. Gaze is often intense. There is, too, an emphasis on social involvement with those one knows.

At the same time, articulateness in spoken and written language is expected as much as admired. There have always been French groups organized to promote the purity and proper use of French, but clarity and precision are admired generally as well. De Gaulle, for instance, was seen as a master. Thus, the attitude is not "talk is cheap," but "attend it skillfully, employ *le mot juste*". Words are telling, appreciated in all their richness (their nuances as well as direct meanings), and influential.

Nature of persuasion
Carefully developed and highly admired, skillful rhetoric touches bases of emotion and of rationality.

This is not the rationality of empirical reason but a rationality that involves logically reasoning from certain universals or principles to particulars. Part of a French person's rhetoric also encompasses the Cartesian qualities of universal doubt and pervasive questionning.

One French writer on negotiation has taken up the subject directly and explicated other French writers' recommendations for offensive and defensive argumentation. They all involve rational aspects: use of deduction, causal reasoning, logical induction, analogy, reduction to the absurd, refutation, and so on. This writer even suggests that a negotiator read Aristotle's *Rhetoric* and works in semiotics.

What actually persuades appeals to certain universal truths (experience) and feelings and preferences (intuition), and carries emotional intensity (*élan*).[33]

Form of agreement
Detailed, legally binding written agreements are preferred.

This practice rests on concerns about documentation and formality, both of which have long traditions in French diplomacy and business matters.

Written confirmation is also undertaken in smaller deals between businessmen. Generally, the individual making the request has the responsibility of drawing up a letter of confirmation for any agreements made orally. If his counterpart does not agree, he writes a counter letter; he does not send a letter when he agrees.

Negotiating with the Japanese

A homogeneous people now numbering 118 million, the Japanese inhabit four major islands collectively the size of Montana. Their history goes far back (30,000 B.C.), but this century was initially distinguished by powerful moves in international politics: acquisition of Formosa (now Taiwan), annexation of Korea (1910), and wars with Russia (1904-05), China (1894-95, 1937) and the Allies in World War II. In August, 1945, two U.S. atomic bombs caused the final physical devastation — as well as a longlasting psychological one — and a September surrender. The U.S. occupied the country until 1952, setting up a new constitution for it along the way (1947). The divine rights that Emperor Hirohito had held for 20 years were replaced with ceremonial duties, and the government now consists of a bicameral parliament (the Diet), six major political parties (the conservative Liberal Democratic Party has dominated since 1955), and a strong prime minister (Yasuhiro Nakasone since 1982). The Japanese had to rebuild their economy after the war and did so with determination and results that established a worldwide reputation. Annual economic growth from 1970-78 averaged 7.8%.

Close government-business ties characterize the economy. The government (the Ministry of International Trade and Industry, in particular) is managing the decline of coal mining, textiles, shipbuilding, and petrochemicals while targeting for growth biotechnology, very large scale integrated circuits, artificial intelligence (the Fifth Generation Project), robotics, and supercomputers. It has thus created Tsukuba Science City, a $5.3 billion "technopolis" with some 7000 scientists. The government and economy are also influenced by key financial leaders (*zaikai*) and huge economic organizations (*zaibatsu*) such as Mitsui and Mitsubishi. These ties have led foreigners to complain about competitiveness and openness (direct investment by foreigners, for example, was illegal until 1980), and that, in turn, has led the Japanese to institute some "liberalization".

Perhaps the most salient aspect of Japanese-American business is a Japanese trade surplus of $21.7 billion out of a total volume of $65.5 (Japan is the U.S.'s second largest trading partner). The figure derives from heavy flows of consumer electronics (Matsushita, parent of Panasonic and Quasar, is the world's largest maker) and automobiles, which are now limited by voluntary export quotas. There are other features of the relationship, however. Some 40 joint ventures between Japanese and U.S. companies exist in the U.S. (General Motors-Toyota, Toshiba-Westinghouse). In 1983, Japanese investment in the U.S. reached $10.5 billion, a 20% increase over the 1982 total. Fujitsu has bought into Amdahl; Nippon Kokan bought into National Steel Corp. And there are some 309 Japanese-owned companies in the U.S. (e.g. Sony in San Diego, Nissan in Tennessee, Honda in Ohio). Hitachi's search for IBM secrets hit the news, as did Lockheed's bribes in Japan. Finally, in 1983, Merck and Company bought a controlling interest in Banyu Pharmaceutical, thus becoming the first foreign company ever to buy control of a blue-ribbon company on the Tokyo Stock Exchange.

Americans are coming into contact with the Japanese more and more, through travel, by both groups, and through a profusion of literature. The greatest contact, however, is with Japanese artifacts: a decorative plate of *sushi*, sculpted *bonsai* trees, martial arts, even a Technics stereo. But in interacting with the Japanese people themselves, beyond common catchwords like "face" and "collectivism," there is much to learn.

Basic concept of the negotiation process
Contingency bargaining. Dysfunctional, nonzero sum. Indirect, avoidant. Collaborative.

Maintaining harmony (*wa*) in relationships is an important ideal for the Japanese, one that is reinforced by norms concerning obligations to others (*giri*) and duty (*on*) and by the importance attached to others' attitudes and benevolence (*amae*). Application of this ideal practically precludes open conflict: an inferior is expected to defer automatically to his superior. The inferior knows his proper station in life but also benefits from the superior's guidance and understanding. Open conflict would shake the legitimacy of this structure. One non-native writer has argued that "harmonious cooperation" is one of two ideals of conflict resolution: the other is a "warrior ethic" (*bushido*) of assertiveness and persistence. The latter furthers understanding of some aspects of Japanese negotiation, but harmony seems to be the predominant goal and guide.

In this light, negotiation in a formal setting with each party advocating its own positions is rather undesirable. Unplanned compromises, submission to threats, admission of inconsistencies, and other such possibilities make it a face-threatening event. The Japanese prefer to use such settings to "ceremonially adopt what has already been worked out".

They see negotiation as a generally irrational, fluid process, and their assiduous preparations notwithstanding, they often wait for counterparts to present their positions first. (Buyers, especially, will do so, since they are treated with deference and greater respect than salesmen in Japan.) Some writers maintain that Japanese negotiators will not ask for much more than they need (although they will offer less than they can eventually offer). In any event, instead of addressing issues directly and openly stating positions and counterproposals (the *erabi* style), they prefer the *awase* style of having to infer parties' positions.

To some foreigners, this behavior appears distributive. The Japanese often repeat positions, use highly ambiguous language, and employ practices in one situation but not another. The last of these reflects a pragmatic emphasis on the particulars of a situation rather than application of general rules. The first two traits probably have less to do with the foreign counterparts than they do with the Japanese negotiators' responsibilities to internal, consensus-built groups.

For them, the goal of this process is a "just, proper, and fair" deal and more generally, a long-term relationship.[34]

Most significant type of issue
The Japanese concentrate on relationship-based issues but also keep in mind elements of the three other types.

The sincerity and good intentions (together, "good faith") of counterparts are considered very important. Emotional sensitivity is also valued. The significance of these and other relationship issues is demonstrated by the initial use of go-betweens (who can, among other things, vouch for negotiators' reliability); gift-giving, entertaining at night, and other initial and ongoing attempts to develop close and personal working relationships; and the value accorded to loyalty and long-term relationships. During Toyota's joint venture negotiations with General Motors, Toyota's chairman told the press that his company was assisting GM in its time of need. That he would even offer this idea reflects his view of what mattered, whether to him or to his audience.

With respect to substantive issues, the Japanese tend to offer a price close to what they need and often resist adjusting it. That resistance does not stem from a profit motive so much as a felt responsibility to constituents and superiors. As a result of the internal bargaining that takes place before a negotiation, the Japanese offer what they see as "correct, proper, and reasonable." (Note that these "positions" tend to be fused with personal issues such as "face.") Foreigners' development of fallback positions in advance struck one anonymous Japanese diplomat as indication that they know their first offers are "unreasonable."

With respect to procedure, a deliberate proposal-counterproposal approach tends to be difficult for the Japanese. Because consensus must be built within the team and organization, they often take what foreigners see as a long time to respond to new proposals. Some observers strongly advise against attempts to split up a Japanese negotiating team.[35]

Selection of negotiators
A team of individuals is selected on the basis of status (sex, age, seniority) and knowledge.

Within Japanese culture generally, status is an important element of relationships and interaction. It determines language use, for one thing. An intensive, nation-wide examination system for students reflects some concern for ability, but personal associations still seem paramount. The university one attends often determines one's career. (Graduates of Tokyo University tend to enter the foreign ministry, for example.) In business, company name is more prestigious than an important title, especially if one works for a *zaibatsu*. At the same time, titles play a significant enough role to have warranted the adoption of a standard status system by 40% of all major companies.

With respect to negotiator selection, the Japanese usually designate a team of males, at least one of whom serves as the symbolic head. More specifically, according to two researchers, a Japanese business negotiating team typically consists of five positions: 1) an individual who introduces the parties initially and facilitates the signing ceremony; 2) operational staff; 3) middle managers; 4) the chief executive officer; and 5) a mediator for any disputes. Other writers contend that a CEO generally joins a team only to arbitrate; that middle level managers perform tasks done by higher officers in the U.S.; and that the most talkative individual does not necessarily have decision-making authority. In government and business negotiations, the presence of a leader with status (seniority, age) is often considered important.

The qualities admired and sought in Japanese negotiators include commitment ("great efforts"), persistence (strength of will), ability to gain respect, credibility, listening skill, pragmatism, and a broad perspective (knowledge).[36]

Individuals' aspirations
For foreigners, collectivism stands as the quintessential trait of the Japanese, but its omnipotence seems to be changing slowly.

Anthropologists consider traditional rice cultivation procedures a major cause of this attitude, but whatever the origins, one can see much evidence and reinforcement of collectivism today. Consider the intensive, group training of employees selected when they are young; group advancement (up to a point); office layouts that consist of desks for all ranks in a large space without walls; consensus decision-making; the fostering of competition between rather than within groups; lifetime employment (in some 40% of the major companies); and so on. An adage makes this orientation appear even more powerful: "The protruding nail is hammered down" (*"deru kugi wa utareru"*).

In a recent advertising campaign, however, Sony adopted the following message: "It is said that a protruding nail is struck on the head. But it is such people that Sony needs. We are seeking protruding people." Usual working conditions have also been altered for the specialists involved in artificial intelligence (the Fifth Generation Project) in order to foster creativity. In short, Japanese in business and government have become concerned about and are reacting to constrictive features of collectivism. Changes seem to be taking place in the culture at large. The president of a biochemical laboratory in Japan recently said:

> If the person is over 40 years old, I tell him he should do something because it is first good for Japan, good for the company, good for his family, and finally good for him. If the person is under 40, I tell him he should do it because first it is good for him, good for his family, good for the company, and finally good for Japan.

This Western idea seems to be drawing an increasing audience, but it is difficult to see now how penetrating it is or will be.[37]

Decision-making in groups
Consensus-building is the norm.

One writer has suggested that "direction-taking" may be a more fitting term for the process than decision-making because the latter does not capture the Japanese process and suggests a "finite and isolated" act by executives. Indeed, in Japan, initiatives are taken by those likely to be directly affected (middle management) and are prepared carefully for acceptance (the concept of *nemawashi*). In government, this bottom-up process involves preparation (*jumbi*), fusion via informal understandings and ministerial conferences (*goketsu*), and decision by the appropriate group (*kettei*), e.g., the cabinet. In business, it is the well-known *ringi* system.

Ringiseido literally means "a system of reverential inquiry about a superior's intentions." To solve a problem, a manager typically obtains his department's support then consults the other departments concerned until he has sufficient supporting information for his plan and an informal agreement among all of the departments involved. Then a formal document of request that outlines the plan is drawn up, circulated, usually approved (with some 10-12 managers' seals of approval), and sent up to top management for a final go-ahead. By this point, to decide is to implement.

For the sake of thoroughness here and with the Lockheed scandal not too historically removed, it seems important to add a contrasting observation: "Wheeling and dealing, bribery, coercion, collusion, threats and violence (including assassination) are as much a part of Japanese politics as they are of Japanese life."[38]

Orientation toward time
The Japanese have a long time horizon, but they can be punctual in some areas and unconcerned in others.

Punctuality is tightly adhered to in some areas, such as appointments and train schedules. Business lunches are passed up in favor of socializing after hours because of the time they take. Yet the Japanese do look at the long term: they may offer a price reduction for a business partner in hard times because they look to the future and the broad picture. Similarly, product quality and other criteria may be considered more important than a deadline. One U.S. business-man said, "Their time values are a great deal more lax than ours, and if you press them into agreeing to schedules that are not realistic from their viewpoint, it is your fault when they don't follow through." Remember that the Japanese do not believe that everything (nature, circumstances) is within their control.[39]

Risk-taking propensity
In general, the Japanese seem averse to uncertainty and risk.

In the cross-cultural survey by Hofstede, the Japanese ranked fourth highest among 39 cultures — high above the mean — in their avoidance of uncertainty. This result seems consistent with concerns about face, among other things. One scholar of Japanese diplomatic negotiations has identified risk-avoidance (*kiken kaihi*) as one of two key principles in Japanese diplomatic and bargaining action.

The period studied, however, was pre-World War II, when Japan entered an arena filled with much more powerful actors. According to the scholar's explanation, the Japanese saw negotiation as face-threatening, an occasion for possible failure; one wonders whether conditions have changed enough in business and government in the years since to mitigate this concern. In contrast, a second study of Japanese businessmen found them high in risk-taking indicators because of their adaptability and openness to change.

This variable clearly deserves further consideration.[40]

Bases of trust
Trust rests on past record and otherwise on intuition.

Mutual trust and respect matter a great deal in Japanese business. In first-time negotiations, the Japanese often attempt to deal with small issues singly at the outset in order to test counterparts' reactions. Night entertainment also serves as an avenue for learning about the personality and character — including trustworthiness — of counterparts.

Trust has to be developed, however, and often comes slowly. The president of an American import-export company in Tokyo has asserted that "It often boils down to the old friend who went to school with you or grew up with you in Osaka." Once a good relationship develops, the Japanese do put trust — and loyalty — into it. Speaking of his American supplier, the president of a Japanese vending-machine company said, "We want to stay with Mr. Karepetian because we respect and we believe in him."[41]

Concern with protocol
Conservative conduct and formal politeness are important.

Relevant rules for conduct in Japan include the use of go-betweens for initial meetings rather than "cold calls"; formal greetings and partings (bows, handshakes, or both among Japanese; handshakes with foreigners); exchanges of business cards (*meishi*) at the beginning of meetings (so rank and status can be determined and guide conduct); conservative dress; and use of titles and last names.

The senior negotiator on a Japanese team generally sits in the middle of his team on one side of the table (rather than at the head). According to one account, those who have authority to make a deal sit to his immediate left and right; those with lesser roles sit at the two ends.[42]

Communication complexity
High complexity describes the context for communication.

"How childish it is, she said to herself, to speak aloud what you think." That line from the fictional but informative *Shogun* is reiterated by a real businessman: "Anyone who can neither read another person's mind nor let the other person read his mind is not worth a damn in Japan." Indeed, reserved and self-controlled in their communication, the Japanese have traditionally relied on indirection and reading between the lines.

The Japanese do distinguish between what is said publicly (*tatemae,* meaning "truthful") and what they think (*honne*, meaning "true mind"). The former is intended to facilitate positive interaction. So is an openly acknowledged communication strategy called *haragei* that entails use of vagueness, ambiguity, and certain paralinguistic cues (e.g., the "pregnant silence," "*sho ga nai*" ["It can't be helped"], and sucking in breath through the teeth [indicating consternation and worry]).

The Japanese language itself is complex. One generally omits references, for example, as in "*Ikimashita*" (roughly, "Went"). The listener must determine by context whether it is "I went," "He went" or "They went".

For negotiators, positive and negative responses merit special attention. One Japanese businessman advises: "Never take a smile for yes. Never take yes for an answer." A smile often indicates embarrassment, and "yes" simply signals comprehension. It can also be the result of a reluctance to offend by saying "no," although a more common one is the expression "It is difficult" ("*Muzukashi desu*"). For an actually positive response, the Japanese often say "I agree" and proceed to elaborate.

Some nonverbal patterns include dislike of open displays of emotion, limited touching, preference for space between speakers, and sometimes restricted eye contact due to deference. Many of the traits above complement a basic concern for minimally disruptive, generally harmonious interaction. Some writers point causally to times when extended families lived in one house in which walls were no thicker than rice paper. Today, however, younger people are evidently showing less skill in the ways of *haragei* and tending toward more direct conversation.[43]

Nature of persuasion
The Japanese see logic as "a bit cold, sterile, and impersonal."

The very idea of persuasion in negotiation seems to run against the grain for Japanese. They place more emphasis on the provision of extensive, detailed information, especially when they are the buyers in a negotiation. Exposition, rather than argument, also characterizes internal negotiations. Individuals sense the direction of group opinion as it evolves.

In a sales presentation, a seller typically begins by discussing the background of the interaction then goes on to present some of the thoughts and feelings of the people involved and an account of major actions or events. Then he expresses sorrow or regret for a request and finally, makes the request.

In terms of the values suggested earlier for this variable, one might emphasize intuition, experience, and emotion (sensitivity, not passion).[44]

Form of agreement

The Japanese tend to prefer brief, written agreements that set forth basic principles, but a gentlemen's agreement often has even more force than a legal contract.

One writer said it very well:

> The Japanese view is that a contract is a piece of paper and people are human beings. Should there be an obligation of one person to another person, then society expects the obligation to be honorably discharged. The penalty for failure ... is dishonor of oneself, one's name, and one's family, perhaps for generations to come.

After all, contracts can be nullified or abrogated by the impersonal, legal process. Thus lawyers' roles are kept to a minimum. An understanding between the parties and mutual trust seem to be much preferred.

Whereas American agreements can run some 100 pages, Japanese firms keep theirs to 2-3 pages. The agreement primarily contains comments on the principles that the parties have agreed to use to guide their relationship. Parties may thus respond to any changes in conditions that later occur.[45]

Negotiating with the Mexicans

"The history of Mexico," as one native has written (Paz 1962:20), "is the history of man seeking his parentage. He has been influenced at one time or another by France, Spain, the United States, and the militant indigenists of his own country ...". A major revolution (1910) and prolonged civil strife marked the early 1900's, but a federal republic was established in 1917 and with it, the Partido Revolucionario Institucional (PRI) that still monopolizes political life. Some writers have called it the most stable political system in Latin America, a system bolstered by the oil boom of the 1970's. Since then, however, social and economic conditions have deteriorated to *las crisis*: high income inequality, annual unemployment of 26-28%, heavy migration to the cities (Mexico City has a population of 16 million), and annual inflation of 63% in 1984 (81-117% in 1983). These problems, along with a history of government corruption and the stirrings of the first viable opposition parties, were among those taken on in 1982 by the new president, Miguel de la Madrid.

De la Madrid has described his approach to the economy as "state rectorship." It is a mixed economy, with government control extending to financial institutions and such basic industries as petrochemicals and steel. Some 800 companies are state-run. National development plans have set forth priority sectors and regions as well as strict regulations on foreign investment. The Computer Decree of 1981, for example, stipulates Mexican majority ownership and various performance requirements for joint ventures with foreigners. A foreign debt of $88 billion has forced some modifications, though, especially to accommodate foreign investors with desired technology and plans to source locally and to export.

Economic ties between Mexico and the U.S. are well established. Their trade volume hit $26 billion in 1983, which made Mexico the U.S.'s third largest trading partner. Americans supplied 68% of all foreign investment in 1983, and U.S. banks hold one third of Mexico's foreign debt. Over 2900 U.S. companies have operations in Mexico, and this figure will continue to rise as those with labor-intensive production take advantage of low wage rates. Companies making recent investments include Ford, Hewlett-Packard, Apple, and Sheraton.

Over the last few years, U.S. residents have heard much about the heavy flows of Mexicans across the countries' shared 2000-mile border and about their work in the U.S. Various impressions have been formulated in the process. (Mexicans have their views, too, one of them captured in the popular expression *"Pobrecito Mexico - tan lejos de Dios, tan cerca a Los Estados Unidos"* ("Poor little Mexico, so far from God, so close to the U.S.")). The North American views of Mexican culture that seem to have the longest history, however, center on the relaxed attitude toward time, and the spontaneity and liveliness of *fiestas*.[46]

Basic concept of the negotiation process
Distributive bargaining. Zero-sum. Indirect, avoidant. Competitive.

"The Mexican views life as combat . . .," the writer Octavio Paz has suggested. "In the United States man does not feel that he has been torn from the center of creation and suspended between hostile forces. He has built his own world ... To us a realist is always a pessimist. And an ingenuous person would not remain so for very long if he truly contemplated life realistically." So Mexicans seem to adhere to the concept of "limited goods" and to assume competitive postures.

That does not necessarily entail openly, honestly verbalized disagreements, however. According to one observer, Mexicans see diplomatic negotiations as formal occasions for distinguished rhetorical performances concerning "grand ideas" and general principles. In business negotiations, they expect counterparts to socialize with them for a time before getting down to business. Still, Mexicans apparently see little value in frank exchange, prefer behind-the-scenes bargaining, and believe *"manas son mas fuerte que fuerza"* (roughly, "tricks are greater than force"). One Mexican explained:

> . . . all of us Mexicans have something to hide. Maybe a bribe given or taken, or taxes that we owe. Take my dear old aunt: she goes to Mass daily but drives her car without a license. When a policeman stops her, she says, "This is your chance for a good deed today." She gets away with it.

A broad generalization, yes, but consider the implied attitudes.[47]

Most significant type of issue
For Mexicans, relationship-based and personal-internal issues tend to predominate and affect other types of issues.

Mexicans emphasize the social and personal aspects of their relationships (e.g., trust) with people they encounter — businessmen included. At the outset of a meeting, for example, conversation is social. As one saying goes, "One works to live; one does not live to work."

With regard to North Americans, many Mexicans resent what they see as a long history of unfair treatment. This attitude is bolstered by the importance Mexicans generally place on good relationships and by their tendency to evaluate new relationships intuitively and often quickly.

These social ways of business and the culture tend to bring to the fore issues such as personal honor and dignity. To some observers, they make the bargaining within a Mexican team even more difficult than that with foreign counterparts. Much is expected of leaders, so much, for example, that their seeking information from or consulting subordinates can be criticized. At the same time, the leaders, too, have concerns about reputation and self-esteem.

Selection of negotiators
Negotiators are selected primarily on the bases of status (political affiliation, relatives) and personal attributes.

Among Mexicans, family, political, and personal ties greatly influence an individual's position, power, and advancement in business and government. Loyalty is an important personal attribute in that it is often valued more highly than expertise. This general penchant is both allowed constitutionally and realized in current politics, de la Madrid's "technocrats" notwithstanding. By constitutional mandate, the President appoints the Mayor and the Chief of Police of Mexico City and the heads of state-owned companies. For the oil company Petroleos Mexicanos (Pemex), former President Lopez Portillo selected his associate, Jorge Diaz Serrano, a man later indicted for bribery and now replaced by Mario Ramon Beteta. The leader of the country's largest union, Fidel Velasquez, has held his position for over 40 years and has so much power within the government that he was one of three or four people to approve of de la Madrid as the PRI's presidential candidate. Hence the importance of *ubicacion* (where one is plugged into the system).

The individuals with whom American business people negotiate tend to be high level (a Mexican preference in negotiating), male, and well-connected. They are also able rhetoricians and tend to call effectively on the force of their personalities.[48]

Individuals' aspirations
Whether Mexicans are individualistic or collectivist seems to depend on the social arena.

In business and with other men generally, Mexican men tend to be very competitive, set on pursuing individual goals and needs for recognition. Leaders understandably display these traits; Mexicans expect them to do so. Employees and others also display them, for while they owe loyalty to their *patron*, they also seek to project publicly an aura of personal significance and power. An image of success, decisiveness in one's personal affairs, and the aforementioned traits all relate to *machismo*.

In family and social relationships, though, there seems to be a strong collective orientation. In Hofstede's cross-cultural study, for example, Mexico ranked even lower than collectivist Japan in level of individualism (defined as the importance of having a job that allows sufficient time for a full personal or family life).[49]

Decision-making in groups
Decision-making is highly centralized.

In government, in companies, and within negotiating teams, leaders in Mexico tend to make decisions without concern for consensus. Subordinates' abilities are not highly valued. At the same time, subordinates accept leaders' broad use of power. In the study of 39 cultures, Mexico ranked second highest in acceptance of power distance (hierarchy, inequality, etc.). Consider also such complementary variables as individuals' aspirations and bases of trust.

Decision-making power does not simply come with position, however. Individuals with *palanca* (leverage) tend both to be well-positioned and have expressive, forceful personalities.

La mordida (payoffs for traffic violations) and bribes in general also continue to influence decision-makers despite de la Madrid's crackdown.[50]

Orientation toward time
There is a relaxed, polychronic attitude towards time.

Although time is a concern, Mexicans do not allow schedules to interfere with experiences involving family and friends. Even with business acquaintances, they take time to talk and socialize. In short, the culture is people rather than task-oriented.

The *siesta*, a regular two or three hour break in the afternoon (2:30-5:00 p.m.) of a work day, illustrates this popular orientation. Even business and government people who do not take a *siesta per se* take 1 1/2-2 hours at that time to lunch and to socialize.

Risk-taking propensity
Mexicans tend to avoid risk more than Americans do.

As stated in an earlier quote, Paz has noted: "To us a realist is always a pessimist." Hofstede's study supports that view: Mexico ranked 11th out of 39 in avoidance of uncertainty. France ranked higher, and Japan higher still.[51]

Bases of trust
Evaluations of trustworthiness are based initially on intuition, then on past record.

Among themselves, Mexican men suspect others who are not relatives, according to Paz. Other native observers contend that negotiations often take place within a generally trusting atmosphere. However, if one party harms the other personally, financially, or socially, trust is completely lost.

In their encounters with North Americans, Mexicans do tend to be especially suspicious. Trust must develop through a series of frequent and warm interpersonal transactions. Remember that its importance is underscored by the personal issues often at stake (honor, self-esteem, etc.) and that much business goes on between individuals who have close relationships.[52]

Concern with protocol
Protocol is important to know and to follow.

As one observer put it, "social competence" is more important than "technical competence" in Mexico. He continues:

> They [Mexicans] like to see themselves as more reserved, able to maintain dignity, not like the Americans, who, they say, are like frogs — every time they open their mouths they expose everything inside.

Mexicans value form and ceremony, due perhaps to their Spanish heritage.[53]

Communication complexity
Communicative context is formed by body language and emotional cues, not just diction.

Mexicans communicate with hand movements, physical contact, and emotional expressions. Social distance is closer than in the U.S. The comparison is not lost on the Mexicans. They have a saying that "Americans are cold in feelings and in conversation."

Insofar as words themselves are concerned, frankness and openness should not be taken for granted. As Paz explains it: "The Mexican tells lies because he delights in fantasy, or because he is desperate, or because he wants to rise above the sordid facts of his life." In negotiation specifically, he will also "tell lies" if circumstances call for them.[54]

Nature of persuasion
Emotional bases tend to be especially persuasive.

"The Mexican succumbs very easily to sentimental effusions." This contention of Paz's goes along with American observers' notes that Mexicans' arguments seem overly dramatic, emotional, and patriotic. Along these lines, there is the concept of *proyectismo* (constructing plans without critical analysis and assuming them to be accomplished fact). Perhaps much of this stems from the twin origins of Mexican culture: the Indian, based on magic and superstition, and the Spanish, based on imposition, dogma, and faith.

With respect to negotiations with foreigners, especially at government and corporate levels, Mexicans may be persuaded more by the rhetoric of experience than emotions. Paz writes that "North Americans want to understand, we want to contemplate." So one can see in Mexicans' rhetorical styles emphases on general aspects of a negotiation and general principles to apply to specific problem areas and minimization of evidence and protracted, critical analysis.[55]

Form of agreement
Mexicans tend to prefer implicit agreements.

Laws and legal instruments have been manipulated through payoffs and other means to such an extent that Mexicans have little faith in them. Oral agreements with close, personal acquaintances are preferred. But written agreements and contracts are bound to be sought from foreigners.

Negotiating with the Nigerians

This West African region was a colony of Great Britain from the late 1800s to 1960, when it became a federal republic. Over 300 tribes with their own languages live in the country (making it the most populous in Africa), and its territorial boundaries often split them up. Three tribes predominate: the Hausa-Fulani, a tradition-bound, ultraconservative group of Sunni Muslims residing in the north; the Yoruba, Christians and non-Christians in the west who have provided a large portion of the national elite — highly educated politicians, judges, senior civil servants, and wealthy entrepreneurs; and in the east, the Ibo, a very competitive, Christian tribe stressing individual initiative and achievement. The Ibo and Hausa-Fulani clashed violently from 1967-1970 (Biafran War). During and after it, various military factions staged *coups d'état* and took over the government. In 1979, a new constitution was completed, and a civilian, Alhaji Shehu Shagari, was elected president. Blamed for rampant corruption, he was overthrown in December, 1983, by Major General Mohammed Buhari, who heads a Supreme Military Council. His government is the most northern and Islam-oriented of recent times.

The country has a mixed economy in which the government controls or owns companies dominant in public utilities and basic manufacturing. A member of OPEC, Nigeria has drawn at least 33% of its GDP and 80% of government revenues from petroleum. Shortages of skilled labor, a weak infrastructure (especially in ports, power, land transport, and communication) hindered development during the oil boom. Shagari pushed a return to self-sufficiency in food production and promoted industrial development through foreign investment (Fourth National Development Plan, 1981-1985). Joint ventures are regulated by the Nigerian Enterprises Promotion Decree of 1977, which sets aside areas exclusively for Nigerians (oil production, business management services, advertising, etc.); areas for at least 40% equity (e.g., high technology), and areas for companies with 40% or less Nigerian equity interest (drugs and tobacco manufacturing). Nigeria also participates in the West African economic community ECOWAS.

With the United States, total volume of trade reached $4.7 billion in 1983 (Nigeria imports more from Great Britain and Germany). Some 40% of its exports go to the United States, most of it oil. Nigeria is the U.S.'s third largest supplier. IBM located there, but pulled out in the late 1970s.

Described by an American journalist in the 1960s as "Texas on the Guinea Gulf, a raw masculine country — sincere, well-meaning, brawling, and lusty," Nigeria is a country Americans seem to know little about. Some details about the government are emerging as Americans, like others, are caught in its "War Against Indiscipline" and its harsh penalties. The country's diversity makes spurious any attempt to talk about Nigerian culture as a whole, though, and there is little information available about specific tribes. The discussion below is based on the Yoruba and Ibo.

Basic concept of the negotiation process

Distributive. Functional, zero-sum. [Indirect? Avoidant?] Competitive, individual gain.

With foreigners, the Ibo and Yoruba have a marketplace attitude toward negotiation: they see it as a means of achieving limited objectives through compromise and bargaining. Experienced foreigners are expected to deal with customers directly. The inexperienced usually go through middlemen: a triangular relationship is set up in which middlemen provide the contact and bargain with state officials and businessmen.

One foreign executive observed: "This is a beautiful place for business, because everyone keeps talking ... everything is in flux, everything is negotiable. That's why you need a hustler, an expeditor." Another remarked: "This [Nigeria] is the most corrupt country in the world ... therefore, it's necessary to buy protection [and influence]." In 1976, Lockheed, for example, admitted paying $3.6 million in "dash" [under-the-table payoffs] for a $45 million deal. Although going rates exist, the amount of dash or the "mobilization fee" is often the primary matter negotiated with foreigners. They almost universally range from 50-100% of the value of the contract sought.

Among the Yoruba and Ibo themselves, disputes arising out of business tend to be settled at home, through arbitration by a mutually respected authority figure. Resort to courts is infrequent and signals the end of a business relationship.[56]

Most significant type of issue

Relationship and personal-internal issues seem to predominate.

Relationship concerns overshadow the competitiveness of prices, quality of product and other substantive issues for a number of reasons: the pivotal role played by middlemen, an emphasis on short term rather than long term gains, and the omnipresence of dash. With Americans in particular, Nigerians generally seem repelled by pushiness and a strong task orientation, which are considered manifestations of the U.S.'s superiority complex. A style that reflects respect, empathy, and sincerity is preferred. Friendships facilitate business dealings.

These issues are heightened by the paramount significance attached to individual prestige and by Nigerians' generally proud attitude toward their country's role in Africa. Elders, among others, are to be respected, for age is equated with wisdom.

Selection of negotiators

The primary criteria are status and personal attributes.

Mentor relationships and tribal ties have strongly influenced the placement of individuals in government positions. However, some businessmen evidently refuse to hire members of their own tribe because they think it encourages demands for favors and undercuts good performance.

Personal bearing and image are also highly regarded. Hence, in part, the importance attached to educational credentials. In the British tradition, the individual with a generalist, literary education is considered more capable than one knowledgeable about a particular industry. A Ph.D. carries great weight: "Without a Ph.D., you of course cannot get an article published in the newspapers, not even a question or letter to the editor."[57]

Individuals' aspirations

The extent of individualistic behavior depends on the context because ethnic collectivism continues to run strong.

Many Nigerian businessmen — perhaps the Ibo, in particular — have been described as "get rich quick" men. This orientation flows from both the political system and tribal emphases. Note the earlier references to prestige, power, and wealth. The dominant elite in Lagos, the capital city, pursues them with a broad range of political favors and sanctions.

But for many, ties to the tribe remain strong. When government administrations have changed leadership, the new leader has often brought in members of his own tribe. By some accounts, stealing within one's own tribe is condemned, while stealing from outsiders is condoned, particularly if some of the wealth is brought back to the tribe. More generally, businessmen may simply try to arrange agreements that have benefits for their extended families or tribes.[58]

Decision-making in groups
Decision-making is highly centralized.

Powerful individuals make the decisions and they tend to do so without having delegated much to subordinates or consulting others. In short, the patronage and power associated with a high position is not easily shared. As one Nigerian has written, "It is common practice in purely Nigerian organizations ... to postpone decisions on very urgent matters just because the incumbent official is on leave and no one else can act for him." A final decision will depend on the personalities of the individuals involved and the personal gains they see. Furthermore, any business venture of significance must involve government officials. These patterns may be traced to autocratic traditions.

Orientation toward time
Time is generally treated casually.

Even the simplest transactions require a great deal of time by American standards and the attention of a senior employee. This is more than a fact of bureaucratic life; time is simply considered flexible. Lateness to meetings (even of several hours) is common. In the same vein, the foreigner who hurries through a negotiation — even after a very late start — will often be suspected of cheating. Punctuality is becoming more important in some of the larger cities, though.

Risk-taking propensity
At least among Ibo and Yoruba, individuals do not seem risk averse.

These groups have taken great risks for large short-term gains. This willingness persists, as evinced by the continuing corruption in the government and in business. Several governments have attempted to eliminate it by threatening severe punishment, but those efforts have yet to succeed. Bear in mind, nonetheless, that the current administration is the most conservative of modern times.

Bases of trust

An essential element of successful negotiation in Nigeria, trust is based largely on friendship (past record).

Nigerians generally attempt to get to know their counterparts before making business transactions. They look to one's credentials (advanced degrees) and expertise, but middlemen usually establish initial contacts. Once friendships have developed, even a foreigner will be considered a member of the family and looked upon with favor during negotiations.

This tendency toward personal bonds is reinforced by the pervasiveness of corruption in recent governments. Legal sanctions do not offer a guidepost for confidence or trust.

Concern with protocol

Certain rules and expectations are very important.

Initial introductions must be made by middlemen. Titles, including one's degrees, are used widely. For example: "Chief the Honorable Alhaji Igun Wagaba, M.A. (Oxon), Ph.D. (Harvard). F.R.S.C.. Q.C.E.. O.B.E. Director." Titles generally reflect power. Formal invitations and appointment-making are not common, however.

Communication complexity

Nigerians generally place a lot of emphasis on nonverbal communication, but exact nuances differ from tribe to tribe.

The official language is English, and many Nigerians that come to the U.S. come across as eloquent rhetoricians. In Nigeria, however, words apparently do not mean much. Meanings are subtle and internalized, and there is more-over a high tolerance for ambiguity.

Nature of persuasion

Emotion, experience, and intuition more than empirical reason are the persuasive bases of argument.

Many of the traits cited above reflect these bases: the emphasis on tribal loyalty, force of personality, and aggressiveness. Even the mystical is invoked when dealing with compatriots.

A foreigner should also recognize the dearth of detailed, reliable information in the country. The margin of error for reported unemployment figures, for example, has ranged from 25-50%.

Form of agreement
Generally, agreements are written but regarded as flexible.

Although Nigerians do pursue written agreements, a practice encouraged by the British, many agreements are spontaneous and verbal. The key to commitment is not legal enforceability but "an understanding" under which obligations of each party are clearly defined and matched with respective rewards.

Negotiating with the Saudis

Like the Chinese, Mexicans, and Nigerians, the Saudis have experienced a major revolution in this century: a social and technological one. Within the last 20 years, they have become one of the richest peoples in the world and have shifted from a longstanding nomadic (bedouin) existence to urban settlements equipped with the most modern of available technologies. The Saudis were pulled together formally by Ibn Saud, who had spent 30 years consolidating contiguous territories and in 1932, established the Kingdom of Saudi Arabia. Since then, the people have been governed by a monarch selected by and from among the 3000 princes and princesses comprising the royal family. There is a council of 21 ministers under the King's leadership; there are no political parties. Even the royalty, however, follows the fundamental, defining characteristic of the Saudis: their religion, Islam. Their daily affairs as well as government practices adhere to the Islamic holy book (the Koran) and more specifically, to Islamic law (the Shariah). Even tax and legal systems are based on it. The Saudis, moreover, are keepers of the two places holiest in Islam: Mecca, the birthplace of the Prophet Muhammed, and Medina, the city of the Prophet's burial ground. Amidst these traditions, the Saudis, whose national population numbers 8.7 million (36% of whom are resident foreigners), continue to see changes: new schools, universities, and medical facilities, free medical care, and much more. Oil production dominates the Saudi economy.

The first discoveries were made in the 1930s, and large scale production began after World War II. Saudi Arabia is now the second largest producer in the world and the largest exporter. Some 89% of government revenue derives from these exports. The government's development plans in the 1970s addressed infrastructure. The third plan, for 1980-1985, continues infrastructure development but emphasizes education, in order to reduce dependence on foreign labor, and expansion and diversification of the productive sectors of the economy. Two large industrial cities, Jubail and Yanbu, are being developed as part of that effort. The government has also provided incentives and policies to the growing private sector (industry, agriculture, banks, construction companies) and is encouraging foreign investment, particularly through mixed ventures.

With respect to Americans, total trade between the two countries reached $11.7 billion last year. Saudi Arabia is the U.S.'s sixth largest market worldwide. For the U.S., Saudi Arabia has been a reliable source of oil (in mid-1982, it was providing 13.2% of U.S. crude oil and petroleum products), and U.S. oil companies have been heavily involved there. ARAMCO, for example, was originally owned by Exxon, Socal, Mobil, and Texaco. Bechtel is overseeing construction of Yanbu and Jubail. Petrochemical plants there are being built jointly by Sabic (Saudi Basic Industries Corp.) and Mobil, and by Sabic and Exxon. From 1970-82, the Saudis entered some 1260 joint ventures with Western firms (a tenfold increase) and invested some $156 billion in the West from 1973-83.

Some 65,000 American workers and their dependents live in Saudi Arabia but Americans as a whole know little about the country and people. Perhaps the most commonly known cultural trait has to do with dress and segregation of the sexes. As with each of the five preceding cultures, however, there is much more for an American negotiator to consider.

Basic concept of the negotiation process

Joint problem-solving (and nondirective discussion) mixed with distributive bargaining. Dysfunctional. Indirect, avoidant. Collaborative.

The Saudis are very sensitive to criticism, open confrontation, and directness and tend to respond to it indirectly. Faced with a conflict, they offer reasons for delays which eventually are insurmountable. The Koran (or *Qur'an*) advises inattention to "ignorant" people who taunt and cause difficulties and forgiveness of those who insult and injure.

With respect to negotiation, consider the following passage:

> The qualities it [the Koran] demands first of a negotiator are understanding and sympathy, mildness and moderation, love and understanding as opposed to force and compulsion, arrogance and conceit, intimidation and coercion. It inculcates persuasion as against the display of strength and severity. The other qualities ... are patience and perseverance. One must proceed slowly and cautiously, one must show tolerance and possess a readiness to understand the point of view of one's opponent; one must aim at winning over his heart.

These beliefs complement some of the ways and patterns discussed below. A European manager said, "It took several months for me to realize that what looked and sounded like social talk and playing around was in fact the most preferred mode for Arab managers to discuss business, solve problems, or make decisions."

On the other hand, one non-native writer has underscored the conflict proneness of Arabs and "age-old virtues of manliness, aggressiveness, bravery, heroism, courage, and vengefulness." He quotes one informant as saying: "They fight first, and then inquire as to the cause of the fight. This is our way of life in Yemen." Whether or not these generalities hold for Saudis, the Saudis do not necessarily follow the ideals above. They bargain — compromising and standing fast. Some writers contend that the Saudis enjoy the dynamic of bargaining and to support that view, point to a history of trading and to bedouin ways.[59]

Most significant type of issue

Relationship-based issues are paramount, but personal-internal issues are also significant.

In general, Saudis take a personal rather than task orientation. Their negotiations reflect it: before any direct discussion of business, time is spent socializing. Then, as one European executive put it, "... you may bring out the subject in an 'incidentally' or 'by the way' manner, even though the problem at hand is an important one ..." This may be traceable to bedouin patterns for within-group relations, but the Koran, as interpreted by one writer, also reinforces it:

> ... he [the Muslim] is gentle and courteous and in fact forgiving while dealing with friends and foes. He avoids all vain discourse, he invites and argues in

> ways most gracious, his words are gentle, his manner is graceful, he is
> unfailing in courtesy, and he says what is best, without hurting the suscepti-
> bilities of any person or party.

The Saudi's loyalty to his family, his placing it above much else, again speaks
to the importance of relationships to the Saudis.

Strong societal norms of hospitality have fused business, social, and
personal life, so it is not uncommon for close friends to drop into an office for
non-business talks over tea. Similarly, business — especially government
negotiation — is often conducted in public, so one's competitors may sit in on
the discussions.

In addition to relationship concerns such as trust, there are personal issues
such as manliness, pride, reputation, and honor (*sharaf*). And substantive
issues — prices, specifically — have become more important to Saudis as a
result of previous negotiations in which they felt others took advantage of
them. They seek a fair deal. Often they have several different asking prices,
each with a different meaning, and negotiation pivots on one of them. One
should know market price.[60]

Selection of negotiators
*In government and in business, Saudi negotiators tend to be males selected on
the basis of status (family and personal ties) and loyalty.*

The predominance of these criteria shows up readily in the government,
specifically with respect to the royal family, and its members become involved
in business negotiations as government representatives but also as private
businessmen. Indeed, for major projects, American business negotiators will
probably negotiate with a member of the royal family. But even other Saudi
negotiators are selected for their ties and loyalty.

These criteria follow from the paternal, hierarchical family structure in
Arabia, the predominance of obligations to one's family, and traditional
aversions to organizational procedures and systems. Extreme importance is
placed on honor, especially family honor, and it can be affected by relatives as
well as oneself. Hence the critical import of trustworthiness and loyalty. As
one writer puts it, "The attitude of 'loyalty first, efficiency second' within
organizations seems to be in accordance with the larger societal values of
group loyalty, nepotism, and paternalism."[61]

Individuals' aspirations

Generally, the Saudis accept and pursue individual aspirations, but they exist within a strong family-oriented context.

A major attribute of Arabs, according to one writer from the Middle East, is strong familism: "the centrality of the family in social organization, its primacy in the loyalty scale, and its supremacy over individual life." There is also the supporting conviction that Allah determines one's destiny. And yet, another observer contends that deference to authority and acceptance of externally imposed discipline has always been balanced by a "sense of equality" that allows individuals to assert their own interests.

The Koran also advises loyalty to oneself. If one is true to oneself, it says, one will be true to others. The hardships of nomadic life would seem to have instilled an individualistic orientation as well.

Some businessmen have noted that Saudis prefer to work alone rather than in a team and take sole credit for accomplishments while passing on blame for failures to others.[62]

Decision-making in groups

Decision making is highly centralized but consultative.

Within the culture generally, a strict hierarchy exists which places ranking males with families in a position to make decisions. Thus "[an individual] may not make decisions without consulting his near relatives and the senior members of his group. He lives in a compact organization in which everyone knows everyone else's business. His every utterance or deed goes through the censorship exercised by his group." Similarly, in business, subordinates are consulted informally, on a one-to-one basis, but the leader always makes the final decision.

The Saudis tend not to delegate responsibility. They feel that only the top man can get things done, and they search him out for meetings. As one president of a large company said, "They [clients] insist on my presence during negotiations. They are offended if I'm not personally involved ..."[63]

Orientation toward time
The Saudi attitude toward time is casual.

"Tomorrow" (*buqra*) is a common attitude among Saudis, so scheduling and keeping appointments are matters of low priority. The Saudis take time during the day for prayers (there is also an annual month-long religious observance called *Ramadan*), consider important the opportunity to get acquainted with prospective associates, and pay social calls to friends in their offices during the business day.

According to one writer, "Arab executives are deeply concerned with the low value and respect that people in their business community place on time." On the other hand, they feel Americans clearly overemphasize its value.[64]

Risk-taking propensity
The Saudis seem to have a propensity to avoid risk but accept some uncertainty.

According to American executive Bill Thomas, president of a firm providing risk management for development of the Jubail and Yanbu industrial complexes, insurance is proscribed by Islamic law. It is considered gambling and for a long time, was not even available. Insurance is now available through companies registered abroad.

As Thomas puts it, "The religion says if it is God's will that something happen, it will happen and it's your destiny to recover from it." This fatalism implies at least some acceptance of uncertainty.[65]

Bases of trust
An extremely important factor, trust depends on personal friendship.

The Saudis place trust and confidence in individuals rather than organizations. As one Muslim writer has said:

> ...a Muslim looks at life as a trust from God — a trust which was offered to the heavens and the earth and the mountains but which they declined to accept. Man accepted and in so doing he undertook heavy responsibilities... And the keeping of trust is not limited to money or property ...it embraces the whole field of our dealings — financial legal, political and moral... A person who betrays a trust, said the Prophet, is devoid of all faith, and a man who fails to

> keep his word is bereft of all moral values. A person who is capable of once betraying a trust loses his title to confidence for he can do it again.

Trust may be extended intuitively at first, but the predominance of Islam and social sanctions (threat to one's honor) also seem to be effective bases.[66]

Concern with protocol
Saudis consider protocol extremely important.

Their conduct is guided by strong social norms of hospitality together with adherence to the Koran. One Muslim saying is "Honor the guest, even though he be an infidel." Upon arrival, guests are usually immediately served food and drink (especially coffee), and this practice carries over to the office, in business negotiations, as well. It initiates an attempt to establish a bond of friendship. Typically, negotiators then discuss topics of mutual interest but not details of personal lives (discussion of female relatives is out of the question). Such talk may last 2-15 minutes. To do otherwise is considered impolite.

Honor, dignity, and respectfulness are all important guidelines of an interaction. The first person to enter a room has the highest rank, the last has the least. Greetings and partings are also significant events that involve kisses and soft handshakes. Titles are used. Swear words, jokes, and strong and disparaging language tend to insult rather than draw parties closer. And apparently, if one admires a Saudi's possession, hospitality requires that he offer it as a gift.

The Koran specifies other aspects of proper conduct, and its precepts are enforced by religious police. There are five 20-minute prayers a day: at dawn, midday, later afternoon, dusk and evening. Friday is a holy day. (The Saudi weekend is the American's Thursday and Friday.) In public places, the sexes are strictly segregated in areas designated for families (including single women) and bachelors.[67]

Communication complexity
Saudis communicate in a context of high complexity.

With respect to verbal messages, one observer points out that Arabs (and, by extension, Saudis) purposely "give greater weight in thought and speech to wishes rather than to reality, to what [they] would like things to be rather than to what they objectively are." Thus speech often contrasts with actions. The same observer goes on to underscore a tendency toward exaggeration. Note also that Saudis tend to avoid refusing a request especially from superiors or others held in esteem; a refusal would be impolite. Bluntness, criticisms, and friendly banter are also considered undesirable and are left out of many conversations.

Various essays on Saudis' communications suggest contrasts difficult for a Westerner to reconcile, and the emotional arena presents some of them. "The very same Arab whose character is hostile and quarrelsome, who shows extreme emotionalism in easily aroused anger and sorrow does not ordinarily demonstrate his joys, fears, and weaknesses. These feelings are not given vent, they are checked from positive overt expression..." An Arab "yells and squabbles" when bargaining in the marketplace and freely expresses his pain when hurt, according to one author. At the same time, the Koran admonishes those who lose their tempers and use strong words: "Be modest in thy bearing and subdue thy voice. Lo! the harshest of all voices is the voice of the ass." Perhaps, then, the Koran proposes the guiding principle, but actual behavior may differ and be accepted when compelled by the force of circumstances.

Several aspects of nonverbal communication are meaningful. Hand gestures, especially with the left hand, and crossing one's legs to expose the sole of one's shoe tend to be taken as insults. The left hand is used for personal hygiene, and the sole is considered the most inferior part of one's body. On the positive side, Saudis tend to stand close together in conversation (10-15 inches versus the American norm of 30), maintain direct eye contact (eyes are the "window to one's soul"), and even talk breath to breath in their discussions. They will touch an arm or hand to emphasize a point. And as for their attitude toward silence, there is a saying that "Allah gave man two ears and one tongue, so he could listen twice as much as he could speak."[68]

Nature of persuasion
The bases of persuasion seem mixed: emotional, but also intuitive, experiential (traditional), and ideological (the Koran).

Empirical reasoning is considered an alien, Western system. It is considered more important to follow the tenets of the *Shariah*. To the extent that it follows the Koran, these guidelines would include brief arguments, clear communication of one's thoughts, avoiding ornamentation, and ending a meeting without ill feelings if the argument fails to be convincing. A basic fatalism, which is reflected in the omnipresent expression "If God wills" (*In sha'allah*) overlays any argument or plan. Religion may not only guide behavior but provide bases for persuasive appeals.

When honor and face are involved, however, the Saudis are known for arguing emotionally. They have also been known to ramble and flatter, and to admire eloquence. To confuse the matter further, consider the following American executive's impressions: "They're clever, precise, and accurate, and know what they want."

In short, more information is needed in this area.[69]

Form of agreement
Bound by their words, the Saudis prefer to cement their agreements orally.

Given its preeminence in social life, an individual's honor serves as a strong incentive to keep agreements and at the same time, as a restraint against writing up agreements. (To ask for a written document may be to insult a counterpart.) As indicated under *Bases of trust*, the Koran treats a Muslim's commitment to another individual as equivalent to a "covenant with God." It is one's duty to fulfill one's obligations.

Despite these strong incentives, one Muslim writer argues that memories are so faulty that individuals should write up agreements. Considering the scale of many projects in Saudi Arabia, today's Saudis probably do write up most agreements. That does not necessarily diminish the importance they attach to commitments and obligations, however. Indeed, having to write agreements may accentuate the commitments.[70]

Conclusions and prospects

From the Chinese emphasis on friendship to the Saudi concern for honor, this paper has touched on aspects of negotiation in six cultures other than the American. Indeed it has only touched on them and left out other aspects. Still, however briefly, this paper has uncovered and presented similarities and differences between the cultures.

One might protest that people are more alike than different, but this paper is not designed to and does not argue the antithesis. It surveys and attempts to provide introductory "understandings" of similarities and differences, and implies that some cultural differences are likely to keep naive negotiators from interacting as satisfactorily and productively as possible. An American who expects and prepares for distributive bargaining from the French or Saudis is probably in for a shock and failure. Generally, it is striking that each of the six cultures studied places more importance on relationships, the complexity of communication, and trust than Americans do. Such "hurdles" are in themselves significant.

What are the implications?

For practitioners, specific cultural influences have been outlined and preliminarily probed. The next question to face concerns appropriate responses. For a long time, we have simply assumed "When in Rome, do as the Romans do." One can easily debate the success of non-Romans in doing so. But a student in one of the author's negotiation classes (who happens to be Italian) contended that one should not even attempt to do so. In his view, a cross-cultural situation presents a unique opportunity for the particular negotiators involved to create jointly a very special interaction. This point of view has some attractive features. That is another discussion, though, and regardless of the avenue a negotiator chooses, some knowledge of a counterpart's cultural background should prove beneficial.

For researchers, this paper touches only lightly some complex, pervasive aspects of negotiating behavior. It does pose important questions, propose a broad, organizing framework, and illustrate some differences between cultures. A real challenge lies ahead: differences need to be studied empirically and evaluated for their significance if we are to go farther down the road toward understanding and ameliorating the negotiating experiences of American business people abroad. This paper sets us on our way.

Notes

1. These figures are attributed to the U.S. Department of Commerce in "The Manners of Foreign Markets," *Philadelphia Inquirer*, June 22, 1984. The article also mentions that some 73,500 U.S. companies conduct business abroad and maintain 200,000 employees overseas at any one time.

2. Alternatively, "Culture consists of patterns, explicit and implicit, of behavior acquired and transmitted by symbols constituting the distinctive achievements of human groups, including their embodiments in artifacts; the essential core of culture consists of traditional ideas and especially their attached values" (Kroeber & Kluckhohn in Terpstra, 1978).

3. For existing but wanting literature on the subject, see Fisher (1980), Graham (1983), Gulliver (1979), Posses (1978), and Smith & Wells (1976).

4. Some of these questions are addressed subsequently in this paper. Others simply lie beyond its scope.

5. They are working propositions meant to focus and stimulate discussion. We welcome your comments. For the sake of manageability, North Americans are treated as one group, but we do wonder about the nature and magnitude of ethnic influences on these cross-cultural interactions.

6. With this level of generality, some operational usefulness is lost. But we question whether a more specific definition exists that is valid across cultures.

7. For instance, the verifiability issue raised in U.S.-Soviet arms control talks is to a great extent a relationship-based issue.

8. Recall that President Carter appointed Hamilton Jourdan to negotiate with the Iranians despite his limited diplomatic experience.

9. Note that the matter of credibility in negotiation is related but not identical to trust.

10. See, for example, Hegstrom, T. G., "Message Impact: What Percentage is Nonverbal?", *The Western Journal of Speech Communication*, 43, Spring 1979, 134-142.

11. For more on argument across cultures, see Glenn (1966, 1981). Nature of persuasion and decision-making in groups also concern information-gathering, evaluation, and use. This, too, may be a fruitful area for cross-cultural comparisons but we leave it for future work.

12. The propositions that follow for each culture are based on perceptions of general cultural characteristics. We recognize the dangers of stereotypy and prejudice and have tried to avoid their extreme forms. This is an introductory piece, though, and one intended to stimulate discussion.

13. This figure and all others for trade in this paper are from the International Monetary Fund's *Direction of Trade Statistics, 1984*. The introductions to each culture are also based on *Background Notes* by the U.S. Dept. of State, Bureau of Public Affairs, and assorted periodicals.

14. See de Pauw (1981:70), Pye (1983:87), Salisbury (1984:52), Wren (1984). Thanks are due to Ying-Zhi Gu, Ernest Liu, Ling Shen, and Robert Wing for their comments on "Negotiating with the Chinese."

15. See de Pauw (1981:64) and Weiss-Wik (1981).

16. See Lall (1968:2ff), Pye (1983:17), and Wren (1984).

17. See Pye (1983:16,89).

18. See de Pauw (1981:55,63) and Pye (1983:73).

19. See "The Scramble ..." (1978).

20. See "The Chinese Abroad ..." (1984) and de Pauw (1981:64).

21. See de Pauw (1981:65), Kapp (1983:71), and Pye (1983:80).

22. See Kapp (1983:38,39), Lall (1968:28), and Pye (1983:73).

23. See Bloom (1977), Kapp (1968:66), Lall (1968:28ff), Pye (1983:42,52,89).

24. See "A China Treaty ..."(1984), Kapp (1983:61), and Pye (1983:78).

25. See Fisher (1980:19), Dupont (1982:270), Plantey (1980:75). Thanks are due to Bertrand Bellon for his useful comments on "Negotiating with the French."

26. See Ardagh (1977:695) and Fisher (1980:50).

27. See Ardagh (1977:21) and Fisher (1980:24).

28. See Hofstede (1984:158) and Inzerilli & Laurent (1983:113).

29. See Ardagh (1977:689), Inzerilli & Laurent (1983), and Lewis (1983).

30. See Ardagh (1977:25-27), Hofstede (1984), cf. Bass & Burger (1979).

31. See Ardagh (1977:695).

32. See Crozier in Ardagh (1977:689).

33. See Dupont (1982:86-89) and Glenn (1972).

34. See Blaker (1977:4-7), Fisher (1980:17), Mushakoji (1972), and Graham & Sano (1984).

35. See Blaker (1977:50,82), Graham & Sano (1984), and Holusha (1983).

36. See Blaker (1977:30,43,50), Fisher (1980:22), Graham & Sano (1984:43) Imai (1975:51), McCreary & Blanchfield (1984).

37. See Imai (1975:3-9), Hofstede (1984:158), Lohr (1984), and Sethi, Namiki & Swanson (1984:9-11).

38. See Blaker (1977:82), Fisher (1980:32), Sethi, Namiki & Swanson (1984:19,34).

39. See Demente (1972).

40. See Bass & Burger (1979), Blaker (1977:11), and Hofstede (1984:122).

41. See Kotkin (1984:181,182) and McCreary & Blanchfield (1984:35).

42. See McCreary & Blanchfield (1984) and Graham & Sano (1984:61).

43. See Barnlund (1975), Clavell (1975:324), Graham & Sano (1984:23), Imai (1975), and McCreary & Blanchfield (1984:15,18,22).

44. See Graham & Sano (1984:22), McCreary & Blanchfield (1984:37), and Sethi, Namiki & Swanson (1984:38).

45. See Graham & Sano (1984: 93) and McCreary & Blanchfield (1984:31).

46. Thanks are due to Raul Lopez Martinez for his comments on "Negotiating with the Mexicans."

47. See Fisher (1980:20), McDowell (1984:149), and Paz (1962:20,22,31).

48. See Riding (1984).

49. See Hofstede (1984:158).

50. See Hofstede (1984:156ff).

51. See Hofstede (1984:122).

52. See Paz (1962:30).

53. See Fisher (1980:20,25).

54. See Paz (1962:23).

55. See Fisher (1980:20,51) and Paz (1962:24).

56. See Ampofo (1984), Biersteker (1983), and Diamond (1984:906).

57. See Ampofo (1984).

58. See Onyemelukwe (1966).

59. See Iqbal (1975:82,92), Muna (1980), Patai (1973), and Sen (1981).

60. See Iqbal (1975) and Patai (1973:283).

61. See Muna (1980).

62. See Iqbal (1975:129), Patai (1973:282), and Lee (1980:13).

63. See Hamady in Patai (1973:284) and Muna (1980).

64. See Muna (1980).

65. See Mulligan (1981).

66. See Iqbal (1975:95).

67. See Lee (1980).

68. See Hamady in Patai (1973:159), Lee (1980), Isbaq (1975:83ff,88), and Sen (1981).

69. See Milligan (1981) and Patai (1973).

70. See Iqbal (1975:97).

References

Note: These references consist of 7 parts, one general part and six parts referring to the six nations discussed.

Bass, Bernard M. and Philip C. Burger. 1979. *Assessment of Managers: An International Comparison*. New York: Free Press.

Beliaev, Ed, Thomas Mullen, and Betty Jane Punnett. 1984. "Understanding the cultural environment: U.S. - U.S.S.R. trade negotiations". Mimeo (New York University).

Bock, Phillip K. 1970. *Culture Shock*. New York: Alfred A. Knopf.

Brislin, Richard W. 1981. *Cross-Cultural Encounters*. New York: Pergamon.

Condon, John and Fathi Yousef. 1974. *An Introduction to Intercultural Communication*.

New York: Bobbs-Merrill.

England, George W. 1975. *The Manager and His Values*. Cambridge, Mass.: Ballinger.

Fayerweather, John. 1959. *The Executive Overseas*. New York: Syracuse Univ. Press.

Fayerweather, John and Ashook Kapoor. 1976. *Strategy and Negotiation for the International Corporation*. Cambridge, Mass.: Ballinger.

Fisher, Glen. 1980. *International Negotiation: A Cross-Cultural Perspective*. Yarmouth: Intercultural Press.

Fisher, Glen. 1979. *American Communication in a Global Society*. Norwood: Ablex.

Glenn, Edmund. 1966. "Meaning and behavior: communication and culture". *Journal of Communication*, December.

Glenn, Edmund. 1981. *Man and Mankind: Conflict and Communication between Cultures*. Norwood: Ablex.

Graham, John. 1983. "Brazilian, Japanese and American business negotiations". *Journal of International Business Studies*, Spring-Summer, 44-61.

Gulliver, P.H. 1979. *Disputes and Negotiations: A Cross-Cultural Perspective*. New York: Academic.

Hall, Edward T. 1959. *The Silent Language*. Garden City, N.Y.: Doubleday.

Harris, Philip R. and Robert T. Moran. 1983. *Managing Cultural Differences*. Houston: Gulf Publishing Co.

Harris, Philip R. and Robert T. Moran. 1982. *Managing Cultural Synergy*. Houston: Gulf Pub. Co.

Heady, Ferrel. 1984. *Public Administration: A Comparative Perspective*. New York: Marcel Dekker, Inc.

Hofstede, Geert. 1984. *Culture's Consequences*. Beverly Hills: Sage.

Ikle, Fred, C. 1964. *How Nations Negotiate*. New York: Harper and Row.

Kluckhohn, Clyde and A.L. Kroeber. 1963. *Culture*. New York: Vintage.

Kluckhohn, Florence and Fred L. Strodtbeck. 1961. *Variations in Value Orientations*. Evanston, Illinois: Row Peterson.

Landis, Dan and Richard W. Brislin, eds. 1983. *Handbook of Intercultural Training*. Vols. 1-3. New York: Pergamon Press.

Lee, James L. 1966. "Cultural analysis in overseas operations". *Harvard Business Review*, March-April, 1966, 106-114.

Nader, Laura and Harry F. Todd (eds.). 1978. *The Disputing Process: Law in Ten Societies*. New York: Columbia Univ. Press.

Posses, Frederick. 1978. *The Art of International Negotiation*. London: Business Books.

Raiffa, Howard. 1982. *The Art and Science of Negotiation*. Cambridge, Mass.: Harvard Univ. Press.

Smith, David N. and Louis T. Wells, Jr. 1976. *Negotiating Third World Mineral Agreements*. Cambridge, Mass.: Ballinger.

Sperber, Philip. 1979. *The Science of Business Negotiation*. New York: Pilot Books.

Spradley, James P. and David W. McCurdy (eds.). 1971. *Conformity and Conflict: Readings in Cultural Anthropology*. Boston: Little, Brown, and Co.

Terpstra, Vern, ed. 1978. *The Cultural Environment of International Business*. Cincinnati: Southwestern Pub. Co.

Ting-Toomey, Stella. 1983. "A cultural analysis of conflict". Paper presented at annual conference of Society for Intercultural Education, Training and Research (Italy).

Triandis, Harry C. and William Wilson Lambert. 1980. *Handbook of Cross-Cultural Psychology*. Vols. 1-6. Boston: Allyn and Bacon, Inc.

Walton, Richard E. and Robert B. McKersie. 1965. *A Behavioral Theory of Labor Negotiations*. New York: McGraw-Hill.

Selected works of the author

"Analysis of complex negotiations in international business: The RBC perspective". *Organization Science*, 1993, 4(2):269-300.

"Negotiating with 'Romans': Part I". *Sloan Management Review*, 1994, 35(2):51-61.

"Negotiating with 'Romans': Part II". *Sloan Management Review*, 1994, 35(3):85-99.

"International business negotiations research: Bricks, mortar, and prospects". In: *Handbook of International Management Research* (Ed. B.J. Punnett and O. Shenkar). London: Blackwell, 1996:209-265.

Negotiating with the Chinese

Bloom, Alfred. 1977. "Linguistic impediments to cross-cultural communication: Chinese hassles with the hypothetical". *Journal of Peace Science*, II(2), 205-214.

Bonavia, David. 1980. *The Chinese*. New York: Lippincott and Crowell.

"The Chinese abroad — rich not red". *The Economist*, April 28,1984:80-81.

"A China treaty the President didn't sign". *Businessweek*, May 14, 1984:55.

Dean, Arthur H. 1966. "What it is like to negotiate with the Chinese". *New York Times Magazine*, October 30.

Dennis, Robert and Shipley Munson. 1983. "Trading with China: A boon for some... a disappointment for many". *Management Review*, May, 13-20.

De Pauw, John W. 1981. *U.S.-Chinese Trade Negotiations*. New York: Praeger.

Freeman, Charles W., Jr. 1975. "Notes on Chinese negotiating styles". East Asian Studies Institute, Harvard Law School, mimeo.

Kapp, Robert A. (ed.). 1983. *Communicating with China*. Chicago: Intercultural Press.

Lall, Arthur. 1968. *How Communist China Negotiates*. New York: Columbia Univ. Press.

Pye, Lucian. 1983. *Chinese Commercial Negotiating Style*. Cambridge, Mass.: Oelgeschlager, Gunn and Hain.

Salisbury, Harrison E. 1984. "Retracing Mao's long march". *New York Times Magazine*, November 18:42ff.

"The scramble to exploit China's oil reserves". *Business Week*, October 30, 1978: 155-156.

Weiss-Wik, Stephen. 1981. "Communication in diplomacy: an examination based on the West-Orient interface". Mimeo.

Wren, Christopher. 1984. "Hot tempers? Chinese say, 'Don't sue, mediate'". *New York Times*, April 12:2.

Negotiating with the French

Ardagh, John. 1977. *The New France*. London: Penguin.
Ardagh, John. 1983. *France in the 1980's*. London: Penguin.
Dupont, C. 1982. *La négociation: conduite, théorie, applications*. Paris: Dalloz.
Fisher, Glen. 1980. *International Negotiation*. Yarmouth: Intercultural Press.
Harnett, D.L. and L.L. Cummings. 1980. *Bargaining Behavior: An International Survey*. Houston: Dame Publications.
Inzerilli, Giorgia and Andre Laurent. 1983. "Managerial views of organization structure in France and in the USA". *International Studies of Management and Organization*, XIII(1-2), 97-118.
Lewis, Paul. 1983. "French socialism stubs its toe". *New York Times*, July 31.
Louche, C. 1978. "La négociation comme processus interactif: revue critique". *Psychologie francaise* (23:3-4), 261-267.
Plantey, Alain. 1980. *La négociation internationale: principes et méthodes*. Paris: Editions du centre national de la recherche scientifique.
Zeldin, Theodore. 1983. *The French*. London: Vintage.
(There appears to be popular literature on negotiation in France like that in the U.S. We have an unscreened list of about 12 of these books.)

Negotiating with the Japanese

Aonuma, Y. 1981. "A Japanese explains Japan's business style". *Across the Board*, February, 18(2), 41-50.
Barnlund, Dean C. 1975. "Communicative styles in two cultures: Japan and the United States". In: *Organization of Behavior in Face to Face Interaction*. Eds. Kendon, Harris, and Key. The Hague: Mouton.
Blaker, Michael. 1977. *Japanese International Negotiating Style*. New York: Columbia University Press.
Clavell, James. 1975. *Shogun*. New York: Atheneum.
Demente, Boye. 1972. *How to Do Business in Japan*. Los Angeles: Center for International Business.
Fisher, Glen. 1980. *International Negotiation*. Yarmouth: Intercultural Press.
Glazer, Herbert. 1968. *The International Businessman in Japan*. Tokyo, Japan: Sophia University.
Graham, John. 1983. "Brazilian, Japanese and American business negotiations". *Journal of International Business Studies*, Spring-Summer, 44-61.
Graham, John. and Yoshihiro Sano. 1984. *Smart Bargaining: Doing Business with the Japanese*. Cambridge, Mass.: Ballinger.
Graydon, R.J. 1979. "Negotiating with the Japanese". *Industrial Development*, May-June.
Hahn, E.J. 1982. "Negotiating with the Japanese". *California Lawyer*, 2, 21-59.
Harnett, D.L. and L.L. Cummings 1980. *Bargaining Behavior: An International Survey*. Houston: Dame.

Holusha, John. 1983. "Toyota on G.M. deal: Giving aid to opponent". *New York Times*, March 22.

Imai, M. 1975. *Never Take Yes for an Answer*. Tokyo: Simul Press.

Janosik, Robert Joseph. 1983. "Negotiation Theory: Considering the Cultural Variable in the Japanese and American Cases". Ph.D. dissertation in Politics, New York University.

Kazuo, Ogura. 1979. "How the 'inscrutables' negotiate with the 'inscrutables': Chinese negotiating tactics vis-a-vis the Japanese". *China Quarterly*, September, 530ff.

Kotkin, Joel. 1984. "Going through customs". *INC.*, December.

Lohr, Steve. 1984. "To modern times for Japanese, add the social ills". *New York Times*, May 9:2.

McCreary, Don R. and Robert A. Blanchfield. 1984. "The art of Japanese negotiation". In: *Languages in International Perspective*. Ed. Nancy S. Nicholson. Norwood: Ablex.

Moran, Robert. 1984. *Getting Your Yen's Worth: How to Negotiate with Japan, Inc.* Houston, Texas: Gulf Pub.

Mushakoji, K. 1975. "The cultural premises of Japanese diplomacy". *Trilateral Commission Papers: Social and Political Issues in Japan*, 17-29.

Mushakoji, K. 1972. "The strategies of negotiation: An American-Japanese comparison". In: *Experimentation and Simulation*. Eds. J.A. LaPonce and P. Smoker. Toronto: University of Toronto Press. pp. 109-131.

Sethi, S. Prakesh, Nobuaki Namiki, and Carl L. Swanson. 1984. *False Promise of the Japanese Miracle*. Boston: Pitman Publishing Co.

Seward, Jack. 1975. "Speaking the Japanese business language". *European Business*, Winter.

Sullivan, Jeremiah et al. 1981. "The relationship between conflict resolution approaches and trust". *Academy of Management Journal*, December, 803-815.

Tung, Rosalie. 1984. *Business Negotiations with the Japanese*. Cambridge, Mass.: Lexington Books.

Van Zandt, Howard E. 1970. "How to negotiate in Japan". *Harvard Business Review*, Nov/Dec, 45-56.

Negotiating with the Mexicans

Fisher, Glen. 1980. *International Negotiation*. Yarmouth: Intercultural Press.

McDowell, Bart. 1984. "Mexico City: An alarming giant". *National Geographic*, August, 138-185.

Paz, Octavio. 1962. *The Labyrinth of Solitude*. Trans. by Lysander Kemp and Toby Talbott. New York: Grove.

Riding, Alan. 1984. "Corruption, Mexican style". *New York Times Magazine*, December 16.

Negotiating with the Nigerians

Ampofo, Kodwo E. 1984. "Cross-cultural conflict: A ZZZ internal handguide to doing business in the Nigerian cultural environment". Mimeo.
"Business around the globe: Nigeria, Texas on the Guinea Gulf". *Fortune*, April, 1964.
Cronje, Susan, M. Ling, and G. Cronje. 1976. *Lonrho: Portrait of a Multinational*. London: Penguin and Julian Friedmann.
Diamond, Larry. 1984. "Nigeria in search of democracy". *Foreign Affairs*, Spring, 905-927.
Koehn, Peter H. 1982. "The evolution of public bureaucracy in Nigeria". In: *Administrative Systems Abroad*. Ed. Krishna K. Tummala. Washington, D.C.: Univ. Press of America.
Nafziger, Wayne E. 1977. *African Capitalism: A Case Study in Nigerian Entrepreneurship*. Stanford, California: Hoover Institution Press.
Onah, J.O. and P.N.O. Ejifor. 1978. *Nigerian Cases in Business Management*. London: Cassell Ltd.
Onyemelukwe, C.C. 1966. *Problems of Industrial Planning and Management in Nigeria*. New York: Columbia Univ. Press.
Panter-Brick, Keith. 1978. *Soldiers and Oil: the Political Transformation of Nigeria*. London: Frank Cass and Co., Ltd.

Negotiating with the Saudis

Alghanim, Kutayba. 1976. "How to do business in the Middle East". *Management Review*, August.
Iqbal, Afzal. 1975. *The Prophet's Diplomacy: The Art of Negotiation as Conceived and Developed by the Prophet of Islam*. Cape Cod, Massachusetts: Claude Stark.
Lee, Eve. 1980. *The American in Saudi Arabia*. Chicago: Intercultural Press.
Mulligan, John W. 1981. "Saudi risk management: A lesson in irony". *Business Insurance*, August, 17:10.
Muna, Farid A. 1980. *The Arab Executive*. New York: St. Martin's.
Patai, Raphael. 1973. *The Arab Mind*. New York: Scribners.
Rand, Edward J. 1976. "Learning to do business in the Middle East". *The Conference Board Record*, February.
Sen, Sondra. 1981. "The art of international negotiating: Doing business in the Middle East". *Art of Negotiating Newsletter*, 11(3), December.
Ward, Thomas Edward. 1965. *Negotiations for Oil Concessions in Bahrain, el Hasa*. New York.
Wright, P. 1981. "Doing business in islamic markets". *Harvard Business Review*, 59(1): 34ff.

III. The Cultural Context

Power and distance as cultural and contextual elements in Finnish and English business writing

Hilkka Yli-Jokipii
University of Turku, Finland

0.   Introduction

Not long ago I ran into a business message written by an importer to a manufacturer. In the message, the importer listed a number of complaints concerning the quality of the product, inadequate attention to detail, the delivery arrangements, etc. The conclusion to the message read as follows: *If you do not give a shit about your product, why should I*? Such a message is hardly to be found in textbooks and is hardly recommended by expert consultants in business communication, because these sources are eager to recommend conventional and unconditioned politeness, achieved, for example, by means of fixed formulae, indirectness, and hedging. Their version of the above request to improve quality control would perhaps be in the form of an apology, such as: *We regret to inform you that there seems to be something wrong with the quality control and delivery arrangements of these products.*

The juxtaposition of these two messages raises a number of questions. The first set of questions is concerned with the contextual conditions around the messages, such as the history of the relationship between the companies involved. How long has the writer's company been dissatisfied with the merchandise? What kinds of messages and how many of them has the writer's company sent to the same effect before this? What is the relationship between the writer and the recipient of this request? Perhaps they have a long history of dealing with each other and they therefore know each other well enough to give vent to such outbursts as illustrated by the first message.

Another set of questions related to these examples concerns the element of power. The buying firm has written both messages, and therefore possesses power over the receiving firm on the basis of the professional context in which the request is issued. In addition to this, the message contains linguistic elements which convey that the issuer of the request assumes power over the addressee.[1] Power is, however, closely intertwined with distance, as Hofstede (1980:92-152) showed with reference to the merely social side of the business profession, and Brown & Levinson ([1978] 1987:74-84) have suggested in their study of politeness. This is certainly the case with the linguistic aspects of the business profession and especially with the manifestations of requests.

Business communication textbooks, those meant for non-native speakers of English in particular, may not observe the contextual and cultural issues that tend to bring linguistic variation to business writing. This claim is well supported by the findings of a study (Yli-Jokipii 1994) in which some textbooks were compared against real-life writing strategies. Likewise, Richardson & Liggett (1993:115), who are both academics teaching business writing and also writing consultants to US corporations, observe that textbooks do not reflect the kind of power relations that occur in workplaces. We also have evidence showing that the received knowledge of textbooks and consultants may not match the real-life demands of writing (Hagge & Kostelnick 1989; Anson & Forsberg 1990), or the real-life conditions of spoken negotiations in organizations (Williams 1988; Tuffs 1995), where the distribution of power, in particular, plays an influential role.

As Bhatia (1993:38 39) and others have noted, business writing, especially the genre of letters, has not received much socio-cultural attention from scholars, who have, with good reason, been interested in studying spoken business contexts, such as negotiations. Recent studies with an intercultural focus include Halmari's (1993) analysis of Finnish and US telephone negotiations, and Ulijn & Li's (1995) comparison of Dutch, Chinese, and Finnish encounters with the focus on interruptions and the tolerance of silence. Neumann (1995) deals with German and Norwegian request strategies in negotiations. As far as I know, Yli-Jokipii (1994) carried out the first corpus-based study on authentic, non-simulated and non-elicited requests in real-life business writing, in which both cultural and contextual elements are included as variables explaining linguistic occurrences.

1.   Purpose of the paper

The present paper attempts to illustrate the role that power and distance play in business writing in two cultures and languages. The cultures involved are British and Finnish and the languages English and Finnish. A further aim is to consider how these factors influence the outcome of the messages and the rhetorical profile of the texts. This will be done through requests because they are sensitive to cultural, contextual, and linguistic variation. Specifically, this paper seeks to find answers to the following questions:

1. How do power and distance occur as contextual elements in business writing in Finnish and English?
2. How do the nature of distance and power, respectively, affect the way requests are issued in Finnish and English business writing?

The underlying hypothesis behind the first question is that linguistic variation may to some extent, but not totally, be explained by cultural issues, as Ulijn & Li (1995:604-605) point out. Other extra-linguistic, social, and contextual matters are expected to influence linguistic variation as well. Power and distance are only two examples of these.

Seeking an answer to the second question presupposes that a stand is taken as to how power and distance may be apparent in linguistic choices. This entails assigning values to linguistic items in terms of the power or distance which they portray. The hypothesis then is that certain linguistic choices signal power, or lack of it, while certain others signal a sense of distance and lack of involvement.

2.   Power and distance

2.1 *Power*

2.1.1. *Power in organizational contexts*
Power is a social phenomenon. Historically, it derives from the possession of coercive rights and of the methods with which coercion can be effected. In this historical sense, power may be defined with respect to the degree to which an individual's freedom is controlled (Fairclough 1989:3-6).

Power therefore reflects social hierarchy at large, but it also emerges in professional settings, and is related to the status of employees in their institutional roles. This has been pointed out by linguists from time to time, primarily with reference to face-to-face encounters. It has been suggested that power influences, for example, topic control (Bogoch 1994:73-76) and interruptions, which partly determine the holder of the floor in negotiations (Ulijn & Li 1995:619). As Richardson & Liggett (1993:113-116) point out, power has primarily been approached in research and education as if it were a choice that an individual may make. However, in organizations, an individual interacts and communicates in terms of his or her role, and not as an individual, and the communication needs to fulfil an organizational goal.

Power issues in organizational contexts are present in internal as well as external operations. The internal issues are connected with the personnel of the organizations in three ways, downwards, upwards, and horizontally. The downward direction is connected with how the management and other superiors behave — linguistically or non-linguistically — towards their subordinates. The upward issues are concerned with how subordinates behave towards their superiors. Moreover, in business organizations, there is also interaction between individuals on the same hierarchical level. Research on institutional communication has shown that the interactants tend to adjust their communication so as to accommodate the imbalance in the social status, whether from superiors to subordinates (Odell, Goswami & Herrington 1983:232) or from subordinates towards superiors (Cherry 1988; Moore 1992). Power may be an issue even in seemingly egalitarian settings such as the academic world, where administrators may obscure their power with exaggerated politeness realized with ambiguous messages (Graham & David 1996).

In external corporate operations, power is connected with the roles of the interactants and with the stages of the transactions at hand. The primary distinction is to be made between the buying and selling party in the transaction. This distinction is contained in the Social Exchange Theory (Roloff 1981). The social exchange theory claims that the party in possession of the resource has power over the other, and the interactant in need of the resource has not. These are labelled as *positive* and *negative power,* respectively. This view gives the buyer the positive power status, because the buyer's company has the resource that the selling company is looking for, i.e. the potential purchasing resource of the merchandise. This view can be applied quite extensively to cover all trading situations, regardless of the nature of merchandise, whether visible or invisible. Figure 1 shows the distribution of power qualitites along different transactional stages and situation types during the business deal.

Transactional Stage	Situation Type	Power	Writer Role
Pre-deal	Inquiry	+P	Buyer
	Request for a Quotation	+P	Buyer
	Offer	-P	Seller
	Quotation	-P	Seller
On-deal	Order	+P	Buyer
	Acceptance of Order	-P	Seller
	Shipping	±P	Buyer/Seller
	Payment Arrangements	±P	Buyer/Seller
Post-delivery	Reminder	-P	Seller
	Complaint	+P	Buyer
	Adjustment	-P	Seller

Figure 1. Power quality incorporated in the roles of writers at different stages and with different situation types during a business deal. +P = positive power quality, -P = negative power quality, ±P neutral or undefinable power quality (Yli-Jokipii 1994:53)

The process of transaction consists of three stages with respect to the closing of the deal. These are the stages preceding the deal, the stages occurring during the delivery of the merchandise, and those potentially following the delivery. These may be labelled *pre-deal*, *on-deal*, and *post-delivery* stages, respectively. The pre-deal stages cover inquiries and requests for quotations as well as replies to these, i.e. offers and quotations. The inquiries and requests are made by the potential buyers who, therefore, possess the positive power quality. The writers of offers and quotations try to sell their merchandise and, correspondingly, possess the negative power quality.

In on-deal situations the power quality is clearly identifiable only in the stages where the order is placed and acknowledged, but in other on-deal situations, which cover the routine shipping and payment arrangements, the power quality is not a clearly identifiable static issue at all. It may have no relevance in the situation or may be established on a dynamic case-to-case basis. The post-delivery stage is concerned with problems arising from the quality of the merchandise — in the case of complaints and adjustments — or from disturbances in payment. In these contexts too the buyer possesses power over the seller.

The foregoing model depicted the concept of power as a dynamic or static property of interaction. In spoken discourse, the dynamic quality of power is easily highlighted, because the possession of power can be negotiated and may switch from one interactant to another during the encounter or conversation, as analyses of, for example, business negotiations have suggested (Tuffs 1995). In writing, the distribution of power is naturally not clear, either, but the professional roles of buyers and sellers give interactants certain macrolevel power qualities, which may override other considerations in the interaction.

The reference to the social exchange theory already indicated that power is related to the costs and benefits involved in the situation (Leech 1983:123-127; Shelby 1986:12). Roughly speaking, the party who stands to benefit from the situation may be seen to possess less power than the party who faces costs in the situation.

2.1.2. *Power in linguistic choices: requests*

In the foregoing discussion, power was approached as a social notion and was defined in terms of the right and means of coercion. We will now be concerned with how power may be encoded and decoded in discourse, and will focus our attention upon requests as linguistic means of exercising and interpreting power. In the ensuing discussion, the examples of requests may seem to be treated in isolation from their discourse context, but this is not the case. On the contrary, they will be viewed in their social and textual context in a pragmatic, discourse-analytical manner, as explained in Section 4.3. below. For reasons of discretion towards the authentic sources, it is not possible to show large stretches of genuine texts here.

There is a connection between power and requests, and requests are especially sensitive to power distribution (Brown & Levinson 1987:74-84; Fairclough 1991:55). A request may be roughly defined as an expression of a need, and therefore it gives its issuer a negative power quality at the outset. In business, the need for something is frequently the reason for writing to the other party, and the purpose of the request is to indicate to the reader that the writer expects a response. The response may be in the form of a physical, verbal, or cognitive act. A physical act may be e.g. sending the items requested, such as catalogues, price lists, etc. A verbal act provides the answer requested, while a cognitive act involves a state of mind favourable to the writer. Examples (1) to (3) cover these, respectively[2]:

(1)   *your immediate and personal intervention would be appreciated* (BrV 29)

(2)   *we will need to know the name and address of your bank so as to ...* (BrV 43)

(3)   *I hope you find the case interesting and I would like to thank you for your co-operation* (BrV 47).

Example (1) is a request for action (*intervention*), example (2) elicits a verbal response, while example (3) may be interpreted as a request for cooperation. In the latter case, such an interpretation is possible on the basis of the shared knowledge of the interactants. There has been no previous cooperation in this case, and therefore the reader does not consider it appropriate to interpret this message at its face value of a thanking act. Instead, the reader interprets this message as manipulative persuasion and understands the message as a request for a benevolent outlook which results in cooperation.

A request thus places obligations on the addressee, and so threatens the addressee's face. Brown & Levinson (1987) call such impositions 'face-threatening acts', or FTAs. Because of the potential face threat incorporated in the request, its issuer tries to mitigate the message, i.e. tries to make it more "polite". The mitigation may be realized with single lexical items, such as *please*, or past modal auxiliaries (*could, would, should*), or with conventional, even fixed formulae (*we would be grateful/we look forward to*). They may also be quite indirect, dressed as hints, and thus open to interpretation, because the linguistic form used may allow the reader to choose not to understand the message as a request at all. If a business professional writes: *the quality control of these products must be improved*, he or she cannot be said to have asked the reader, or the reader's company, to do so, although in certain contexts the message is meant to be interpreted as *you must improve your quality control*. Similarly, the writer of example (3) cannot be said to have asked for the reader's cooperation on grounds of the linguistic form alone.

Requests are thus sensitive to indirectness and implicitness and give their issuer room for considerable creativity. This was already suggested with the foregoing examples, but let us look at another message, which represents an even more implicit way of requesting.

(4)   *I have costed this title according to ... latest price list dated ...*
       which allows for a reprint reduction on work that is transferred to
       yourselves. **I assume that there will also be a slight reduction on**
       the printing of the cover *as it is 3 colours and not 4 as on the scale*
       (BrT 19)

This example illustrates a difficult and sensitive communicative situation for
a business writer, because he or she needs to ask the recipient's company for
an extra reduction in price. The indirectness in this example is first achieved
with the declarative form, and the request is given as a statement *I assume ...*
The word *price* is only mentioned in the passage preceding the core of the
request. The core of the request (emphasized with boldface here) is effected
with a nominal form (*a reduction*), which is downsized by the adjective *slight*.
The action is diluted with an inconspicuous generic expression *there is*. This
makes it possible to avoid mentioning the readers or writers in this request at
all. The writer has created an impression that the writers and readers have
nothing to do with allowing and receiving a reduction in price. There is very
little interpersonal involvement in this message, and the participants are kept
at a distance. This indirectness and distancing thus saves both interactants
from loss of face.

2.2. Distance

2.2.1. *Language-internal focus*
Like power, the concept of *distance* may be approached from a language-
internal and language-external focus. The language-internal aspects of distance are concerned with the means by which it can be effected. These are, as
example (4) already suggested, primarily interpersonal elements, connected
with the action of the message, and with the participants in the action. The
variation of the reader or writer orientation in particular has a major role in the
creation and interpretation of the degree of distance embedded in the message.

To use the example of quality control again, the writer has several
options in coding distance. He or she may choose a writer-oriented approach
only: *we are not satisfied with the quality control of these products*, or may
add a reference involving the reader: *we are not satisfied with the quality
control of **your** products.* The inclusion of this reader orientation reduces the
distance considerably, but at the same time increases the face threat and

directness coming through the message. The writer may further choose to use the passive form, which does not entail the involvement of either of the parties: *the quality control of these products must be improved*. This version represents the most distant variant of this request. In addition, the substitution of *your* for *these* reduces the distance and increases the impositive force and face threat of the message also in this passive version.

2.2.2. *Language-external focus*

We now turn our attention to the language-external manifestations of distance. The notion of distance is then used here as showing in the level of acquaintance between the writer and the reader. The term *writer* in this context is to be understood as the person who is responsible for the message conveyed in the text and, correspondingly, the term *reader* refers to the person who is responsible for decoding the message.

The concept of the level of acquaintance, therefore, tells about the interactants in their institutional roles and in their professional work, and does not tell anything about their relationship as private individuals.

The level of acquaintance between the writer and reader is apparent in English in the mode of address in the greeting or salutation part of the text. The choices are between the *T* or *V* level of address. These terms come from Brown & Gilman (1960), and derive from the Latin second person singular *Tu* and second person plural *Vos*. In Finnish, we usually do not have a greeting in business letters at all, but the choice of person shows in each inflected verbal form.

3. Business writing

Business writing occurs in various forms, but the present investigation focuses on interactive written business communication. The term *interactive* comes from Östman (1987), who uses it to illustrate the reciprocity in communication. The interactive nature of written correspondence is also pointed out by De Rycker (1987), who was able to employ principles of conversation analysis to such writing. I call the documents concerned *letters*. However, this term is not used here just in the traditional sense of a piece of paper sealed in an envelope and carried by mail and postman, but a letter is defined as *a written element in business interaction, in which the recipient is identified in the greeting and the person responsible for the message is identified in the signature.* A letter is then a theoretical term, referring to a genre. Physically, it can be transmitted by post, or via the fax machine, or even electronically (Yli-Jokipii 1994; see also Louhiala-Salminen 1996).

3.1. *The genre of business letter*

The term *genre* is employed here as a notion concerning full texts and operating on the level of discourse structure (Couture 1986:82). According to this view, genre sets conditions on different parts of text, such as its beginning, body, and ending. As Berkenkotter & Huckin (1995:1-24) observe, the concept of genre is useful in professional communication, because it enables us to refer to media which are used to communicate with peers. They claim, quite correctly, that understanding the genres of written communication which are available in an individual's professional field is an essential professional qualification. A business letter thus forms a genre of its own, which may vary in format and visual arrangement. Genre correlates highly with the likelihood of certain types of linguistic occurrences and, therefore, the concept of genre is useful in making statements on linguistic variation in business settings (Bhatia 1993:45-75). The view on genre adopted here is somewhat milder from that presented by Swales (1990:42), who argues that genre "acts as a determinant of linguistic choices". Berkenkotter & Huckin (1995:13) talk about *genre knowledge* as "part of the conceptual tool kit of professional writers".

The notion of genre knowledge may be associated with the concepts of *frame* and *script* (see Brown & Yule 1983:238-245) in the sense that genre may derive from the frame of discourse which, in turn, helps in setting up the appropriate script manifested in the genre. For example, the frame of discourse might be an official offer, a potential selling situation. The situation affects and might even determine the kind of genre employed, e.g. whether a letter needs to be written to provide "black on white", or whether a telephone call will suffice. A script may be explained as a set of mutually shared principles drawing on conventional norms (Nyyssönen 1990:20). The proper script of an offer, which materializes e.g. in a letter, might conventionally require the employment of certain rhetorical approaches, such as interpersonal, informative, and persuasive. The interpersonal aspect is realized as a sign of appreciation for the interest shown in the products, the informative element comes out in the detailed account of terms of trade, and the persuasive aspect might be realized in the prompt for an order. By comparison, a different script, within the same frame of an offer, would be called for in the genre of a phone call.

3.2. *The letter in business organizations*

The role of the letter in business organizations seems to vary to some extent from culture to culture. The choice of medium in Finland seems to be different in domestic relations from its use in international trade. The letter is infrequent in home trade, because the telephone is the major medium of communication between the Finnish companies operating in Finland. The practice appears to be different with regard to international communication in Finnish business organizations. For example, the employees of the marketing department of a medium-sized company reported that the number of letters they wrote daily had increased towards the end of the 1980s (Luoma 1993:6). A recent study on the types of English-speaking messages sent and received by Finnish business professionals indicated that these subjects sent nearly one third (27%) of outgoing international messages by traditional mail, and nearly fifty per cent (48%) via the fax machine, while a third (33%) of the incoming mail came by traditional mail and 45% via the fax machine (Louhiala-Salminen 1995:68-70). The study did not indicate what genres were transmitted via the fax machine.

What are the situations in international contexts that cause a written message to be preferred over a spoken contact, such as a telephone call, and a properly staged letter to be preferred over a casual memo? These are complex issues and encompass e.g. the equivocality of the message (Trevino et al. 1990:177) and the time pressure, as well as time differences caused by the geographical locations of companies. Moreover, with the diffusion of the fax machine, written messages may have gained ground over telephone contacts in those international situations in which the interactants are not very proficient in the language used, since using a written form may reduce the risks of miscommunication (Luoma 1993:72). In addition, respect for the written word may have some influence on the choice of medium.

Although the more "disposable" modes of exchanging messages may be more frequent than the letter in daily professional activities, the respect felt for the letter is shown in the fact that it is chosen as the medium for messages involving managerially weighty situations. This seems to be more obvious in the United Kingdom than in the Nordic countries, for example. In fact, it is claimed that Britain is a writing society, as opposed to some other countries, such as Greece, where transactions are dealt with orally (Sifianou 1989:540). Finnish export managers attempting to create contacts in Britain soon find that a prospective British customer still expects the initial approach to be made in writing (Hallenberg 1990:9-10). Although the phone and the computer are the major media of communication in the United States, letters and memos as items of managerial communication are objects of constant interest, especially in education (for details, see Russ, Daft & Lengel 1990).

4.   The study

4.1. *Data*

This paper is an elaboration of certain aspects incorporated in my recent study on business writing (Yli-Jokipii 1994), for which I compiled a corpus of over 500 British, American, and Finnish business documents. Nearly 400 of these were authentic business letters and telefax messages, and 150 texts came from teaching material. The present paper refers to only the British and Finnish data from this corpus. Of these 225 texts, 150 are authentic British letters or telefax messages and 75 are authentic Finnish letters.

To obtain the material, various business companies were invited to submit samples of their interactive writing, letters or telefax messages. The companies concerned represent approximately twenty branches of business, ranging from clothing to construction and from metal and heavy industry to foodstuffs and travel. The samples were requested and released on the understanding that the contents would be treated with proper discretion, whole texts would not be reproduced and any items that might identify the companies would be erased. Some companies required a written promise of this.

In order to investigate the role of social distance in the linguistic profile, the data were compiled so that half of the British material was that exchanged between familiar interactants, apparent in the first name occurring in the greeting, while 75 were written to readers who were greeted by last name or no name was identified at all. The texts in which the reader is identified by using the first name are henceforth referred to as the T level texts, and correspondingly, the term V level refers to texts in which the addressee is identified by last name or by no name at all.

The Finnish data consisted of 75 documents written by Finnish business professionals to their colleagues in Finnish. The Finnish data represent only the formal, V level discourse, because it turned out that there was no written correspondence available on the familiar, first name basis between Finnish companies in Finland that would match the definition of the genre set for this study. It seems that there are few situations that would entail written messages between familiar interactants in Finnish domestic trade, which is what the Finnish data represent. The phone may be a more likely medium of communication in Finnish companies operating in Finland.

4.2. *Requests*

The identification and analysis of requests was based on their definition as stretches of language which seek a verbal, physical, or cognitive response. They were approached as messages in discourse, and not as isolated speech acts. Requests were invariably looked at and assigned a meaning in relation to their context. Similarly, the letters in which they occurred were treated as elements in interaction and not as texts in isolation.

The analysis of the 225 texts in the two British and one Finnish group produced a total of 832 requests, of which 302 occurred in the British T level texts, 283 in the British V level texts, and 246 in the Finnish V level texts.

4.3. *Theoretical framework*

The present approach is *eclectic,* which means that we are not confined to one individual theory but employ several approaches to achieve our purpose. It is also *discourse analytical* in the sense that messages are regarded as elements in the text and not as isolated sentences. Moreover, messages are viewed as components in interaction, and the contextual and cultural, user-oriented elements are brought into the investigation as well. This gives the work a *pragmatic* outlook. Further, I believe that language operates on several levels simultaneously, such as the textual, logical, and interpersonal level. This claim is in broad agreement with Halliday (1973), who calls these levels language metafunctions.

The present approach is also in agreement with those scholars who claim that *description* alone is not satisfactory in a linguistic study, and that there should be an *explanation* of the findings as well (Candlin 1987:23-25; Nyyssönen 1992:320; Bhatia 1993:10-12; see also Fairclough 1991:26, who identifies an interpretive stage between description and explanation). Explaining the findings concerning requests requires the scholar to look for reasons for the linguistic directness and indirectness, which derive from the discrepancy between the communicative function and the linguistic form employed to realize that function.

Brown & Levinson's (1987) work on politeness universals offers valuable insights for explaining linguistic indirectness. The theory sets out from the assumption that the degree of indirectness derives from the options available to the addressee in order for him or her to maintain 'face'. The more a linguistic act threatens the addressee's face, the more likely the speaker or writer is to choose a strategy that minimizes the face-threatening effect. 'Positive politeness' is oriented towards the positive self-image that the addressee wishes to have. This strategy is normally employed between intimates, while 'negative politeness' is characterized by expressions of linguistic deference and is easily associated with formality and restraint. The strategy employed must be in proportion to the degree of the imposition, i.e. what is requested, to the familiarity between the interactants, and to their hierarchical position in relation to each other (Brown & Levinson 1987:74-84). Thus, the notions of distance and power were used as social variables in the present study and were treated quantitatively, while it was not possible to place the degree of imposition, i.e. the weight of the request, into rigid categories. The weight of the request is, namely, a sensitive notion from both a cultural and a contextual point of view.

The words *polite* or *politeness* are also culturally sensitive. They deserve a definition here, because these notions have created much confusion, controversy, and misinterpretation among scholars, especially when used across cultures (see e.g. Matsumoto 1989; Watts, Ide & Ehlich 1992; Wierzbicka 1991:67-130). These concepts will, first of all, be employed here in the social and cultural sense of the words as referring to all conventionally well-mannered, civil, and considerate behaviour normally expected from a well-behaved individual in a given society or user group. The use of the word polite(ness) then does not presuppose a commitment to what such behaviour is like. On the contrary, it will be used as meaning *polite(ness) as the society or user group concerned may define it.*

5. Findings

5.1. *British and English*

Distance

The observations concerning the British data will be given first and these will be followed by an account of the findings based on the material in Finnish.

The T level texts in the British data occur primarily in on-deal contexts, which cover the transactional situations after the order and are then mostly connected with packing, transport, and delivery or payment arrangements. The need for making requests on the T level is greater than on the V level, and so is the density of requests in texts. The high density of requests in the familiar level texts, compared to the formal level, shows that the former contain little redundant discourse and persuasive rhetoric.

Making requests to familiar, T level readers is a problem for the British business writer. Interactive business writing in English lacks the repertoire which would be suitable for making impositions on people at a reduced social distance. The familiar choices belong to spoken discourse, which again involves the problem of social distance. For example, the modal initial fomulaic requestive phrases (*can/will you; would/could you do X*) in writing seem too authoritative to be comfortably employed in writing to familiar interactants. However, as Brown & Levinson (1987:70) point out, such conventionalized indirectness should be the very choice for making requests between familiar interactants.

The problem of making requests on the familiar level emerges in different ways. One of them is the use of evasive ways of making requests. Evasion is an indirect strategy which offers the addressee options for not understanding the message as a request. In Brown & Levinson's (1987:69) terms, the request is given off record. The evasion is effected primarily on the interpersonal level of language, by failing to indicate who should perform the action requested, as examples (5) and (6) will show.

(5) *It is very much hoped that you can see your way to supporting us in the presentation of our equipment at [the exhibition]* (BrT 3)

(6) *it is important that the samples in the ... reflect* (BrT 42)

Another evasive method is the use of a performative verb which does not entail naming the reader as the actor of the request. This can be effected with a reader-oriented perspective, as illustrated in example (7).

(7)   *we are sending you ... and would ask you to credit ...* (BrT 38)

A further indirect way of requesting emerging in the British T level data is the use of the phrasal verb *something is to be done*. This occurs quite frequently in routine contexts in which the writers give instructions regarding production, packing, etc. Examples (8) and (9) illustrate this.

(8)   *All prints are to be reduced to 87%* (BrT 15)

(9)   *All running heads are to be deleted* (BrT 20)

The scarcity of conventional formulae in making requests is a characteristic of T level requests in the British data. The conventional formulae, such as *routine declaratives*, which are typically recommended by British textbooks, are avoided by real-life British writers.[3] The term *routine declarative* refers to requests which are issued in a declarative form, containing e.g. an anticipation statement (*look forward, hope*), need statement (*need, require*), self-obligation statement (*grateful, obliged, appreciate*), a performative verb (*request, ask*), or a modal of necessity (*must, should, ought*). It is possible that these are too conventionally polite, as it were, for a reduced social distance. Too much politeness, when it is not expected — as is the case in the T level context — intensifies the show of power and this may not be the writer's intention.

The evasive orientation and the indirectness effected through writer orientation illustrate respectful discourse strategies, which Brown & Levinson (1987) label *negative politeness*. Such strategies use linguistic items which are open to interpretation, and, in the case of requests, make it possible for the reader to choose not to understand the message as a request at all.

Power
Power is embedded in at least two sets of linguistic choices. The first concerns the syntactic form. The imperative form is richest in its force of signalling power because it leaves the addressee no options. Certain interrogative forms, especially wh-questions, have the same challenging property. The more indirect forms do not signal power because they do not contain a linguistic challenge. The avoidance of linguistic challenges may then be interpreted as refraining from signalling coercion which would display power. Linguistic challenges occur in this British data in power-neutral situations, but diminish

in asymmetric situations, while the negative power situations contain fewest direct requests. Likewise, modal-initial forms, which represent the highly routinized formulaic forms of requesting, seem to be considered less suitable for negative power situations in the British T and V groups alike. This is strange, because the conventional indirectness of modal-initial forms is judged to represent the most polite forms of requesting in some studies with more limited or no contextual elaboration.

A notable finding is the low frequency of the passive orientation in negative power situations. It is possible that the passive voice in requests, while it brings indirectness and, therefore, should sound polite in Brown & Levinson's terms, brings a distancing effect to the message at the same time, as example (10) may indicate. Distance, in turn, might easily be associated with power and authority.

> (10) *[products] are required on [date]. To be packed in parcels of 20 [pieces]* (BrT 20)

The passive form in requesting obviously encompasses two conflicting qualities. If the focus of observation is on the scale of explicity and implicity, these messages tilt towards the implicit end because the actor of the request is generally not mentioned at all. Such requests contain a minimal threat to the addressee's face and should be considered acceptable also in negative power situations. On the other hand, if the focus is on the distancing effect of the message, it is obviously regarded as unsuitable. Coding linguistic distance, in Britain at least, seems to be avoided in negative power situations. This may derive from the historical reasons explained by Richardson & Liggett (1993: 118-120), as the linguistic illusion of distance was intentional in the discourse of the ruling classes.

5.2. Finnish

Distance

Social distance is a more static issue in Finnish business writing than it is in English. There are two reasons for this. First, in Finland business letters, as defined for the purpose of this study, occur only on the formal, V level, as explained in Section 4.1. These letters tend to occur in official, even legally binding situations, such as quotations or orders, which do not invite communicative creativity. The messages are seen as exchanges between companies and the individuals have no major role in the composition of the text. Where requests are concerned, the Finnish writer primarily has a repertoire of writer-oriented or evasive phrases to indicate a request.

Power
The Finnish data do not contain linguistic signs of power even in those situations in which the writer possesses positive power in the role of buyer. The Finnish texts contain few linguistic challenges, such as imperatives or interrogative forms. In fact, only two per cent of the 246 requests in the Finnish data had the imperative form, and even these occurred in messages which involved benefit to the addressee.

Another characteristic of Finnish writing on the formal level takes us to the interpersonal area of discourse. There is a distinct absence of reference to *other*. The Finnish writer also avoids referring to *self* by the first person singular reference, which in Finnish could be done with a pronoun plus suffix, or with a suffix alone. Exclusive *we* (*me* or *-mme*) occurs primarily with the performative verb (*pyydämme*, request-we, 'please'). The focus of action may also be on non-animate items such as the name of the writer's or reader's firm, or the transactional situation. Examples (11) and (12) will illustrate this.

(11) *Hinta on ilmoitettava liikevaihtoveroineen* (FinV 2)
       Price is quote-must value-added-tax-with
       'Please include VAT in the quoted price'

(12) *Tarjouksesta tulee ilmetä* (FinV 16)
       Quotation-of shall to-show
       'Please include the following details in your quotation...'

These examples also show that the strategies employed in them have a distancing effect on discourse because of the absence of a reference to the writer or the reader. We might indeed wonder whether some of the reserved quality attributed to the Finnish culture derives from native English-speakers' experiences of situations in which Finnish people have transferred their native language strategies to their English. Not only do the Finnish speakers and writers try to avoid pinpointing the person in impositions, such as requests and apologies, but the Finnish language is also well stocked with means of avoiding personal reference (Hakulinen 1987:142). The avoidance of mentioning the reader, especially, is certainly a characteristic of formal business writing in the Finnish language and culture.

6. Conclusion

This article discussed the concepts of power and distance in business writing, and explained how these concepts are manifested in British and Finnish business organizations. Both distance and power were approached from the linguistic and non-linguistic point of view. The non-linguistic focus illustrated how social power and social distance serve as components in the corporate context. The linguistic part of this article introduced certain items which seem to signal power and distance, and reported findings of a study which investigated the linguistic variation which may be explained by the quality of social power and with the social distance between the interactants. The linguistic observations were based on the realizations of requests because they are sensitive to both the extra- and intra-linguistic aspects of power and distance. The data came from an extensive corpus of authentic business letters and telefax messages.

The cultural part of the article was thus concerned with authentic business writing in Britain and in Finland. The linguistic part had a contrastive nature, because it focused on native English and Finnish speakers' writing. The two languages are quite different. English belongs to the Indo-European language group, and is related to several other European languages, such as French, German, and the other Germanic languages spoken in the Nordic countries, i.e. Swedish, Danish, and Norwegian. Finnish, however, is a non-Indo-European language, which operates on totally different principles from the Germanic languages.

Social, contextual power and distance appear differently in these two cultures and languages. The Finnish writer is sensitive to the power quality which prevails in the transactional situation. Even in situations with positive power quality, the Finnish writer seldom uses linguistic devices which would assume power. There is, by convention, a distinct sense of distance in Finnish business writing, and the writers have little room for the kind of creativity in issuing requests that their British colleagues have. In Britain, social distance is a source of variation, which appears on the contextual level as well as in linguistic terms. Compared to the clear variation effected by the social distance of the interactants, British business writers seem to be somewhat oblivious to the contextual power qualities. This occurs also in situations in which the distribution of power is quite clear, and the discourse produced by the interactants in their roles as buyers and sellers would be expected to show signs of consciousness of the imbalance in power.

Writing between familiar interactants, at least as far as issuing impositions such as requests is concerned, seems to intensify linguistic problems for English-speaking business professionals. The problems are related to this genre in particular, and to the distinct character of interactive business writing in society. The familiar, T level writing occurs, namely, in business in such situations in which the context would entail using the linguistic repertoire assigned for discourse between well-acquainted individuals. Yet the repertoire available for such situations belongs to spoken discourse and is appropriate in writing only between family members and relatives. We must remember that professional writing has developed for formal situations, and the need for informal register in professional writing is so recent that no comfortable and indisputable linguistic stock has had time to develop. It may be argued that the Plain English Movement and the textbook advice to adopt the you-attitude for example, entail everyday style, and such argument is naturally quite justified. But it is these delicate, face-threatening situations, with underlying professional demands, that contain predicaments for the English-speaking business writer.

A further cultural observation arises from the findings reported here. In Finland and in Finnish, distance is a characteristic of business writing on both extra- and intra-linguistic accounts. Much of the distance derives from the conventions of the genre in Finland, because the letters are written in formal situations to document the information concerned in the transactional stage. The genre thus bears some resemblance to legal writing, and as such there is little room for creativity and individual preferences. If transferred to English, the discourse used by Finnish writers may seem oddly distant, and the English-speaking reader may decode a sense of exaggerated avoidance. Some readers may even read withdrawal and alienness into such discourse. There is, therefore, a danger of linguistic and cultural ethnocentricity in assigning universal or even cultural values to linguistic strategies without well grounded evidence. There is also a danger in the set-up of the framework for a cross-linguistic analysis. Fortunately, business scholars and teachers are increasingly aware of the dangers of making sweeping generalizations about the characteristics of cultures and languages with too limited focus and too little evidence.

There is much room for future research into interactive business writing in general, as everyone involved in such research knows. In particular, power and distance are such complex issues that the present report is only the tip of an iceberg. We need to ask further, for example, how clear the cultural differences are in coding power. Is it perhaps possible that the Finnish writer codes social, contextual power with linguistic distance, and not with linguistic challenge and directness? These are among the questions that deserve further research with a differently controlled material and perhaps complemented with user interviews. Finally, there is the vast number of questions connected with the genres of business writing which deserve scholarly attention. The more "disposable" genres borne by the electronic exchange of messages in the business environment are among the foremost of these.

Notes

1. The question form *why should I* is an example of the exercise of power. Another is the use of an obscene word *shit* which degrades the addressee and leaves the impression of the unworthiness of the recipient firm.
    The second example is written in the same situation in which the writer possesses power brought about by the transactional situation, but linguistically, the message does not contain elements of power. On the contrary, the writer uses language which seems to give power to the addressee. Choosing the form of an apology is one way of submissive linguistic behaviour, using the very neutral word *inform* is another, and using the hedging *there seems to be something wrong* rather than saying bluntly that there is something wrong, are examples of how the writer may decline from linguistic expressions which assume the power of the writer. Finally, the generic expression *there is* and the avoidance of all references to the recipient's firm may in some contexts be indications of avoidance of power.

2. When the examples used in this paper represent the data of the study, the sources are indicated as follows: Br = British data; Fin = Finnish data; V = formal, V level text; T = familiar, T level text. The distinction between the formal and familiar texts is explained in Sections 2.2.2. and 3.1.

3. The percentage of these routine declaratives in the British T level material was 29, and in the British V level material 38. By comparison, 41 per cent of the British textbook requests investigated in Yli-Jokipii (1994) were realized with a declarative form of the type *we hope to hear from you, or we look forward to ...*

References

Anson, Chris M. and L. Lee Forsberg. 1990. "Moving beyond the academic community: transitional stages in professional writing". *Written Communication* 7: 200-231.
Berkenkotter, Carol and Thomas N. Huckin. 1995. *Genre Knowledge in Disciplinary Communication: Cognition/Culture/Power.* Hillsdale, N.J.: Lawrence Erlbaum Associates.

Bhatia, Vijay K. 1993. *Analysing Genre: Language Use in Professional Settings*. London/ New York: Longman.

Bogoch, Bryna. 1994. "Power, distance and solidarity: models of professional-client interaction in an Israeli legal aid setting". *Discourse & Society* 5: 65-88.

Brown, Gillian and George Yule. 1983. *Discourse Analysis*. Cambridge: Cambridge University Press.

Brown, Penelope and Stephen C. Levinson. 1987. *Politeness. Some Universals in Language Usage*. (Studies in Interactional Sociolinguistics 4.) Cambridge: Cambridge University Press. First published in: Esther N. Goody (ed.), *Questions and Politeness: Strategies in Social Interaction*. Cambridge: Cambridge University Press [1978], pp. 56-289.

Brown, Roger and Albert Gilman. 1960. "The pronouns of power and solidarity". In: Thomas A. Sebeok (ed.), *Style in Language*. Cambridge, Mass.: MIT Press, pp. 253-276.

Candlin, Christopher. 1987. "Beyond description to explanation in cross-cultural discourse". In: Larry Smith (ed.), *Discourse Across Cultures; Strategies in World Englishes*. New York: Prentice Hall, pp. 22-35.

Cherry, Roger D. 1988. "Politeness in written persuasion". *Journal of Pragmatics* 12: 63-81.

Couture, Barbara. 1992. "Categorizing professional discourse: engineering, administrative, and technical/professional writing". *Journal of Business and Technical Communication* 6: 5-37.

De Rycker, Teun. 1987. "Turns at writing: the organization of correspondence". In: Jef Verschueren and Marcella Pertuchelli-Papi (eds.), *The Pragmatic Perspective: Selected Papers from the 1985 International Pragmatics Conference*. Amsterdam: Benjamins, pp. 613-647.

Fairclough, Norman. 1989. *Language and Power*. London/New York: Longman.

Graham, Margaret Baker and Carol David. 1996. "Power and politeness: administrative writing in an organized anarchy". *Journal of Business and Technical Communication* 10: 5-27.

Hagge, John and Charles Kostelnick. 1989. "Linguistic politeness in professional prose: a discourse analysis of auditors' suggestion letters, with implications for business communication pedagogy". *Written Communication* 6: 313-339.

Hakulinen, Auli. 1987. "Avoiding personal reference in Finnish". In: Jef Verschueren and Marcella Bertuchelli-Papi (eds.), *The Pragmatic Perspective: Selected Papers from the 1985 International Pragmatics Conference*. Amsterdam: Benjamins, pp. 141-153.

Hallenberg, Juha. 1990. "Liikemiehenä Englannissa" [Doing business in England], *Horisontti* [Horizon]. Lontoon suomalaisen merimieskirkon & Suomen kirkon killan uutislehti [Journal of the Finnish Church Guild & the Finnish Seamen's Mission in London], 9: 9-10.

Halliday, M.A.K. 1973. *Explorations in the Functions of Language*. London: Edward Arnold.

Halmari, Helena. 1993. "Intercultural business telephone conversations: a case of Finns vs Anglo-Americans". *Applied Linguistics* 14: 408-430.

Hofstede, Geert. 1980. *Culture's Consequences. International Differences in Work-*

Related Values. Beverly Hills/London: Sage.

Leech, Geoffrey. 1983. *The Principles of Pragmatics*. Harlow: Longman.

Louhiala-Salminen, Leena. 1995. *"Drop me a fax, will you?": A Study of Written Business Communication*. (Reports from the Department of English 10.) Jyväskylä: University of Jyväskylä.

Louhiala-Salminen, Leena. 1996. "The business communication classroom vs reality: what should we teach today?" *English for Specific Purposes* 15: 37-51.

Luoma, Sari. 1993. "Correspondence - korrespondens: writing tasks in English and Swedish in the marketing section of a middle-sized Finnish manufacturing company". In: Kari Sajavaara and Sauli Takala (eds.), *Finns as Learners of English: Three Studies*. (Jyväskylä Cross-Language Studies 16.) Jyväskylä: University of Jyväskylä, pp. 1-18.

Matsumoto, Yoshiko. 1989. "Politeness and conversational universals - observations from Japanese". *Multilingua* 8: 207-221.

Moore, Patrick. 1992. "When politeness is fatal: technical communication and the *Challenger* accident". *Journal of Business and Technical Communication* 6: 269-292.

Neumann, Ingrid. 1995. "Realization of requests in intercultural negotiations: on pragmatic method". *Hermes* 15: 31-52.

Nyyssönen, Heikki. 1990. "Lexis in discourse and the acquisition of socio-cultural competence in the target language". In: Heikki Nyyssönen, Leena Kuure, Elise Kärkkäinen and Pirkko Raudaskoski (eds.), *Proceedings from the 2nd Finnish Seminar on Discourse Analysis*. (Publications of the Department of English 9.) Oulu: University of Oulu, pp. 14-26.

Nyyssönen, Heikki. 1992. "Linguistic study in its socio-cultural context", in: Heikki Nyyssönen and Leena Kuure (eds.), *Acquisition of Language, Acquisition of Culture*. (Publications de l'association finlandaise de linguistique appliquée 50.) Jyväskylä, pp. 309-322.

Odell, Lee, Dixie Goswami and Anne Herrington. 1983. "The discourse-based interview: a procedure for exploring the tacit knowledge of writers in nonacademic settings". In: Peter Mosenthal, Lynne Tamor and Sean A. Walmsley (eds.), *Research on Writing: Principles and Methods*. New York: Longman, pp. 221-236.

Östman, Jan-Ola. 1987. "Implicit involvement in interactive writing". In: Jef Verschueren and Marcella Pertuchelli-Papi (eds.), *The Pragmatic Perspective: Selected Papers from the 1985 International Pragmatics Conference*. Amsterdam: Benjamins, pp. 155-178.

Richardson, Malcolm and Sarah Liggett. 1993. "Power relations, technical writing theory, and workplace writing". *Journal of Business and Technical Communication* 7: 112-137.

Roloff, Michael E. 1981. *Interpersonal Communication: The Social Exchange Approach*. Beverly Hills, CA/London: Sage.

Russ, Gail S., Richard L. Daft and Robert H. Lengel. 1990. "Media selection and managerial characteristics in organizational communications". *Management Communication Quarterly* 4: 151-175.

Shelby, Annette. 1986. "The theoretical bases of persuasion: a critical introduction". *Journal of Business Communication* 23: 5-29.

Sifianou, Maria. 1989. "On the telephone again! Differences in telephone behaviour: England versus Greece". *Language in Society* 18: 527-544.

Sims, Brenda R. and Stephen Guice. 1992. "Differences between business letters from native and non-native speakers of English". *Journal of Business Communication* 29: 23-39.

Swales, John. 1990. *Genre Analysis: English in Academic and Research Settings.* Cambridge: Cambridge University Press.

Trevino, Linda K., Robert H. Lengel, Wayne Bodensteiner, Edwin A. Gerloff and Nan K. Muir. 1990. "The richness imperative and cognitive style: the role of individual differences in media choice behavior". *Management Communication Quarterly* 4: 176-197.

Tuffs, Richard. 1995. "The language of meetings: are we meeting the need?" In: John Bennett (ed.), *Towards the next millenium: Challenges and Opportunities in Language Training, Business and Multicultural Contexts.* s.l.: University of St. Gallen, pp. 126-135.

Ulijn, Jan M. and Xiangling Li. 1995. "Is interrupting impolite? Some temporal aspects of turn-taking in Chinese - Western and other intercultural business encounters". *Text* 15: 589-627.

Watts, Richard J., Sachiko Ide and Konrad Ehlich (eds.) . 1992. *Politeness in Language. Studies in its History, Theory and Practice.* Berlin/New York: Mouton de Guyter.

Wierzbicka, Anna. 1991. *Cross-Cultural Pragmatics. The Semantics of Human Interaction.* Berlin/New York: Mouton de Gruyter.

Williams, Marion. 1988. "Language taught for meetings and language used in meetings: is there anything in common?" *Applied Linguistics* 9: 45-58.

Yli-Jokipii, Hilkka. 1994. *Requests in Professional Discourse: A Cross-Cultural Study of British, American and Finnish Business Writing.* (Annales Academiae Scientiarum Fennicae. Dissertationes Humanarum Litterarum 71.) Helsinki: Suomalainen Tiedeakatemia.

Cultural values and
Irish economic performance

W. Fred Scharf and Séamus Mac Mathúna
University of Ulster, Northern Ireland

0. Introduction

In this paper we proceed from the understanding that national and organisational cultural values held by managers, administrators, and workers affect
the ways in which they behave, and that these values have an important
impact on factors such as motivation, initiative, job satisfaction, and patterns
of interaction (McClelland 1961; Baumol 1968). We suggest that in the
Republic of Ireland there has been a readjustment in the emphasis attached to
those cultural values which appear to contribute to the creation of a favourable environment in which economic expansion can occur. In the case of
Northern Ireland, we suggest that the circumstances are of such a nature as to
have led to emphasis being placed on cultural characteristics which detract
from the creation and development of conditions favourable to growth. In
order to test the validity of these assumptions, we begin by briefly setting out
both the recent and present economic trends in both parts of the island and
proceed thereafter to discuss factors such as individualism and collectivism,
uncertainty avoidance, and high-context/low-context discourse and communication.

In our discussion of cultural factors, we draw in particular on the work of
Hofstede, who carried out research on the attitudes and behavioural patterns
of employees in different countries who worked at a variety of levels in
subsidiaries of the multinational corporation IBM (Hofstede 1980, 1994).
Hofstede identified four cultural dimensions on which countries could be
plotted, namely, power distance, individualism versus collectivism, masculin-

ity and femininity, and uncertainty avoidance. Long-term versus short-term orientation was added later as another important dimension. Due to the paucity of information presently available, the assessment of these values in respect of the Irish experience is quite difficult and complicated and much more research needs to be carried out before definite conclusions can be reached with regard to their effect on economic performance (Murray 1981; O'Farrell 1986; Hirschman 1965). In addition to Hofstede's work, we also draw on other cultural and management studies and on our own observations.

1. Economic trends

In recent years the Republic of Ireland has witnessed a period of record economic growth, and it is probable that the criteria for joining the European single currency in January 1999 will be met. The political decision to join has already been made. While the global market dictates for the most part the present circumstances of Ireland's small open economy, the policies adopted by successive governments since the middle of the 1980s have made a not insignificant contribution to the turnaround in Irish economic affairs and the present ongoing success. These include the provision of a stable environment for foreign investors in the form of certainty in regard to low corporate taxation, which has been gained by imposing a level of personal taxation much higher than that in Great Britain, three-year social contracts with employers and workers which trade cuts in personal taxation for moderation in pay increases, low inflation rates, major injections of capital from the European Union's social and structural funds which have been invested in large scale modernisation of the infrastructure, and a qualitatively better educational system than in the past (Fitzgerald 1997).

Despite the opening up of the economy at the end of the 1950s, and the subsequent improvements in living standards, economic performance since the formation of the state had not been particularly successful when compared with other developed West European countries. Ireland was still towards the bottom of the European Community economic league at the end of the 1980s. The economy, however, had developed from one largely dependent on agriculture and a single export market, the United Kingdom, to a scenario in which living standards were rising and the country was becoming a global player in terms of export destinations. As Kennedy (1993:16) points out:

At independence, over 90 per cent of Irish exports went to the UK. No other European country was so heavily dependent on a single market, and this dependence proved to be a disadvantage given the poor performance of the UK this century. (See Table 1)

Table 1. Composition of Irish merchandise exports (%)

	1929	1950	1991
Commodity			
Food and drink	86	80	23
Manufactures		7	70
Other	14	13	7
Total	100	100	100
Destination			
UK	92	88	32
Other EC	3	7	42
US	2	2	9
Other	3	3	17
Total	100	100	100

Source: Statistical Abstract of Ireland and Trade Statistics; Kennedy 1993:17

Due to this trade dependence on the UK, Irish economic performance was generally compared with the former and not with the rest of Europe. As Table 2 shows, the increase in GDP per worker between 1973, when Ireland became a member of the EC, and 1990 was quite impressive. This increase in productivity and the improvement in export trade was due primarily to the contribution of overseas firms which located in Ireland. This in turn led to substantial income flows, reducing the GNP per worker accordingly. When the high level of unemployment, which in 1990 was the highest in the EC at 31 per cent, is added to the equation one arrives at a figure for GNP per head of population which had hardly changed during this period. In terms of living standards, therefore, Ireland had fallen behind all the major EU member states with the exception of Portugal and Greece.

Table 2. Productivity and income per capita in Ireland relative to the European community

	1973	1990
	EC 12 = 100	
GDP per worker	69	89
GNP per worker	69	80
GNP per head of population	59	62

Sources: EC Annual Economic Report 1991/92 and OECD Labour Force Statistics, 1970-90; Kennedy 1993:19.

Since the beginning of the 1990s to date, Irish economic development has been quite remarkable. Real GDP growth in 1995 was 10.3 per cent compared with the EU average of 2.5 per cent and the forecast growth for 1996 was 7.3 per cent in comparison with a EU average of 1.6 per cent. The inflation rate of 1.7 per cent for 1996, which was also the predicted rate for 1997, was also well below the EU average of 2.6 per cent in 1996. Unemployment, although still quite high, at 13.1 per cent in 1995 and 12.3 per cent in 1996, is moving down in comparison to a slight upward trend in the rest of the EU, from 11.2 per cent in 1995 to 11.4 per cent in 1996 (Central Bank of Ireland, 1996).

Assessments of the Northern Irish economy tend to be rather gloomy. Hutton (1994:1), for example, argues that 'Northern Ireland is locked in an unrelieved downward economic spiral', while Munck (1993:64) is even more pessimistic: 'Northern Ireland does seem to be reaching the end of the road as a viable economic entity'. When economic growth lagged behind Great Britain's in the mid-1980s, it appeared that the economy was irredeemable and would forever be dependent on subsidies and government support. Gudgin (1994) has argued recently, however, that 'manufacturing firms grew rapidly towards the end of the 1980s boom in the UK. They have weathered the national recession better than their counterparts in Great Britain, and are expanding faster in the recovery from recession'. He has to admit, however, that 'many serious economic problems remain' (1994:21). In 1994 the GDP was Stg £13.2 billion, which represents only 2.3 per cent of the total UK GDP. GDP per head of population was the lowest in the UK at Stg £8,025, the UK average being £9,763.

One of the conclusions which can be drawn from a comparison of the two economies is that foreign direct investment (FDI) has grown much faster in the Republic than in the North. Since both parts of the country share a cluster of similarities, including the provision of incentive packages to investors, conflict and instability are clearly the single most important factors militating against the attraction of inward investment and the growth of the economic sector in the latter. Woelger (1994) estimates that political unrest has cost Northern Ireland 50,000 jobs.

The weaknesses of the private sector are cushioned by an inflated public sector: the latter is the largest by far of any region in the UK, accounting for over a third of total employment in Northern Ireland. In the Republic, on the other hand, less than a quarter of employment is public sector based. Furthermore, in the manufacturing sector, output has grown much faster in the Republic than in the North. Between 1985 and 1993, this amounted to an annual growth rate of 7.5 per cent in the Republic, compared with 1.9 per cent in Northern Ireland. The fastest growing sectors in the Republic were high technology industries, such as Electrical Equipment (including computers) at 14 per cent and Chemicals at 12.6 per cent per year. In fact, one fifth of all greenfield industrial investment in Europe located in the Republic in 1995. In Northern Ireland, low technology labour intensive sectors performed strongly, particularly Textiles and Clothing, which employs approximately a quarter of the total workforce in the manufacturing sector.

The recent paramilitary ceasefires and the ensuing Peace Process have had an enormous impact on business confidence. There are great expectations that Northern Ireland may be entering into a new phase of economic development which will be underpinned by a shift to a more enterprising culture. The resumption of hostilities would undoubtedly have a negative effect on economic prospects. Peace and stability alone, however, do not guarantee success, as is clear from the experience of the Republic and other small economies. Northern Ireland has a particularly conservative and inward-looking culture which adversely affects the situation. Due to the conflict, or 'The Troubles' as they are known in Ireland, this conservatism has become more accentuated and has led to an over-emphasis being placed on values which have a negative affect on the ability to react to global market trends and forces. The people of the Republic of Ireland, on the other hand, have enthusiastically embraced the ideal of closer integration of the European states and have displayed the characteristics of conciliation, co-operativeness, good neighbourliness, and friendship towards their partners. These characteristics have helped in fostering positive attitudes on the part of foreign investors and in securing financial support from the other states of the Union.

2. Individualism and collectivism

Individualism may be defined as pertaining to countries in which individuals are loosely bound together and are expected to look after themselves and their immediate family; collectivism pertains to countries in which people are bound together in strong cohesive ingroups which protect them in exchange for unquestioning loyalty (Hofstede 1994:51).

Society in early and medieval Ireland was rural, tribal, hierarchical, and collective. Group activities were dominant, responsibility was shared between members of the kin group, and the emphasis was on shared ingroup beliefs and co-operation. While isolated individual performance was secondary, the individual was nevertheless a personalised microcosm of the greater universal totality, linked in popular cultural orientation and practices to the rest of life. The breakdown of the old political and social order in the seventeenth century brought about a fragmentation in the collective practices and strengths of the community, leading to the emergence of deep ambiguity and lack of security. This manifested itself in various ways, such as in the relationship between landlord and tenant, farmer and labourer, and the interplay between the Irish and English languages, the former being the language of the vast majority of the people, the latter that of the new power mandarins. As a colonised people, the Irish lost control of economic, political, and administrative power. Upward mobility in society depended on the acquisition of a new tongue and a new set of cultural values; religious and linguistic discrimination were rife. Since the Reformation had failed to take hold, Roman Catholicism became the dominant cultural symbol which bound people together. Collective mentality manifested itself at the national level in the nineteenth century in the exercise of political power in order to achieve the emancipation of Catholics and the reacquisition of the land. The rise of political nationalism, underpinned by a redefinition of cultural considerations and values, eventually led to the formation of the Irish Free State (now the Irish Republic) in 1922 and Northern Ireland, a constituent part of the Government of the United Kingdom.

The long and bitter struggle for the land, together with the principle of inheritance to the eldest son, not only contributed to the already dire problem of emigration but accentuated the conservatism and localism of the traditional culture and led to an obsession with what has been called 'the possessor principle' (Lee 1989:392ff.). This expressed itself in an extreme attachment to the land, which was equated with security. Individualism, in the form of rights to tenure, far outweighed the performance ethic. Prestige and rank in society depended on possession, not on the productive output which might result from ownership. The policy of protectionism and the cultivation of the rural ideal which were followed by successive governments between the 1930s and the 1950s tended to underpin the possessor ethic. Lethargy and inefficiency were endemic to large sections of the socio-economic system. Although individualism was strong, it was grafted on to typical elements of the collectivist ethic in which neighbourly co-operation, networking and kinship favours dominated. The family farm and the family firm ruled supreme (Lee 1989:393).

In Hofstede's study of IBM employees in 49 countries and 4 regions, the Republic of Ireland was ranked 12 on the individualism index, above Germany (Federal Republic) which was ranked 13 and below France and Sweden ranked 10-11, and Great Britain ranked 3. The USA was ranked 1, Guatemala 53. Given that the remnants of the collectivist ethic were still strong in the Republic until the 1960s, this may be considered by some observers as a particularly high score. It may be explained in part by the fact that the IBM respondents belonged to the middle class, that the standard of living had risen significantly, that the legacy of the possessor principle was still strong and, perhaps most importantly, that Ireland is a strongly humanist country. In comparison with other west European countries and developed systems with a high level of individualism, however, the Republic was poor, had a peripheral economy and was towards the bottom of the rank ordering. Individualism lacked the drive and initiative associated with it in wealthier economies and the fragmentation of the collectivist mentality ensured that business ventures were not linked sufficiently closely with social responsibility and viewed as national assets contributing to the country's wealth and well-being. Not surprisingly, indigenous business could not compete internationally and by the 1980's no significant native managerial cadre had emerged.

On a more positive note, however, there had been a stable form of democratic government since the formation of the state and the new modern industrialised society had been established. The coherence of the inter-dependent parts of the system had now become one of the critical factors relevant to sustaining and developing economic growth and social cohesion. In the second phase of modernisation, from the end of the 1950s until the 1980s, individual initiative was reflected in a willingness to work hard within established frameworks, such as those of the state and existing management structures, but not to experiment and develop new initiatives. As Fogarty (1982:37f.) points out, there was 'a tendency to assume that it is leaders' business to lead, that "strong" leaders are required, and that, whether at work or at home, it is a citizen's business to get on with his or her own life rather than to initiate new things.' This view of leadership is connected both with Hofstede's dimension of power distance and with that of individualism versus collectivism. It is similar to the Anglo-American model of management, which relies heavily on leadership, team-building, and individual achievement. This model does not, however, necessarily encourage and promote co-operative attitudes. In Germany, on the other hand, participation is formally built into the organisational system: consultation, worker representation, and task-orientation are all institutionalised to a greater or lesser extent and underpin the entire organisational and managerial ethic. As Gottfried Bruder of Commerzbank put it to a recent British researcher (Stewart et al., 1994: 187f.):

> In Germany we are far more used to a collegiate, committee-style of decision-making. Our style is more immune to your 'star culture'. The British style, looser with much more responsibility for the top managers, lends itself to people running away with things.

Ireland inherited many British institutional, organisational, and management forms and practices. Some of these fitted naturally into native Irish cultural patterns; others were less suited to the Irish temperament. Although Britain and Ireland are market economies in which bureaucratic structures are weak, personal relationships of great importance, and greater control exercised by people over how they perform their tasks, there are also major differences between the cultures which, because of its generality, Hofstede's study does not address. Co-operative ventures, for example, have played, and continue to play, a more central role in Ireland than in Britain. The growth of the credit union movement is a case in point. Credit unions are 'co-operative organisations based on thrift that are directed at fulfilling human and social needs' (Ferguson & McKillop, 1997). The core values are community self-help aimed at enhancing and regenerating social relations and community identity. The impetus for the development of the movement, which is predominantly rural-based, comes from the Catholic Church. There were 520 credit unions in the Republic of Ireland in 1994. They had one and a half million members and assets of over IR £1 billion. The same year there were 611 such unions in

Great Britain with a total membership of under 350,000 and assets of approximately Stg £250 million. The rate of penetration of this movement is put into context when one considers the respective populations of the two countries, 3.5 million in the Republic of Ireland and 55.5 million in Great Britain, and the fact that the latter includes 152 unions in Northern Ireland with 200,000 members and assets in excess of Stg £180 million.

Co-operation and networking are distinctive characteristics of both strategic planning and day-to-day management in Ireland. Due to the small size of the country, interrelationships of various kinds are widespread. These include family connections, religious and political affiliations, networking based on loyalty to the Irish language, relationships centring on various pressure group and community activities, and the old schoolboy network, which is not as strong in Ireland as it is in England with respect to the acquisition of top management and government posts. The proverbial 'friend of a friend of a friend' is no stranger in Ireland. The extent to which this kind of networking and thinking are commonplace in the highest echelons of Irish industry may be inferred from the following comments by the Director of Industrial Policy in the Confederation of Irish Industry:

> Let us for once think strategically and view our migrant youth as key contributors to an Irish network in Europe which can in the shorter term provide essential marketing and technological links for Irish business and industry and ultimately in the years ahead be the cornerstone for enterprise creation at home. (O'Boyle 1990:96)

Following de Madariaga, the authors Gatley, Lessem & Altman (1995) have recently argued that there are four principal European philosophical types which may be equated with differing managerial forms: pragmatism giving rise to the experiential manager (England, Scandinavia, Netherlands); rationalism giving rise to the professional manager (France, northern Italy, French-speaking Switzerland, parts of Germany); wholism giving rise to the developmental manager (Germany, Austria, Hungary, part of Switzerland); and finally, humanism giving rise to the convivial manager (Italy, Greece, Spain, and Ireland). According to the authors, the positive manifestation of the latter is in its communal nature, its negative expression being in the form of nepotism and corruption. They set out the features of humanism as follows:

Aspect	Attribute
Kindred philosophies	Aestheticism, classicism
Unit focus	Family group; social community
Business outlook	Communal, networked
Managerial orientation	Convivial
Psychological type	Feeling, concretely oriented
Path of evolution	Patriarch/social architect; family business/socio-economic network

Table 1. Features of humanism

Source: Gatley, Lessem & Altman, *Comparative Management* (1995:56)

Cultures in which the humanist ethic is dominant are individualist in that people are inclined to rebel against the chain of collective life. On the other hand, collective life links individual life to a system of gears.

> In such a gear only a small part of each wheel is actually connected at every moment, and playing an active role, while the person of passion is at every moment present with their whole self wherever they are. Such a man or woman of passion lives and works in a highly personalized world. (Gatley et al. 1995:44)

In this world, personal contacts are essential, and in business, if results are to be obtained, a person-to-person relationship is indispensable.

De Madariaga describes the English as taking from an object that which they think is useful to them; the French systematically and rationally investigate it; the Spanish, and other humanist cultures, think by contemplation.

> They wait in an apparent passivity for the object to reveal itself. They let the continuous stream of life pass through them, until chance will suddenly imbue it with new light. In other words, the object contemplated reveals itself all at once in its essence, with all its connections which attach it to the rest of life. (Gatley et al. 1995:44)

On the negative side, this may lead to apparent inertia and arbitrariness, together with inefficiency in work practices.

Humanist cultures have a passion for wholeness and seek universality in a personalised and spontaneous manner which is full of integrity. A sense of hierarchy is totally alien to such a mindset and a subconscious equality permeates life. Small-scale cohesion, of which the family is the first collective sphere, is the natural habitat. Radiating from the self and the small collectives are the larger scale co-operative and collective groupings and allegiances. Not surprisingly, then, Ireland has very low power distance, as is confirmed by Hofstede (1994:26), and a propensity for small collective units.

In more recent times, the Republic appears to be coming to terms with her underlying cultural values and is attempting to hone and focus them in a manner which will be beneficial to overall economic performance. The cult of the rural ideal and the policy of economic protectionism were linked in the early years of the new independent state to the national aim of the restoration of the Irish language as the first language of the people. By the 1960s it was clear that this linkage was not succeeding. Although passive competence in Irish was much higher than at any other time during the century, Government policy had not succeeded in arresting the decline of the language in Irish-speaking areas. Furthermore, since these were the poorest and most westerly parts of the island, the identification of Irish with traditionalism, protectionism, and poverty became increasingly accentuated. By a somewhat warped sense of logic it was felt that the restoration policy was partly responsible for economic inefficiency. Following the reacquistion of the land and the independence of twenty-six of the thirty-two counties of the country, there was a genuine feeling that restoration would go hand in hand with economic development. The fact that neither restoration, economic growth nor the full independence of the country came about exacerbated the sense of failure and the existing inertia which permeated society. Pragmatic integrated planning of the socio-cultural and economic systems, with clearly defined and achievable objectives, was not seriously attempted.

The conclusion seems to have been reached that Irish was not the vehicle by which increased modernity, urbanity, and economic development could be achieved. It was a sacred cow which could be sacrificed in the interests of economic growth. A climate of anti-intellectualism pervaded the culture and the language debate was swept under the carpet. There appeared to be a growing consensus that Irish would die before long anyway and the problem would disappear. The same fatalistic approach applied to a greater or lesser extent to other societal values. In the 1970s Government policy changed from one of idealistic unintegrated intervention on behalf of the language to a more pragmatic and less compulsion-oriented bilingual approach. Due to a great extent to recent economic successes, there is today a greater confidence in the value of Irish as an important symbol of Irish identity and the bilingual approach is somewhat more focussed and less fatalistic. It is becoming integrated into the web of cultural values which make up the Irish way of life and is viewed as being less exclusivist, traditional, and protection-oriented as was previously the case.

Over these past twenty-five years Irish has become an increasingly important cultural symbol for Northern Irish nationalists. For many Protestant Unionists, however, it is deemed to be subversive and they tend to identify it with militant Republicanism. A small percentage of liberally-minded Protestants, it is true, make a distinction between the use of the language as a cultural asset for all of the people and its perceived misuse by Republican paramilitary organizations for their own political ends. This should be borne in mind in international business contacts and negotiations.

The Northern Protestant Unionist was proud in the past of his self-reliance, individualism, and business acumen, giving himself a score of 98 for determination, 94 for business capacity, 91 for courage, 90 for trustworthiness and 70 for generosity (Lee 1989:3f.). The native Irish were, in a typically colonial mindset, deemed to be lazy, indolent, untrustworthy, and lacking in business ability. It is true to an extent that indolence and inertia were not unknown characteristics in the culture of Catholic Nationalism in Northern Ireland, but the reasons for this had more to do with discrimination, lack of educational opportunities, and fatalism than with ethnicity. However, Lynn controversially argues that low anxiety cultures, such as the Republic of Ireland, exhibit characteristics which lead to lack of initiative, achievement, and wealth creation (Lynn 1971). Fogarty's survey of Irish entrepreneurs (Fogarty 1973), on the other hand, suggests that while many members of the Irish business community do not themselves lack initiative, the educational system and dominant cultural values of society have not encouraged innovative thinking and entrepreneurial activity.

The antipathy towards Irish and Roman Catholicism on the part of the Unionist community is ultimately rooted in the colonisation or so-called 'Plantation of Ulster' in the seventeenth century, which was based on the idea of planting settlers in this most recalcitrant part of Ireland with the aim of stabilising English government rule. The plantation covered the counties of Armagh, Cavan, Derry, Donegal, Fermanagh, and Tyrone. Most of the land was to be distributed to English and Scottish settlers, and only a small part, particularly the less fertile land on the hills was to be left for the native Irish. These plans, however, were only partly put into practice and, as a result, the native Catholic Irish, while occupying more land than had been originally allocated to them,

> lost none of their resentment, because they regarded it all as theirs in the
> first place. And the Protestants, less numerous, less dominant than had been
> intended, felt insecure and more like a beleaguered garrison surrounded by
> enemies than masters in their own new homes. (Kee 1980:41)

In a separate development another wave of emigrants from Scotland spread across the north of Ireland, taking in the counties of Down and Antrim. These settlements took a much firmer hold and resulted in a higher proportion of Scottish Presbyterian settlers than English Anglican ones. This dispossession of Irish landowners has been widely interpreted as the event which defined Catholic-Protestant relations in the form that survives to the present day. There is still today in some areas a clearly identifiable 'them and us' mentality, which is a typical element of collectivist cultures. In Belfast, for example, the Falls Road and Shankill Road are synonymous with Catholic and Protestant working class areas respectively. Where shifts in population occur there may be a reluctance to give up territory to the other side (Cormack & Osborne, 1994:79).

Economic factors have played a significant role in population movements. When Belfast emerged as the hub of industry in the region during the nineteenth century it attracted many rural labourers from southern and western counties, resulting in an increase in the Catholic population of Belfast from 5 per cent in 1800 to 35 per cent half a century later. The new arrivals settled mainly in an enclave in the west of the city. This geographic segmentation and the notion of 'hostile' and 'friendly' territory has been used as an explanation for significant imbalances in the workforce, such as the low proportion of Catholic workers in two of the major employers in Northern Ireland, the shipyard Harland and Wolff and the aircraft manufacturer Shorts. Similarly, the low proportion of Protestant workers at Dupont on the Maydown industrial estate in the city of Derry has been explained in the same way. Compton (1991) also uses the geographical factor as one explanation why the unemployment rate among Catholics is higher than among Protestants. He argues that the percentage of Catholics in the population is higher west of the river Bann where unemployment generally is higher whereas the Protestant population tends to be concentrated in the Greater Belfast area which has a relatively favourable unemployment rate. He points out, however, that 'the reason for relative Catholic disadvantage in the job market is a complex matter and is not amenable to simple explanation' (Compton 1991:47).

Complex it may indeed be, but it is undoubtedly the case that, in the past, job discrimination on the basis of religion and tribal loyalty was rife, being particularly blatant in public sector employment in which the most important posts were filled by Protestants who could be relied upon to be unquestionably loyal to the state. The same applied to the private sector, which to the present day has an under-representation of Catholics. A similar tribal loyalty led to a degree of discrimination against Protestants in Catholic-owned small businesses. Job discrimination is now closely monitored by the Fair Employment Commission and the legislation which has been enacted over these past twenty years has had a salutary effect and has succeeded in eradicating many of the more glaring injustices against Catholics.

3.   Uncertainty avoidance

Uncertainty avoidance may be defined as 'the extent to which members of a culture feel threatened by uncertain or unknown situations' (Hofstede, 1994: 113). In the IBM study, the Republic of Ireland scores very low on the uncertainty avoidance index, being ranked 47-48 out of 53, that is, the same as Great Britain (excluding Northern Ireland), below Malaysia, which was ranked 46 and above Hong Kong and Sweden, ranked 49-50. France and Spain have high uncertainty avoidance, ranked 10-15, Germany (Federal Republic) medium, ranked 29. The USA has weak uncertainty avoidance, ranked slightly higher than the Republic and Great Britain at 43. Greece was ranked 1, Singapore 53. As we have previously stated, the culture of the Republic of Ireland exhibits a high level of ambiguity, which is typical of low avoidance cultures in general. High avoidance cultures, on the other hand, reduce ambiguity by having reasonably clear-cut distinctions between the acceptable and unacceptable and 'look for a structure in their organizations, institutions, and relationships which makes events clearly interpretable and predictable' (Hofstede 1994:116). This is generally achieved by having many formal and informal rules and regulations controlling people's behaviour in various socio-cultural spheres of activity. Low avoiding societies tend to have an abhorrence of formal rules and are less anxious about what the future might have in store for them. Hofstede (1994:123) makes the point that these cultures are often innovative and have a greater tolerance for unusual ideas, but have difficulty in implementing innovations, as this requires attention to detail and punctuality. Time in rural Ireland is elastic and circular, a device for orienting oneself and one's relationships, rather than something which must be adhered to punctiliously.

Hofstede notes that cultures which exhibit weak uncertainty avoidance and masculinity deal with conflict by finding compromise but draws attention to the point that neither Northern Ireland nor the former apartheid culture of South Africa seem to fit this pattern. The first thing that needs to be said here is that like its counterpart in the Republic of Ireland, Northern Ireland Protestant culture also exhibits deep ambiguity. While this ambiguity is rather different in the two cultures, it is essentially the same side of the one coin. Formally speaking, since the abrogation of the Stormont parliament in 1972, Northern Protestant and Unionist culture has been stuggling to emerge from its former status of colonial dominance: it is under intense pressure and exhibits many of the signs of deep anxiety. Uncertainty avoidance is particularly high in certain domains of activity. This becomes accentuated in times of tension and is reflected in a tightening of public and private security arrangements and in xenophobia in general. The culture is conservative, parochial, and tradition-bound on the one hand; individualist, pragmatic, and task-oriented on the other. The various elements of the cultural package have not yet struck a healthy balance, the conservative elements being clearly in the ascendancy. Since the culture considers itself to be under siege, and *is* therefore in this state, physical and mental walls have been erected against outside attack and penetration. There is a paranoiac fear that almost all strangers are enemies in league with the Nationalists and that attempts to bring in American and European investment are stratagems aimed at undermining group solidarity and advancing the cause of Republicanism and Roman Catholicism. While this mindset is less marked among members of the Anglican Church of Ireland and more liberal wings of Presbyterianism, when linked with fundamentalist Presbyterianism, which accounts for over one-third of the Protestant population, it appears to be the dominating force.

There is a widespread deep sense of insecurity regarding the possibility of the political system to maintain Protestant culture and hence Protestant individualism tends to be conflictual rather than compromising. This volatile mixture has clearly an adverse effect on business enterprise. The high uncertainty avoidance in regard to politics and culture led in the past to a greater propensity for written and formal rules, regulations, and agreements. This is offset today, however, by a mistrust of government, which is deemed by many

Unionists to be duplicitous. Trust is therefore essential in business dealings in Northern Ireland. Providing that it is clear there is no hidden political agenda lurking behind the scenes, business negotiations can be conducted in a genuine spirit of trust and harmony. The key to success therefore in this area is to steer clear of politics.

The problems facing the economy of Northern Ireland are clearly recognised by the business sector and there is a growing recognition that the culture needs to become much more outward-looking and that the level of xenophobia must be lessened in order to attract investment and increase competitiveness and performance. Roy McNulty, for example, President of Short Brothers PLC and Chairman of Northern Ireland Growth Challenge, argues that innovation and growth are constrained by conservatism and insularity on the one hand, and a traditional reaction by Government to a depressed regional economy on the other (McNulty 1995). This is illustrated graphically below:

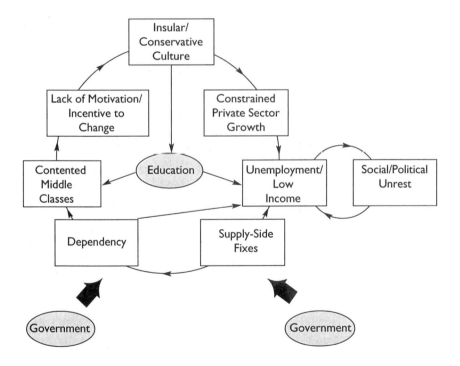

Figure 1. Northern Ireland's vicious cycle, constraining innovation and growth
            (McNulty 1995)

4.   High-context/low-context

Hall (1976) differentiates cultures on the basis of their predominant mode of communication. A high-context culture is one in which the information is in the physical context or internalised in the person; very little information is contained in the explicit spoken or written coded part of the message. In a low-context culture, most of the information is explicitly given. The former is typical of collectivist cultures, the latter of individualist cultures. The Irish are often viewed stereotypically as having the gift of the gab or as having kissed the blarney stone. There is an emphasis on expressiveness, rhetorical flourish, and talk for talk's sake. Speech is often used to bolster and develop personal contacts rather than to initiate and direct tasks. Direct confrontation and refusal to meet the demands of another are avoided. There is a tendency, less marked now perhaps than in the past, of communicating indirectly. Conse-quently modals and tag clauses are frequently employed. The negative indi-rect request is a typical example of the manner in which politeness formulae are used. Rather than saying 'could you confirm this in writing, please?', the structure 'you couldn't confirm this in writing, could you?' is commonplace. Direct requests are less common: the addressee will know from the context what is being requested. Indeed, it may happen that when quizzed as to one's needs, a person may disguise what one really wants: 'no' may mean 'yes' and vice versa. Hence, although one may have refused a request, the request may be repeated several times and many foreigners have been known to have received innumerable unwanted cups of tea and other substances of a more potent nature. This mode of discourse is also linked to the generosity ethic, which remains a central and highly-prized cultural value.

The high contextual nature of Irish culture distinguishes it from other more individualistic cultures and indeed from some cultures which are ranked below it in the IBM study. Although directness is a feature of Northern Ireland's culture, the mode of communication is clearly high-context in private and social interaction. Indeed the use of language reflects the underly-ing societal tension and conflict. At times of high tension, linguistic behaviour becomes rigid and concerns may be either expressed in a volatile emotional manner by public spokespersons or almost entirely suppressed at the private level. Since the use of particular words and phrases, accent and intonational patterns generally betray the community to which an individual belongs, extreme care is taken to avoid detection. It is costly to the individual and to the community to which he or she belongs to open the channel of communication and widen the range of applicability of inherited tribal vocabularly. In Northern Ireland, the saying 'If you say anything, say nothing', tells a great deal about the nature of society. When life and death may be at stake, the value of words increases enormously. At present, 'Sticks and stones may break your bones and words may also kill you'.

Investors and visitors to Northern Ireland should be aware of the subtleties of linguistic communication. For example, the term 'Northern Ireland', which has been employed in this paper, is one of contention. For many Nationalists, its use implies a recognition of the political entity which it represents, and they prefer the terms 'The Six Counties' or 'The North of Ireland'. For the Unionist population, the use of the latter term in particular is deemed to be offensive and tantamount to a verbal non-recognition of the state. The designations 'Ulster' and 'The Province' for the state, which are frequently employed by Unionist and British politicians, are also contentious. Nationalists take the view that these terms refer not to the state of 'Northern Ireland' but to this territory plus the three northern counties of Donegal, Monaghan, and Cavan which are in the Republic of Ireland. As regards the term 'The Republic of Ireland', both Nationalists and Unionists use it, but the latter prefer the terms 'Southern Ireland' or 'Eire', a clear reminder to Nationalists that 'Northern Ireland' exists as a separate and distinct political entity. Nationalists do not call the Republic of Ireland 'Southern Ireland', preferring the terms 'The South', 'The South of Ireland', or 'The Free State'. The city and county of Derry/Londonderry reflect the tension surrounding terminology and territory in microcosm. For Nationalists, the city is Derry; for most Unionists, it is Londonderry. This has led to broadcasters, for whom it can become a problem of nightmarish proportions, giving the city the homely designation 'Stroke City'.

British politicians and some Unionists are inclined to refer to Britain as 'The Mainland', a term which is anathema to a large section of the population. One recent commentator, Professor Foster, the distinguished Irish historian who holds the Carrol Chair of Irish History at Oxford, has argued that the first phase of the Peace Process foundered as Britain's language became too literal (Foster 1996). In his view, the cadences and intonational patterns of the British politicians, rather than the content of what they said, concealed double-dealing. The 'literal-minded and restrictive conditions' increasingly relied upon by John Major, the former British prime minister, and the tone in which they were presented ... ended a process where a joint language was evolving which allowed necessary flexibility and provided a moment for tentative cross-community links at local levels in the North, conceivably presaging a new dispensation. It appears now that what Mr. Major meant by 'election' may have been different to what people thought he meant.

As Foster remarks, 'that has a promisingly Irish sound to it'.

5. Conclusion

In this paper we have suggested that a readjustment in the emphasis attached to certain cultural values is occuring in the Republic of Ireland, which contributes to the creation of a favourable environment for reacting to changing economic circumstances in the modern world. The exercise of the traditional collective values of neighbourliness and communality, together with low uncertainty avoidance, appears to have paid handsome economic dividends which have, in turn, led to a more balanced and initiative-driven individualism. This readjustment is still, however, in its early stages and has not yet permeated organisational structures of management to a degree which will ensure continuing and future success. Our analysis suggests that both culturally and economically Northern Ireland is in deep crisis, caught in a maze of conflicting pathways and values. On the other hand, if properly harnessed and positively focussed, some of these values could be of great benefit in the pursuit of economic development and growth.

References

Baumol, William J. 1968. "The entrepreneur in economic theory". *American Economic Review* 58, 64-71.

Central Bank of Ireland. 1996. *Bulletin. Winter 1996*. Dublin.

Compton, Paul A. 1991. "Employment differentials in Northern Ireland and job discrimination: A Critique". In: Patrick J. Roche and Brian Barton (eds.), *The Northern Ireland Question: Myth and Reality*. Newcastle upon Tyne: Athenaeum Press, pp. 40-76.

Cormack, Robert J. and Robert D. Osborne 1994. "The evolution of the Catholic middle class". In: Adrian Guelke (ed.), *New Perspectives on the Northern Ireland Conflict*. Newcastle upon Tyne: Athenaeum Press, pp. 65-85.

Ferguson, Charles and Donal G. McKillop. 1997. *The Strategic Development of Credit Unions.* London: John Wiley and Sons.

Fitzgerald, Garret. 1997. "How Irish eyes came up smiling". *The Observer Business,* 9 March 1997:4.

Fogarty, Michael P. 1973. *Irish Entrepreneurs Speak for Themselves.* Dublin: ESRI.

Fogarty, Michael P. 1982. "The Irish economy - An outside view". In: *The Economic and Social State of the Nation.* Dublin: ESRI, pp. 25-45.

Foster, Roy. 1996. "Ireland's English troubles". *The Observer Review,* 18 February 1996: 4.

Gatley, Stephen, Ronnie Lessem and Yochanan Altman. 1995. *Comparative Management.* Maidenhead: McGraw Hill.

Gudgin, Graham. 1994. "Pulling ahead: Industrial growth in Northern Ireland". *Irish Banking Review,* Summer 1994: 3-22.

Hall, Edward T. 1976. *Beyond Culture.* Garden City NY: Doubleday Anchor Books.

Hirschman, Albert. 1965. "Obstacles to development: a classification and a quasi-vanishing act". *Economic Development and Cultural Change* 13, 385-393.

Hofstede, Geert. 1980. *Culture's Consequences: International Differences in Work-Related Values.* Beverly Hills: Sage Publications.

Hofstede, Geert. 1994. *Cultures and Organizations.* London: HarperCollins.

Hutton, Will. 1994. *Britain and Northern Ireland, the State We're in - Failure and Opportunity.* Belfast: NIEC Report 114.

Kee, Robert. 1980. *Ireland. A History.* London: Weidenfeld & Nicolson.

Kennedy, Kieran A. 1993. "Long-term trends in the Irish economy". *Irish Banking Review,* Summer 1993: 16-25.

Lee, Joseph J. 1989. *Ireland 1912-1985.* Cambridge: Cambridge University Press.

Lynn, Richard. 1971. *National Differences in Anxiety.* Dublin: ESRI.

McClelland, David C. 1961. *The Achieving Society.* Princeton NJ: Van Nostrand.

McNulty, Roy. 1995. "Northern Ireland growth challenge". *Irish Banking Review,* Winter 1995: 3-12.

Munck, Ronnie. 1993. *The Irish Economy. Results and Prospects.* London: Pluto Press.

Murray, J. A. 1981. "In search of entrepreneurship". *Journal of Irish Business and Administrative Research* 3: 41-55.

O'Boyle, Aidan. 1990. "Ireland within Europe in the 1990s - An assessment". In: David Kennedy and Aidan Pender (eds.), *Prosperity and Policy: Ireland in the 1990s.* Dublin: Institute of Public Administration, pp. 53-101.

O'Farrell, Patrick. 1986. *Entrepreneurs and Industrial Change: The Process of Change in Irish Manufacturing.* Dublin: Irish Management Institute.

Stewart, Rosemary, Jean-Louis Barsoux, Alfred Kieser, Hans-Dieter Ganter and Peter Walgenbach. 1994. *Managing in Britain and Germany.* Basingstoke: Macmillan.

Woelger, Ernestine. 1994. "The economic impact of the Northern Ireland conflict". *Irish Banking Review,* Summer 1994: 23-32.

IV. Linguistic Perspectives

Parallel texts and diverging cultures in Hong Kong

Implications for intercultural communication

Peter Grundy
University of Durham, England

0. Introduction

In this paper I extrapolate consequences for intercultural communication from an analysis of variation in the pragmatic realization of meaning in parallel texts written in English and Modern Standard Chinese[1] for a Hong Kong readership. Since parallel texts are typically intended to convey identical meanings (i.e. to represent the same "distal" context [Mehan 1991]), the kinds of differences revealed in the texts analysed in this paper are hypothesized to be invocations of cultural membership (Schegloff 1987) and orientation to topic.

Pragmatic phenomena function "reflexively" (Lucy 1993) to cue the way in which the propositions to which they are attached are to be interpreted. They are, therefore, significant indicators of the attitudes or membership status of the writers by whom and the assumed readers for whom the texts are created. In single-language intercultural communication, such as occurs in business contexts, it is frequently difficult to know whether perceived pragmatic modulation is the effect of the interlocutor's limited pragma-linguistic (Leech 1983, Thomas 1983) knowledge or whether it is a true reflection of intended meanings. The analysis of English and Modern Standard Chinese parallel texts which follows indicates which pragmatic effects are orientations to cultural affiliation and thus enables participants in single-language business communication involving Chinese or English (speaking) interlocu-

tors to know when same meanings are being encoded from different membership perspectives.

Parallel text analysis of this kind is in principle capable of revealing
prototypical pragmatic modulation for every cultural group.

1. Language and culture

Any study which tries to make sense of cultural phenomena in terms of
linguistic realizations has to consider the theoretical ways in which language
and culture are conceived, as well as the specific properties claimed for
particular languages and cultures.

1.1. *Typological and universal characterizations of language and culture*

Both language and culture may be characterized typologically. Thus syntactic
category and word order patterns across languages, such as those revealed in
Universals of Human Language (Greenberg 1968), enable us to characterize
language types. The following features, for example, occur in Cantonese but
not in English: Cantonese NP's contain classifiers, Cantonese allows the null-
subject option, Cantonese discourse structure favours topic prominence, and
Cantonese categories include a class of particle that marks illocutionary
force.

In cultural typology, the work of Hofstede (1980, 1991) and Hall (1976)
enables us to characterize cultures according to various behavioural and
organizational patterns. Thus, Hofstede's study showed Anglo cultures (Australia, UK, USA) to be small power distance (PD) and high individualism
(IDV) cultures, whereas the Chinese societies included in his survey (Hong
Kong, Singapore, Taiwan) were shown to be large PD and low IDV cultures.

The typological approach to universals is based on the study of particular
languages and particular cultures and adopts a structuralist perspective in
defining each language or culture in terms of its difference from others. This
approach may be contrasted with the universal, or common-property, perspective of generative linguistics, which is also found in some accounts of
language *behaviour*. One of the most carefully worked out of such accounts is
Brown and Levinson's theory of politeness (1978, 1987), which argues that
more or less the same linguistic resources are available to speakers of all
languages but that their functional employment is triggered by culture spe-

cific computations of imposition, and the hierarchical power and social distance differentials between speaker(s) and addressee(s). Thus small PD, high IDV cultures favour positive politeness (language structures used to encode mutual esteem and equality of status) whilst large PD, low IDV cultures favour negative politeness (language structures used to encode respect for ascribed status).

1.2. *Characterizations of Chinese culture*

It often strikes outsiders as surprising that characterizations of Chinese culture typically appeal to historical rather than synchronic events as determinants of contemporary behaviour. Thus the recent, extremely rapid economic development of south-east Asian societies with predominantly Chinese populations is held by many researchers to be based on values established 2,500 years ago, and accounted for by the so-called *post-Confucian Hypothesis*: "Both aspects of the Confucian ethic — the creation of dedicated, motivated, responsible, and educated individuals and the enhanced sense of commitment, organizational identity, and loyalty to various institutions — will result in neo-Confucian societies having at least potentially higher growth rates than other cultures" (Kahn 1989:122).

It is not only Confucian ethics that are appealed to as an explanation of contemporary social organization. Yang claims a still more ancient base for contemporary Chinese social organization. He suggests that "a self-sufficient and self-sustaining agricultural system as a subsistence economy" was formed around 5,000 BC and brought about a set of social values which still determine Chinese social organization:

> (a) hierarchical organization (society mainly organized in terms of, and social power allocated solely according to, vertical relationship defined with respect to seniority, position, and sex); (b) collectivistic functioning (individual required to submit himself to his family, group, or other collectives in social functioning); (c) generalized familization (family as a general model for the organization and functioning of all outside-family groups); (d) structural tightness (social roles and their relationships highly rigid in their prescriptions and enactment); and (e) social homogeneity (social norms stressing local uniformity rather than diversity) (1981, in Bond 1986:150).

Those who live in Confucian cultures are generally held to have a holistic notion of society (Yang 1986:148). In characterizations of these societies, the term "collectivist" is never far away. Yum defines collectivism in terms of its manifestation in interpersonal relations:

> The cardinal principle of Confucianism is humanism, which is understood
> as a warm human feeling between people and strongly emphasizes reciproc-
> ity. As a philosophy of humanism and social relations, Confucianism has
> left a strong impact on interpersonal relationships and on communication
> patterns. The five most important areas of interpersonal relationships influ-
> enced by Confucianism are particularism, reciprocity, the in-group/out-
> group distinction, the role of intermediaries, and the overlap of personal and
> public relationships (Yum 1988:374).

Although Yum's is not an empirical study, her explanations of the five
areas of interpersonal relationships she identifies bring together many of the
observations of other researchers. She argues that *particularistic* societies do
not apply the same rule to everybody, but differentially grade and regulate
relationships. At the same time, Confucianism provides an elaborate moral
code for relationships among known members of *ingroups*, be they family,
friends, or colleagues in the workplace, but it does not provide any universal
rules for others.

In discussing *reciprocity*, Yum notes that in USA relations are symmetri-
cal-obligatory (i.e. as nearly "paid off" as possible at any given moment) or
else contractual (where the obligation is to an institution with whom one has
established some contractual base), whereas in Confucian societies relationships are complementary or asymmetrical, and reciprocally obligatory. In a
sense, a person is forever indebted to others. When different parties are
brought together by *intermediaries*, in Chinese culture these intermediaries
look for common or mutual knowledge between the parties, whilst western
intermediaries tend to be professionals — lawyers, negotiators, etc. And
whereas the Confucian goal is to diminish the *personal life/public life* di-
chotomy, personal privacy is jealously guarded in western societies.

Yum goes on to consider the implications for communication, and concludes that in Confucian societies the main functions of communication are to
develop and maintain social relationships and to maintain face through indirectness, so that meaning depends on the receiver's interpretation.

Although it is obviously very difficult, if not impossible, to measure the
extent to which an act of communication maintains social relationships, this
paper will show that at least to the extent that pragmatic language is sometimes considered to be indirect by virtue of requiring interpretative inferences, the claim that Chinese texts are more indirect than their western
equivalents is inaccurate. On the other hand, this paper will also show that
Chinese texts do favour face maintaining indirect speech acts.

1.3. *Chinese culture and western culture*

Hofstede's study (1980) showed that Anglo societies have small PD and high IDV, and Chinese societies have large PD and low IDV. He also found weak Uncertainty Avoidance and high Masculine values in both Hong Kong and UK. Although we might hypothesize that large PD and low IDV are consistent with a collectivist society, it could be argued that PD and IDV are not culture-free concepts. For this reason, the Chinese Culture Connection, a team of researchers headed by Michael Bond at the Chinese University of Hong Kong, tried to determine a cultural dimension that would reflect Chinese values. The research team identified a set of forty values which their informants rated as particularly Chinese. These values were then scored on a 9-point importance scale by students in 20 countries. The results enabled four factors to be identified as typifying the Chinese Value System, which the research team termed *Integration, Confucian work dynamism, Human-heartedness,* and *Moral discipline*:

Table 1. Chinese value systems as measured by the Chinese Culture Connection.

Integration

+tolerance	+harmony	+solidarity
+non-competitiveness	+trustworthiness	+contentedness
+being conservative	+close intimate friendship	-chastity in women
-filial piety	-patriotism	

(Western countries score high, eastern and underdeveloped score low)

Confucian work dynamism

+ordering relationships	+thrift	+persistence
+sense of shame	+reciprocation	-respect for tradition
-personal steadiness	-protecting your face	

(Hong Kong scores highest, Anglo countries score low)

Human-heartedness

+kindness	+patience	+courtesy
-sense of righteousness	-patriotism	

(Hong Kong, England, USA all score high)

Moral discipline

+having few desires	+moderation
-prudence	+keeping oneself disinterested and pure
	-adaptability

(England and USA score low, Hong Kong near the mean)

The post-Confucian hypothesis is also confirmed in this study, with high Confucian Work Dynamism (CWD) being strongly associated with annual growth rate in both GNP and *per capita* income.

1.4. *Summary*

Whilst it is relatively easy to identify respects in which Cantonese and English differ as languages, it is much harder to identify dimensions of cultural difference. The following "ready reckoner" of perspectives on cultural difference, based on those aspects of the work of the social psychologists discussed above which reveal the greatest differences between Anglo and Chinese cultures, enables us to investigate the extent to which the linguistic differences between the parallel texts which are analysed in the next section of the paper support this typology. The hypothesis is that

Table 2. Contrasting Anglo and Chinese value systems.

Chinese texts encode
Large PD/Low IDV (Hofstede)
High Confucian Work Dynamism (CWD) (Chinese Culture Connection)
Ingroup/outgroup distinction (Yum)
Collectivist stress on needs of ingroup rather than self (Yang)
Indirectness (Yum).

English texts encode
Small PD/High IDV (Hofstede)
Low Confucian Work Dynamism (CWD) (Chinese Culture Connection)
Directness (Yum).

2.   Text, context, and membership

Until relatively recently no one thought to question the assumption that phenomena could be explained in relation to the presumptive contexts in which they occurred. The prevailing view was that "since social structure forms the presumptive context of activities of lesser scale, such as social interaction, it is ultimately the fundamental explanatory resource" (Zimmerman & Boden 1991: 5)[2].

However, there is good reason to be suspicious about the rightness of this position. The ethnomethodologists have shown the value of a no-prior-hypothesis approach. In the field of Conversation Analysis in particular, Schegloff has insisted that relevant orientations to (cultural) contexts need to be demonstrated rather than presumed. Thus if a doctor asks a patient how they are, only a reply such as "Much the same I'm afraid. The pills didn't do any good" and not "Fine thanks! How are you?" treats the doctor's inquiry as orienting to a medical context (Grundy 1995:123).

This paper therefore accepts the ethnomethodological position that it is unprincipled to explain data in terms of what we think we know about those who provide it. At the same time, we need to recognize that the established characterizations of cultural typology which are often appealed to in accounting for behavioural patterns in the social psychology literature may be useful taxonomies for categorizing the effects observed in these data.

2.1. *Hong Kong as a context*

At the time these data were collected, Hong Kong was within eighteen months of returning to Chinese sovereignty. Although Chinese and English are the two official languages of Hong Kong, in case of dispute over the interpretation of parallel text documents, the English version is usually held to be the determining text for legal purposes. The then "majority" language, English, is the mother tongue of two percent of the population, and the then "minority" language, Cantonese, is the mother tongue of 97% of the population. In the 1991 census, 70% of the population of Hong Kong claimed to have no significant knowledge of English, although 92% of secondary school children currently choose English-medium schools. Hong Kong has been characterized as a bilingual state containing monolingual populations (So 1987). For all these reasons, Hong Kong serves as an ideal test-bed for a study of the extent to which parallel texts intended to convey the same meaning to two language populations may invoke diverging membership and cultural affiliation.

2.2. *Hierarchies: A letter from the bank*

The first point to note is that the two versions of the bank's letter are virtually identical in propositional content. This is in fact quite rare in parallel texts and indicates that the bank perceives both its audiences to be in the same relationship to the topic of the letter. There are, however, notable differences in the pragmatic modulation of the propositions which demonstrate the bank's orientation to the membership statuses of their Chinese and their English (speaking) audiences. The analysis focuses on the pragmatic features of the two texts because, following Lucy (1993), are regarded pragmatic markers as diacritic interpretation cues which indicate to the reader the way in which the stated propositions are to be understood. In this way, the encoded propositions are seen as distal contexts and their pragmatic modulation indicates how these contexts are to be understood by the Cantonese and English speaking readers of the letter.

In order to facilitate the analysis, each of the five paragraphs of the original English (E) and translated[3] Modern Standard Chinese (MSC) texts are presented together and commented on.

Paragraph 1

(E text)
Dear Customer,

Standard Chartered Bank is constantly looking for ways in which we can improve the quality and efficiency of the services we offer to you. We are therefore delighted to announce that the Bank has undertaken an initiative for a specialist technology organisation, the Sema Group, to manage the operation of the Bank's data processing centre.

(MSC text)
Dear Customer:

The Standard and Chartered Bank has all along been constantly trying hard to improve for you (honorific form) the service quality and efficiency. In order to achieve this aim, we will appoint the computer technology experts the Sema Group to be responsible for managing the operation of our Bank's computer data processing centre.

In the E text, the reader is left to infer from the second sentence that the bank's initiative in appointing the Sema group will improve the quality and efficiency of the service provided. In the MSC text, this meaning, which was recovered as an implicature in the E text, is achieved propositionally ("in order to achieve this aim"). The E text is also more verbal ("the bank is.. looking for ways in which we can improve..the services we offer to you"), so that in the MSC text there is no equivalent to the three-place predicate "offer" ("the bank has..been..trying..to improve for you the service quality"). The tendency to favour nominal over verbal forms is more presuppositional than assertive and enables agency to go unmentioned. It is also more collectivist in representing meanings as agreed. Brown & Levinson (1978, 1987) associate nominality with negative politeness, since avoiding indicating agency is a means of encoding distance between speaker/writer and audience.

Negative politeness strategies are also evident in the use of honorific second person forms and the use of the powerful first plural form "our bank" in the MSC text, where the E text uses the positive politeness form "the bank". Moreover, the MSC text exercises the option of using the exclusive deictic form for "we" and "our" throughout. The MSC text also uses the modal "will appoint", whereas the E text represents the appointment of the Sema group as a past event and makes the announcement of it a present action.

To summarize, the MSC text favours negative politeness strategies to a greater degree than the E text, indicating that the bank's new initiative is perceived as a greater imposition on their Chinese than on their English (speaking) customers and that the power-distance differential between the bank and its Chinese customers is perceived to be greater than between the bank and its English (speaking) customers.

We might hypothesize that orderly cultures with strong ingroup identity will disfavour implicatures, in which a new logical form replaces that of the original utterance. In contrast, high IDV cultures will favour implicature as a mode of conveying meaning because the understanding is recovered by the audience rather than determined by the speaker/writer. Similarly, cultures where no clear distinction is made between ingroup and outgroup members will need to take into account a more plural audience and allow for the more individualized understandings that implicatures, as context dependent infer-ences, permit. Explicatures (inferences that preserve the logical form of the original utterance [Sperber & Wilson 1986]) are more frequent in texts in high context cultures, and implicatures are more frequent in texts in low context cultures.

These hypotheses raise the issue of whether pragmatic meanings are indirect. How can it be that pragmatic meanings are typically considered indirect, and yet are employed so frequently in Anglo talk in which it is claimed that communication is more direct?

I want to suggest that the real function of pragmatic markers is diacritic. The language we use typically consists of both propositions and cues as to how to interpret the utterances that contain these propositions. Anglo talk contains more of these interpretation cues and hence invites more inferences, not because it is more indirect, but because it allows more variation in the interpretation of the significance of propositions as context creating or invoking. If we distinguish pragmatic inferences (present in virtually all talk and strongly favoured in Anglo talk), propositions (found in almost every example of talk in any culture), and indirect speech acts (as found in the MSC text analysed in the next section of this paper), it is the first two that are expectable and only the third that is actually indirect.

Paragraph 2

(E text) The Sema Group is a leading European technology services company which specialises in the management and support of technology and has extensive experience in managing data processing operations on behalf of many large corporations. Our relationship with such a world-class organisation underlines our commitment to innovation and the improved servicing of our customer's requirements in Asia.

(MSC text) The Sema Group is a company which specialises in managing and supporting computer technology. In the aspect of managing computer data processing for large organisations, (it) possesses rich/extensive experience.

The mention of the European base of the Sema group, its status as "a world-class organization" and the reference to "customer's requirements in Asia" in the E but not in the MSC text all overtly orient to the expatriate status of the bank's English (speaking) customers and remind them of their outgroup status. The placing of the apostrophe before the final "s" in "customer's" is also consistent with orientation to a customer perceived as individualistic.

Paragraph 3

(E text) The new arrangement is planned to take effect within the next few weeks. After the transfer of the management of the Data Processing Centre to Sema, the Bank will continue to maintain the current service levels and strive for ongoing improvement opportunities. In addition, the Bank will safeguard the confidentiality of all customer information. in the same way that we do today. Sema will operate under a strict code of secrecy, complying with the policies and standards imposed by Standard Chartered Bank and Government regulations.

(MSC text) The above new measure is planned to take effect in a few weeks. Besides transferring the computer data processing centre to the management of the Sema Group, our Bank will continuously maintain the usual quality service standards and actively open more development opportunities. Besides, our Bank will as usual adhere strictly to the principle of keeping all customers' information confidential, and the Sema Group also need to operate in accordance with a set of strict confidentiality codes, adhere to the aim and standard of confidentiality stipulated by our Bank and the government.

In this paragraph, the E but not the MSC text abbreviates "the Sema group" to "Sema". This shortened form is a positive politeness indicator consistent with small PD. In the MSC text, the discourse deictic "above", like "in order to achieve this aim" in paragraph 1, shows the intention of the writer to be explicit in connecting each part of the discourse. The occurrence of presupposition (in "more development opportunities") is consistent with the more explicit, less inferential mode of conveying meaning of the MSC text.

Paragraph 4

(E text) To enable the Bank to implement this initiative, the standard terms and conditions of the accounts you hold with Standard Chartered Bank or its subsidiaries will be changed accordingly (please refer to the attached).

(MSC text) To go hand in hand with our Bank's implementation of the above measure, the standard terms and regulations of the different accounts of the respected/honourable customer with the Standard and Chartered Bank or our Bank's subsidiary organisations will need to be slightly revised (please refer to appendix).

The MSC text again exhibits more nominality than the E text ("to go hand in hand with our bank's implementation.." / "to enable the bank to implement.."; "the different accounts of the respected customer" / "the accounts you hold"), as well as discourse deixis ("the above measure"), and the negative politeness strategy of minimizing imposition ("will need to be slightly revised" / "will be changed accordingly"). In avoiding the use of "you", the MSC text makes the customers the illocutionary target without addressing them directly.

Paragraph 5

(E text) This initiative will keep the bank in the forefront of technology which is an essential factor in continually improving our ability to service your banking needs.

Sincerely,
General Manager, Hong Kong & China

(MSC text) This brand-new measure will enable our Bank to keep abreast of the times, with advanced technology to seek ever-improving excellence, to provide you (honorific form) with better service to meet your (honorific form) different financial management needs.

Yours faithfully

In the E text "our ability to service your banking needs" is much more direct and positive-face addressing than the MSC negative-face addressing equivalent.

Overall, the MSC text exhibits several expectable "ready reckoner" features, including large PD, ordered relationships, a more indirect mode of communication (negative politeness), and evidence of collectivist orientation (nominalization). The E text exhibits small PD and a more direct mode of communication (positive politeness)[4].

2.3. *Families: A letter from the President*

The second set of parallel texts analyzed here consist of a letter sent by the Head (President) of a Hong Kong university to all staff members working in the University on the occasion of two disasters in China. This text shows very different orientation from the bank letter. For a start, the propositional content is different in each of the two texts of the letter although the distal context is the same two events. The President of the university, himself Chinese, uses the MSC text to address members of the university staff first as compatriots ("We are the more fortunate descendants of the Chinese") and second as colleagues, whereas the E text addresses members of the university staff only as colleagues ("I now write to appeal for the support of all my colleagues"). Because the President of the university is in different relationships with his Chinese and English (speaking) colleagues, the topic of the parallel texts is no longer the same since their propositional content as well as their pragmatic modulation is different.

Paragraph 1

(E text)
February 7, 1996

Dear Colleagues

Fund-raising for earthquake and blast victims

As you are aware, two recent disasters in China — the terrifying blast in Hunan and the disastrous earthquake in Yunnan — have claimed the lives of hundreds, leaving tens of thousands of victims desperately in need of help.

(MSC text)
All <informal name of institution> colleagues:

I think you all know that recently Chinese compatriots in Hunan province and Shaoyang municipality of Yunnan province have suffered severe casualties as a result of the earthquake and blast accidents respectively. Since hundreds and thousands of compatriots in Yunnan province have their home demolished, they are forced to sleep out in the wind and snow. Natural disasters are merciless. Could anybody who hears about this have no grief?

The MSC text opens with the hedged assertion that "you all know" about the recent disasters in China, yet it goes on to provide what appears to be new information ("Since hundreds and thousands.."). This causes us to re-evaluate the illocutionary force conveyed by "I think you all know" as an indirect speech act, particularly when both "all" and "Chinese" have been lexicalized when they could equally have been recovered as explicatures. Similarly, "respectively" reinforces the extent to which the writer wishes to go on record as observing the Gricean maxim of Manner (although as it happens the earthquake and blast accident are in the wrong order). This suggests that the letter has a directive rather than an informative status. The MSC paragraph ends with a rhetorical question, which again asserts the status of the writer, since rhetorical questions function indirectly as negative assertions. Although in many respects the MSC text is more verbal than the E text, it is notably more indirect on the subject of the death of the victims ("compatriots..have suffered severe casualties" / "two recent disasters..have claimed the lives of hundreds").

It seems therefore that the MSC text encodes larger P than the E text in being more indirectly directive and· smaller D in being more verbal. This is one way in which the head of an organization might be expected to orient to same nationality local and other nationality expatriate employees.

Paragraph 2

(E text) In this connection, I have decided to launch a <informal name of institution>-wide campaign to collect relief fund for the earthquake and blast victims. To kick off this meaningful campaign, the Deputy President, Vice-Presidents, Faculty Deans and myself have collectively pledged a total of $48,000 to support this initiative.

(MSC text) We are the more fortunate descendants of the Chinese. On the past few occasions when mainland China suffered natural disasters, we all have generously donated large sums to our unfortunate compatriots. In face of the unforeseen calamities sent from Heaven, I now sincerely appeal to all of you to extend your compassionate hand again and to give full play to our love for the compatriots. The Lunar New Year is drawing close, I hope that traumatised compatriots will feel the care and concern rendered to them by Hong Kong compatriots and the <informal name of institution> staff.

The Deputy President, Vice-Presidents, Faculty Deans and myself have taken the lead in donating a total of HK$48,000.

The E text exhibits discourse deixis ("In this connection") whereas the MSC text first recalls the past record of generosity and then repeats in a new formulation what was said in the first paragraph ("In the face of the unforeseen calamities sent from heaven.."). Again the MSC text lexicalizes "all of" in "all of you", which would normally have been recovered as an explicature and repeats the reference to past generosity with the presupposing iterative "again" in "I..appeal to all of you..again".

Although the MSC text is more (indirectly) directive than the E text, at the moment at which the appeal occurs, the MSC text is explicitly performative: "I now sincerely appeal to all of you", whereas in the E text "appeal" is embedded in "I now write to appeal for the support of all my colleagues" (paragraph 3). At this point, the larger P and smaller D of the MSC text is particularly clear. The following, "I hope that traumatized compatriots..", in the MSC text is an indirect request for support.

The MSC text exhibits large P in pointing out that senior members of the University "have taken the lead" in donating money, high CWD in attempting to shame potential non-contributors, and strong ingroup appeal to the collective community. The E text letter shows orientation to ingroup/outgroup awareness in taking the high IDV value of the readership into account by explicitly stating that the senior members of the University have acted "collectively".

Paragraph 3

(E text) I now write to appeal for the support of all my colleagues towards this campaign. Your tax-deductible donations, which can be either in cash or by cheque made payable to "<formal name of institution>", should be forwarded via your departmental AO/EO to the Office of Communications and Public Affairs on or before February 12, 1996. The donations raised will then be sent to Mainland authorities via the New China News Agency.

Thank you very much in anticipation of your support and generosity.

<name>
President

(MSC text) I hope that each and every academic department and administrative office can start donating immediately. The donations should then be collected by the departmental officers who will give the donations to the office of Communication and Public Affairs by 12 February. The donations would then be forwarded to the New China News Agency who would handle the donations properly. Donations by cheque should be made payable

to <formal name of institution>. Your donations can also be used for tax deduction purposes.

Would all of you live out the <informal name of institution> spirit by rendering your strong support!

President

<signature>

7 February 1996

Whereas the E text appeals for the support of colleagues, the MSC text is an indirect speech act which amounts to a strong recommendation, if not actually a directive, to "each and every academic department and administrative office" to donate "immediately"[5].

3. Conclusion

In social psychology, data collected over a period that extends back almost twenty years show that it is possible to place cultures on relative scales in relation to the extent to which they distribute power among their members, value individualism, use shame as a means of ordering conduct, are tolerant of outgroup behaviour, and favour (in)directness in communicating meanings.

This paper accounts for the cross-linguistic variability of data occurring in an identical social situation. The analysis of English and Modern Standard Chinese versions of a letter written by a major bank to its customers and a letter written by a university President to members of the university staff reveals the perceptions of the cultural values of the two readerships encoded in the different texts, distinctions which broadly match those that research in social psychology has revealed. This does not guarantee, however, that appealing to diverging cultural memberships will necessarily result in desired outcomes, as the reactions of some English speaking readers of the bank letter and some Chinese speaking readers of the university letter indicate (see note 4).

The relevance of parallel text analysis to the practice of intercultural business communication lies in its ability to reveal which pragmatic modulations of talk or text are orientations to cultural affiliation, so that in the more typical context of single-language communication events, these modulations can be distinguished from those which are event-specific.

The analysis of the bank letter makes a number of observations about Chinese and English pragmatic modulation: comparable observations would be likely to result from an analysis of parallel texts written in other languages. Whilst modulation of proposition may reveal either membership or event-specific meaning, unexpected propositional content indicates that the message originator perceives the audience, and hence the topic, differently from the way 'he' perceives 'himself' and the topic.

Notes

1. "Modern Standard Chinese" is used to refer to the common written form used to represent the different spoken languages (or, as they are frequently termed by native speakers, "dialects") of China, including Mandarin and Cantonese.

2. It should be noted that Zimmerman & Boden expressly disassociate themselves from this viewpoint.

3. The translations of the Chinese texts into English were done without reference to the existing English texts. They attempt to represent as naturally as possible in English the propositions that the original writers intended their Chinese readers to recover.

4. It is of interest that this letter received widespread criticism in the English language media, and a number of the bank's English (speaking) customers closed their accounts in consequence. One might hypothesize that the assumptions implicit in the positive politeness stance of parts of the E text were insufficiently oriented to the negative face of some English speaking customers.

5. Some Chinese members of staff were moved by this letter; some suspected a political motive; some were scathing. One might hypothesize that encoding large P in institutions such as universities will sometimes be counterproductive in dealing with colleagues.

References

Bond, Michael Harris (ed.) 1986. *The Psychology of the Chinese People.* Hong Kong: Oxford University Press.

Bond, Michael Harris and Hwang Kwang-kuo. 1986. "The social psychology of Chinese people". In: M.H. Bond (ed.), pp. 213-266.

Brown, Penny and Stephen C. Levinson. 1978. "Universals in language usage: politeness phenomena". In: Esther N. Goody (ed.). *Questions and Politeness.* Cambridge: Cambridge University Press, pp. 56-311. Reprinted with new introduction and revised bibliography as *Politeness: Some Universals in Language Usage.* 1987. Cambridge: Cambridge University Press.

Chinese Culture Connection (Michael Bond). 1987. "Chinese values and the search for culture-free dimensions of culture". *Journal of Cross-Cultural Psychology* 18:143-164.

Greenberg, Joseph Harold. 1978. *Universals of Human Language*. Cambridge, Mass.: MIT Press.

Grice, H. Paul. 1967. "William James lectures: Logic and conversation". In: Peter Cole and Jerry L. Morgan (eds.). *Syntax and Semantics 3: Speech Acts*. 1975. New York: Academic Press, pp. 41-58. Also in: Davis, Stephen (ed.). *Pragmatics: A Reader*. 1991. Oxford: Oxford University Press, pp. 305-315.

Grundy, Peter. 1995. *Doing Pragmatics*. London: Edward Arnold.

Hall, Edward T. 1976. *Beyond Culture*. Garden City, New York: Anchor Press.

Hofstede, Geert. 1980. *Culture's Consequences*. Beverley Hills: Sage.

Hofstede, Geert. 1991. *Cultures and Organizations*. London: McGraw-Hill.

Kahn, H. 1989. *World Economic Development: 1979 and Beyond*. London: Croom Helm.

Leech, Geoffrey N. 1983. *Principles of Pragmatics*. Harlow: Longman.

Lucy, John Arthur (ed.). 1993. *Reflexive Language: Reported Speech and Meta-pragmatics*. Cambridge: Cambridge University Press.

Mehan, Hugh. 1991. "The school's work of sorting students". In: Zimmerman and Boden, pp. 71-90.

Schegloff, Emanuel A. 1987. "Between micro and macro: context and other connections". In: Alexander, Jeffrey, Bernard Giesen, Richard Munck and Neil Smelser (eds.). *The Macro-Micro Link*. Berkeley: University of California Press, pp. 207-234.

So, Wing-cheung, Daniel. 1987. "Searching for a bilingual exit". In: Robert Lord and Helen Cheng Ngai-Lun (eds.). *Language Education in Hong Kong*. Hong Kong: Chinese University Press, pp. 240-268.

Sperber, Dan and Deirdre Wilson. 1986. *Relevance: Communication and Cognition*. Oxford: Basil Blackwell.

Thomas, Jenny A. 1983. "Cross-cultural pragmatic failure". *Applied Linguistics* 4.2:91-112.

Yang, Kuo-shu. 1981. "The formation and change of Chinese personality". *Acta Psychologica Taiwanica* 23:39-56.

Yang, Kuo-shu. 1986. "Chinese personality and its change". In: Bond, pp. 106-170.

Yum, June Ock. 1988. "The impact of Confucianism on interpersonal relationships and communication patterns in East Asia". *Communication Monographs* 55:374-388.

Zimmerman, Don H. and Deirdre Boden (eds.). 1991. *Talk and Social Structure: Studies in Ethnomethodology and Conversation Analysis*. Cambridge: Polity Press.

Cultural keywords in Chinese-Dutch business negotiations

Xiangling Li
Eindhoven University of Technology

and

Tom Koole
Utrecht University

0. Introduction[1]

In this paper we will argue that word meaning is something attributed to that word by its users rather than a property of the word itself. In a commonly used model, verbal communication is depicted as a process in which a speaker or writer 'encodes' a message in order to 'send' it to a hearer or reader who in turn 'decodes' that message. This coding process would account for the transfer of the message from one head into another. However, research of language-in-use has made it clear that this model, although useful for some practical purposes, is too reductionist to be valuable as a basis for research. The meaning of verbal utterances is not as fixed as this model seems to presuppose. For one thing, meanings are linked to interpretative frames of participants, and, for another, meanings are also produced by the participants in the course of the interaction.

Here we will address the problem of word meaning in the context of Chinese-Dutch face-to-face interaction. The analysis will show how word meaning relies on reference to specific cultural knowledge. The data consist of simulated business negotiations, gathered in an adapted version of the Kelley Game (Kelley 1966), in which English is used as a *lingua franca*. The negotiators are both real-life negotiators with comparable international negotiation experience.

In our analysis we have focused on the Chinese use of the word 'support'. We will argue that the Chinese negotiator uses this word in a way which is specific to his culture, in that he uses it as part of 'aligning actions' (Stokes & Hewitt 1976). We will provide evidence from the interactional context, such as the discursive actions in which 'support' is used and the sequential placement of these actions in the Chinese-Dutch interactions. Moreover, we will attempt to dig out the deep-rooted cultural connotations behind the concept.

Although the use of 'support' by Chinese negotiators was found in several business negotiation sessions, including an authentic Finnish-Chinese session, we will focus our present analysis on a particular one-hour-and-a-half session, since this will enable us to elaborate on the analytically important aspect of the interactional development of the discourse and the sequential placement of 'support' in it.

Before we proceed to an analysis of the interactional data, we will provide a short discussion of relevant research with respect to the relation of word meaning to cultural diversity.

1.   Word meaning and culture

We will not attempt to provide a comprehensive discussion of linguistic relativity (but see the recent volume edited by Gumperz & Levinson, 1996). We will, however, discuss research on the relationship between cultural knowledge and word meaning and the approaches these researchers have chosen to investigate this relationship.

In her book on cross-cultural pragmatics, Wierzbicka (1991) warns against setting universal parameters for the investigation of different cultural practices:

> It seems obvious that if we want to compare different cultures in terms of their true basic values, and if we want to do it in a way that would help us to understand those cultures, we should try to do it not in terms of our own conceptual artefacts (such as the English self-assertion or sincerity) but in terms of concepts which may be relevant to those other cultures as well — that is, in terms of concepts which are relatively, if not absolutely, universal. (1991:71)

Global labels such as directness, self-assertion, distance, intimacy, solidarity, harmony, informality, sincerity, and some others are often believed to stand for identifiable cultural values, but Wierzbicka argues that they cannot be applied to different cultures in the same manner. Research on politeness practices, for instance, points towards a Chinese perception of politeness that differs from that prevalent in the West (Gu 1990; Chen 1993; Song Mei 1993). Among others, imposition as a fundamental concept in the prevalent politeness theory of Brown & Levinson (1987) needs to be redefined in the Chinese context. The assumption that indirectness is a strategy for conveying politeness in requests is shown to be inaccurate for Chinese speakers.

With respect to word meaning Wierzbicka provides the examples of five Australian speech-act verbs and argues that they cannot be explained with reference to universal parameters, but derive their meaning from some characteristic features of Australian culture: the verbs *to hiack*, *to yarn*, *to shout*, *to dob*, and *to winge* are related to the Australian practices of sociability, mateship, and enjoyment of joint activities with one's 'mates'.

This relationship between linguistic elements and cultural practices and knowledge is also the basis of Gumperz' contextualization theory (e.g. 1982; 1992). Gumperz argues in this theory that participants in verbal communication use different types of linguistic devices for signalling to the other participant(s) which interpretative frames (contexts) are relevant for the interpretation of the verbal utterances: "Roughly speaking, a contextualization cue is any feature of linguistic form that contributes to the signalling of contextual presuppositions" (Gumperz 1982:131). This insight has been used by Gumperz and others for the analysis of intercultural communication, and more specifically to explain the occurrence of misunderstandings in communication. Gumperz has shown that 'contextual presuppositions' or interpretative frames can be highly culture-specific, with the result that one linguistic form may signal different presuppositions for speakers from different cultures. In his research, Gumperz has shown that contextualization cues can range from intonation contours and minimal responses to words and phrases.

Koole & ten Thije (1994) have shown that differences in word meaning do not arise solely from differences in national cultures. In their study of meetings in Dutch institutions, they discuss the use of 'institutional key words': "words that have a meaning that is specific of their use in [an] institution or organisation" (1994:139). They use the term *keyword* to emphasise that the knowledge of the keyword's meaning distinguishes qualified from non-qualified institutional actors. Those who enter the organisation or institution will have to learn this meaning to become full members of the institutional or organisational culture. They also point towards the fact that key words may be both 'new' words (like the Australian verb *to hiack*), and also existing words that are given a new meaning. The first type may lead to an immediately repairable *not* understanding, but the latter type carries the greater communicative danger since it may lead to a *mis*understanding which is not immediately recognised for repair.

In the analyses below we will argue that the specific use the Chinese negotiator makes of 'support' has many characteristics of these keywords: in the present discourse it is one of the discursive means with which a distinction is made between the Chinese participant as a member of one cultural group and the Dutch participant as a member of a different one. We will therefore adopt and adapt this terminology and speak of 'cultural keywords' as words that have a meaning specific to their use in a specific cultural context. By cultural context we refer to the culturally specific interpretative frames Gumperz defines in his contextualization approach.

2.   Data analysis

2.1. *The use of 'support' in the introductory phase*

Excerpt (1) is taken from the introductory phase of the negotiation. Although the two companies have been doing business for six years, the negotiators themselves are both new in their present positions. Preceding the excerpt, the Chinese negotiator has thanked his Dutch colleague for organising this meeting. Subsequently the Dutch negotiator has introduced himself and displayed enthusiasm for the rapidly developing Chinese economy. Also he has mentioned that he expects a successful negotiation because of the six-year friendship relationship between the two companies. During this Dutch introduction the Chinese negotiator confines himself to frequent "ja" and "yea" acknowledgements.[2]

Excerpt (1) starts just before the Chinese negotiator takes the floor from the Dutch.

excerpt (1) (see Appendix for transcription conventions)

89	D:	Ehn:: if I add to that the experience that
90		both companies have enjoyed in the past, I
91		think it will be easy
92	C:	((nodding))
93	D:	to come to ehn:: an:: agreement for both of
94		us.=
95	C:	=Ye:ss, (0.8) <I've found thatuh (0.8) our
96		<u>two</u> company have a very <u>goo</u>tuh relationship
97		(.) .hh for quite long ti:me. (1.5) A:nu:h (.)
98		I feel (1.0) CONfident thatuh (0.7) we
99		can come to:: (0.7) a:: a: a: a: (.) a new
100		agreement (.) for my orders. (1.1) But
101		according to the:: to the: to the
102		nego<u>tia</u>tions with mister VanRIce (1.5) I:
103		(0.8) <u>foun</u>t (1.1) er:: from: (.) >this
104		gentleman< (0.7) that there are something
105		(.) er:: (1.2) to: to to (2.0) need your
106		<u>ef</u>forts (.) in improving: (.) your <u>price</u>
107		because of thi:: the compe<u>ti</u>tion (.) at
108		this moment. (1.4) So that's why mister
109		Vanrice lea:ves thi: <u>price</u> negotiation
110		(0.8) >with you<.
111		(1.2)
112		>I <u>think</u> you see< u:h on <u>my</u> hh (.) in <u>my</u>
113		head you see .hhh I <u>think</u> it's necessary
114		>because you see:< (0.8) h/ e: as you
115		saitu:h (.) <u>you</u> a:re (.) >in ye company:<
116		(.) not <u>al</u>so not very LONG (.) so: .hh I
117		thinktnecessary for us to:: MEET a:nuh (.)
118		through our both efforts to settle this .hh
119		<u>price</u> program.
120	D:	Yes↑=
121	C:	=so that we ca: (.) er:: (0.7) mmh <u>leadz</u>
122		zi: >zi PERsonal< (0.5) friendship between
123		us (1.0) to a:: (1.0) to a more (1.5) >to a
124		<u>new</u> stage< (1.1) in which is necessary to
125		develop (.) for the new (.) new bins. >So
126		<u>that</u>'s why:,< (.) °mmh:::° (1.1) >from <u>our</u>
127		side I'll try:< our best to coope<u>ra</u>te. But
128		<u>one</u> thing (.) we need <u>more</u> i:s (.) er:: to
129		have a: sup<u>port</u> (.) from you especially .hh
130		at thiss (.) er: compe<u>ti</u>tion (.) market.
131		(1.1)

132	D:	Right↑=
133	C:	=Yea
134		(0.9)
135	D:	e::h (1.3) I understand from your words,=
136	C:	=>Yea<
137		(0.8)
138	D:	thate:he::h (0.8) you expect uh<u>us</u> (0.9) er:
139		to: give you suppohort,=
140	C:	=Yea
141	D:	(.) butuh we havv (.) done it al<u>ways</u>,
142	C:	>Hn< ((nodding))
143	D:	so e::r I don't think that it isuh <u>reason</u>
144		to (.) have <u>any</u> doubt,
145	C:	yheh
146	D:	that we will <u>not</u> offer you support on
147		different ways (.) to reach this agreement.
148	C:	Yea.
149	D:	E::r (0.9) I: think that it is also well
150		wi:se to mention that (0.9) compe<u>ti</u>tion
151		you're right,
152	C:	[Yea
153	D:	[Is getting (.) e:r in Europe in Western
154		countries=
155	C:	=Yea.
156	D:	e::r indeete:re:r mor:e extensive, (0.7)
157		bute:r you have also seen (.) that we
158		havu:h (.) in<u>ves</u>ted in very <u>so</u>phisticated
159		(0.6) er:: e<u>qui</u>pment with computer-<u>ai</u>ded
160		de<u>si</u>gn,
161	C:	((nodding))
162	D:	Annu:h <thatuh is giving> (.) an ad<u>van</u>tage
163		(.) ffor our products, which you cannot
164		find by the competitors.

In his contribution the Chinese negotiator stresses that efforts will have to be made. He closes his contribution with the following statement: "from our side I'll try our best to cooperate. But one thing we need more is er:: to have a: support from you especially .hh at thiss competition market." (126-130). Through the use of "but" this statement focuses primarily on the second part, that is, not on the Chinese' display of willingness to cooperate, but on his display of need for Dutch support.[3] This focus is also recognised by the Dutch who in his response takes up the topic of support (135-139).

However, this response does not follow immediately. The Dutch seems to be uncertain whether he is to respond at all, and if so, what kind of response is expected of him. The Dutch negotiator waits 1.1 seconds, and when the Chinese does not continue, he produces a "right" (132) which is certainly not a claim to the floor, but still leaves open the possibility of a turn prolongation by the Chinese. This possibility is ruled out, however, after the Chinese produces a "yea" and then pauses again for 0.9 seconds. We can conclude that with his statement in lines 126-130 in which the focus is on the need of support, the Chinese negotiator marks a place after which speaker change should occur (a 'transition relevance place' (Sacks et al. 1974)), or perhaps even projects a specific relevant next utterance in the way that for instance questions project answers (Schegloff & Sacks 1974).

At the same time we can conclude that the Dutch negotiator does not interpret it as a transition relevance place; moreover, he appears to have no idea of any relevant next action. He starts with two hesitation signs: "e::h" and a 1.3 second pause and then produces what Heritage & Watson (1979) have called a 'formulation' in which he displays his understanding of the interaction for the other to assess (135-139). He even makes his uncertainty more apparent by announcing the formulation explicitly as his understanding of the other's words ("I understand from your words" (135)), by which he leaves open the possibility of having misunderstood. In short, the Dutch does not know what to make of the request for support. First he is not sure *if* he should respond, and then he is not sure *what* to respond.

The Dutchman interprets the request for support still hesitantly ("e:he::h", pauses) as "you expect us to give you support". This interpretation becomes even more visible in this response when, with "but" (141), he creates an opposition between the Chinese request and "we havv done it always" after which he concludes "so e::r I don't think it isuh reason to have any doubt that we will not offer you support ...". Thus, the Dutch negotiator interprets the request as a display of doubt on the Chinese side whether the Dutch will support the Chinese. In this way the Dutch negotiator responds to the pragmatic presupposition of making a request (Searle 1969: 'felicity condition') that the requested person will only perform the requested action if requested to do so.

In Chinese, however, the request for help or support is used to show humility and respect for the other person. It is a highly conventionalised sequence used for the initial phase of an interaction and sometimes also for the closing phase. Pye (1992), for instance, reports that leaders of negotiation teams frequently end substantial sessions by saying something like 'we are counting upon you to help us achieve international standards as far as possible'. In the Chinese cultural context the manifestation of humility and respect does not play down the speaker; rather, it elevates the face of the addressee and aims to make him feel important and obliging. We will elaborate on this cultural meaning in section 3.

An example of the use of this request can be found in the introductory phase of a Kelley game conducted by two Chinese business men in Chinese. We here present a translation followed by the original Chinese transcript:

excerpt (2)

1	C1:	Before me, the predecessor, [my predecessor
2	C2:	[Yea, yea.
3	C1:	has had lots of dealings with Campax, and
4		our company has always had favourable
5		treatments from your honourable company.
6		For this I express my gratitude. Yes, for
7		this I express my gratitude.
8	C2:	$ Yea, yea, I'm glad to cooperate with
9		you.$
10	C1:	I hope Mr. Li will offer us more help for
11		the future development of our company.
12	C2:	Don't mention it, don't mention it.
13	C1:	Mutual help, in this way can we make joint
14		efforts for the promotion and sales of the
15		products from your honourable company.
16	C2:	Yea, yea, yea.
17	C1:	Also for the development of our own com-
18		pany.

C1:	在我以前，前任，［我的前任］，
C2:	［对对］，
C1:	已经和 CAMPAX 公司已经有很多的业务往来，而且我们公司一直能从贵公司得到很大的优惠，我对此表示感谢，对此表示感谢。
C2:	$对对，很乐意合作$，
C1:	希望李先生以后也对我们的公司的以后的发展能够多一点多一些帮助，=
C2:	=哪里哪里，=
C1:	=互相帮助，这样的话我们共同为推销贵公司的产品来做出努力，=
C2:	=对对对，
C1:	也对我们自己的公司的发展做出一些努力，

The part we are particularly interested in is lines 10 to 12. In lines 10 and 11 C1 makes a request for help (Chinese: *zhichi*), comparable to the request for support we saw in excerpt 1. In the Chinese context, asking for help is very much synonymous with asking for support, although the former sounds a bit more direct and thus has more face value. C2 responds to this request in line 12 with a repeated "don't mention it": a response which fits a preceding display of thankfulness, or a preceding compliment, rather than a preceding request.

The request for support or help forms the first part of a Chinese sequence which as a second part does not contain a positive or negative response to that request but an acknowledgement of the other's display of humility or respect.

Again this sequence can be understood from a pragmatic presupposition of making a request, only a different one than the Dutch negotiator in excerpt (1) is oriented to. In this Chinese sequence, participants orient to the pragmatic presupposition that the requested person is deemed capable of performing the requested action. It is this ascription of capability to the other which lends this sequence its respect-displaying character. It is ironic that these two presuppositions, which are both present in the action of making a request, can lead to such different interpretations of this action: instead of understanding the request as a display of respect and feeling obliged, the Dutch negotiator in excerpt (1) takes it to be a display of distrust.

2.2. *The use of 'support' to handle disagreement and non-alignment*

In this section we focus on a second use the Chinese negotiator makes of 'support'. We discuss fragments of the negotiation in which the two negotiators are in disagreement as well as in non-alignment. With this latter notion (used by Stokes & Hewitt 1976) we refer to the fact that the discourse often appears to be incoherent. Both participants dwell on separate topics and repeat their arguments without getting closer to a consensus or to an overt acknowledgement of their failure to agree. And in all these fragments the Chinese negotiator attempts to repair both the disagreement and the non-alignment by requesting or claiming support.

2.2.1. *The choice of currency*

In the first phase, the choice of currency for the business deal is discussed. In this discussion the Dutch negotiator suggests using another currency than US dollars because the dollar has much devaluated recently. He argues that using the dollar would force him to increase prices. The Chinese negotiator, on the other hand, argues that they have always paid in dollars, also in times when the dollar as a strong currency was less favourable for the Chinese, and that the currency should not be changed because the Dutch company is now at the unfavourable end of the bargain. A second argument put forward by the Chinese is that the competitors of the Dutch company are also offering their products in dollar prices.

The discussion is too long to be presented in full but for a proper understanding we will present some exchanges in which the two negotiators repeatedly perform a two-part sequence consisting of the Dutch proposing a different currency and the Chinese rejecting this proposal.

excerpt (3)

243	D:	Or do you consider to pay us in the
244		guilders or Deutsch marks.
245	C:	Well, in this respect (.) I have to say (.)
246		usually in all our purchase from abroad we
247		all use US dollars.

excerpt (4)

255	D:	I was trying to offer you=
256	C:	=ahn↓ en↑
257	D:	to pay maybe in another currency than the
258		US dollars, you make the preference for the
259		US dollar.(1.2) ((tapping at the table))
260	C:	No. but you have to consider the compita
261		your competitor is also is is offering the
262		same same currency.

excerpt (5)

285	D:	(.) margin is decreasing of 20%. I have
286		not to tell you that because we are huge
287		production size that we are not making such
288		margin, so we HAVE TO ASK your contribution
289		to increase and to share this increase.
290	C:	I understand you, (.) your difficulty, you
291		have something difficult in your production
292		cost. But you have to consider the: (.)
293		competition in the market and some o:f your

294	competitors in/ also in in in some are in
295	Netherland, some are in in Germany, they
296	are offering (.) still in US dollar. That's
297	a fact.(.) So you have to consider this
298	fact. I HOPE to to hope you to offer (.) in
299	US dollar.

In the last excerpt (5), we see that the Dutch negotiator is changing the topic from 'change of currency' to 'price increase'. He thus appears to concede to the dollar preference of the Chinese and asks him to accept the consequent price increase. The Chinese negotiator's response to this request is negative ("I understand you ... But ..."), but his repeated request to "offer in US Dollar" (298-299) seems to be non-aligned to the preceding Dutch concession. Possibly the Chinese's request for using the dollar is an argument against price increase, or, alternatively, he interprets the Dutch request as yet another try to change the currency.

Following this, the Dutch negotiator explicitly agrees on the use of the US dollar ("I agree we can do it in US dollars.") and then goes on to tell the Chinese that prices will therefore have to be increased. Interestingly, as in excerpt (5), the Chinese negotiator reiterates his seemingly non-aligned plea for the use of dollars:

excerpt (6)

327	C:	Er:: I understand you but I would like to
328		draw your attention to the fact that (.) we
329		always purchasing you er:: in the currency
330		of US dollar since the: ((using hand
331		gesture)) since we have [establish the
332	D:	[that's correct.
333	C:	relationship between our two companies.

Following this excerpt the Dutch negotiator repeats his consent ("we fully agree") on the use of US dollars, and his argument that this means a price increase, this time illustrated with an example. It seems that he interprets the insistence of the Chinese on the use of dollars as a token of not understanding.

The currency discussion is completed in the following way:

excerpt (7)

349	D:	=but therare limits you can not afford to
350		have such a <u>change</u>. Anat <u>that</u> moment <it is
351		wise> (.) that we:uh sit around the table
352		(.) and (I'd) say 'all right (.) we stick
353		to the same currency, <u>fair</u>' but dan the
354		price in US dollar is going to increase.
355		(0.9) So that wer <u>in</u>come (.) will be
356		somewhere (0.7) between hundred fifty and
357		two hundred guilders as we had in the past.
358		(1.3)
359	C:	>Yea<, well, I I I follow you what you
360		mea:n.
361		(1.5)
362		Ehr::
363		(1.4)
364		>yes, we/ since we have< °oo::h° done a lot
365		of biness (0.9) within: (0.8) paste:r e:r
366		six years.
367		(1.2)
368		A:n in that time, during that (.) long
369		period ((shaking head)) we (.) never
370		mention (.) about the:: (.) <u>cu</u>rrency: what
371		should be: a<u>dop</u>ted in our trans<u>ac</u>tion.
372		(1.0)
373		Al<u>though</u> someti:me (.) US currency iss/ was
374		quite <u>strong</u>.
375		(1.9)
376		A::nuh we we we we we still/ >we we a<u>gree</u><
377		to use the e:r US dollar, (.) asu:h/ (.) as
378		a (.) <u>CU</u>rrency.
379		(2.0)
380		A:nuh ((using hand gesture)) ssince (.) e:r
381		<u>bo</u>th of us/
382		(0.9)
383		e:r since e:r bo/ <u>mu</u>tual support and <u>mu</u>tual
384		<u>u</u>nderstanding (.) between us we neve:r (.)
385		argued aboutuh what currency to be used.
386		(0.8)
387		So at this moment, (.) although you facing
388		some: (0.8) something difficult (.) I
389		>hope< you can (.) consider from <<u>lo</u>:ng

```
390         term> (.) >biness relationship< (.) from
391         the development in the ↑future biness.
392         (0.8)
393    I: (.) >HOPE< (1.1) <you to assept my
394         suggestion. (.) To offer (.) °still in US
395         dollar°°>.
```

The excerpt begins with the conclusion of the Dutch negotiator's explanation which is responded to by the Chinese in the following way: he acknowledges the Dutchman's argument (359-360: "I follow what you mean"), and then continues with a repetition of his own argument that the currency must not be changed because it has now become a weak currency. In fact he rephrases an argument presented just before:

excerpt (8)

```
338    C:    sometimes the the the US dollar was quite
339          strong, so at that time we did not ask you
340          to change the currency,
```

It seems that the two negotiators both believe that the other does not understand and therefore take refuge in explanations and repetitions. This is also apparent in the Chinese repetition (fifth occurrence) of the suggestion to use US dollars (393-395). Most interesting, however, for the purpose of our present analysis is the argument the Chinese introduces here. He argues that they have not wanted to change the currency in the past "since e:r bo/ mutual support and mutual understanding" (383-384) and concludes from this ("so" (387)) that therefore the Dutch should not want to change the currency under the present circumstances.

In the first place we can conclude that the Chinese stays with his interpretation that his repeated (four times) arguments in favour of the dollar have not persuaded the Dutch. The placement of the argument of "mutual support and mutual understanding" at this stage of the discussion is an indication of the relative force this argument has for the Chinese. In the five times the Chinese negotiator has pleaded in favour of the dollar, it is only on the fifth occasion that he uses this argument.

Not only is it the fifth occasion, it will also prove to be the last occasion. The discussion goes on like this:

excerpt (9)

428		(2.3)
429	D:	Mister Li=
430	C:	=Yea
431	D:	we already agreed on that point.=
432	C:	=Yea ((nodding))
433	D:	Here we have already (0.6) no argument. The
434		only thing is that I uhuhe:r tryto explain
435		you (.) thate: oruh uh price quotation will
436		be higher, (.) than in the pahast, (0.7)
437		((C sits back)) <because of the US DOllar.>
438		(1.5)
439		That ise:r thi consequence of it. ((using
440		hand gesture))
441		>I agree with you:,< and then (.) we can
442		still (.) consider that (.) IF it goes fur-
443		ther down (.) or mu:modify, (.) we can
444		think about some some solution that it will
445		bring compensation to you (0.8) and your
446		company as well as to us. We coultuh all
447		tink about of/ s imagint (.) <THAT> (.) the
448		US dollar (.) gets 20%=
449	C:	=Yhah, [yhah ((nodding))
450	D:	[higher
451	C:	>yhah<
452	D:	that you get dan a lower price in US dol-
453		lar.
454	C:	Yhah, yhah, yha, yha
455	D:	And in this way we trying to be fair for
456		both parties.
457		(1.5)
458	C:	We:ll actually: it's nonsense forus to
459		disuh (.) cuss (0.9) about what currency to
460		be: used in our transactions.
461		(1.8) ((using hand gesture))
462		To argue the: (0.7) Currency, actually is
463		the argument of price.
464		(0.8)
465	D:	Yes,=
466	C:	=Yea,

In his reply the Dutch negotiator shows his uncertainty as to what he should respond. Apart from his hesitating 2.3 seconds (428) before responding, this uncertainty is also manifest in other aspects of his speech. He performs a 'formulation' in which he states his interpretation of the discourse-so-far. This action is an alignment device, and its content clearly shows that it is triggered here by the non-alignment experienced by the Dutch negotiator. In other words, he makes an attempt to repair a not-understanding which exists on his part at least. At the same time he also hints at not-understanding on the part of the Chinese negotiator by stressing that he *tries* (or *tried*) to explain (434), thereby implying that he did not succeed in explaining.

It is also interesting that, after the Chinese has made his request for support and the Dutchman has reacted in this way, the Chinese aligns to the topic of his Dutch partner. The utterance in which the request for support was made appears to be the last attempt the Chinese makes to argue the choice of currency. After this attempt has failed, he switches the topic to price ("To argue the: (0.7) currency, actually is the argument of price." (462-463)), thereby hinting that his currency arguments were actually price arguments, and that there was no non-alignment on his side. In any case, from that moment on he explicitly takes up the discussion of the proposed 20% price increase. We will look at this discussion in the next section.

For the moment we can say that the Chinese negotiator uses the argument of support after a sequence of repeated non-aligned actions. When also this argument fails to establish alignment, he makes his interpretation of the non-alignment explicit (currency is price) and explicitly changes the focus of his line of argument from 'currency' to 'price increase'.

2.2.2. *Dollar fluctuations and inflation*
This discussion shows some interesting parallels with the discussion on currency in terms of both disagreement and non-alignment and a concluding Chinese request for support.

In the discussion of price the Chinese negotiator introduces the argument of different rates of dollar fluctuation:

excerpt (10)

492	C:	((using hand gesture))
493		>Well you see mister Verwee:l<, (0.9) er:
494		talking about the currency, I would like to
495		draw another fact/ (.) draw attention to
496		another factor in China. >Well you see<,
497		you said thi: US dollar is devaluated a

498		lot. (.) By: twenty percent. (0.9) In:

498   lot. (.) By: twenty percent. (0.9) In:
499   comparison with the: gui̲lders.
500   (.)
501   D: °Yea:h°
502   (1.1)
503   C: >But you see<, WE ARE still facing: the
504   difficult (.) °in Chinese currency°°. The
505   ra̲te (.) between US dolla:r (.) to: Chinese
506   Renminbi̱: (1.9) er:: (.) it's: l/ only/ US
507   dollar is <only devaluated aboutu̱:h>
508   (0.8)
509   °how can° (.) °°mmmmhh°°
510   (1.6)
511   <abou:t>
512   (1.0)
513   >one̲ percent°<.
514   (1.6)
15   That's the trouble°
516   (1.5)
517   that's the trouble°.
518   D: ↑Mh↓hh
519   (1.3)
520   C: °°Ah°°
521   (.)
522   So (.) that (.) ((using hand gesture)) if
523   you̲ use̲ in US dolla:r (0.9) in our co̱:st
524   (.) you said you have devalu/ US dollar has
525   devaluated (.) by °twenty percent°°.
526   D: °°Hnn°°
527   C: But the co:st (1.0) e:r in U/ Renminbi it's
528   only (1.1) LESS.
529   (1.4)
530   °One percent°°.
531   (1.9)
532   >So that'suh< ( )/ that'suh trouble wu/ we
533   are facing °now°.
534   (0.9)
535   D: >All ri̲ght<
536   C: yeah
537   D: Butu:h one of the reason why you are
538   facing: th:is, (0.8) <is because you are
539   subje:ct in China,>
540   C: >Yah<
541   D: to a very huge in̲flation.

The Chinese argues that the dollar may have devaluated 20% in relation to the Dutch guilder, but only 1% in relation to Chinese Renminbi. A 20% price correction because of the dollar fluctuation would thus mean a real increase for the Chinese. Before he proceeds to draw this conclusion (following 'So' (532)) he uses several means to present this argument as a problem: he calls it 'difficult' (504), repeats the phrase 'that's the trouble' (515, 517), and also the prosodic features of his speech display the problematic nature of this information. For instance, the volume decreases in 'that's the trouble', and he produces a soft sigh (°°Ah°° (520)) following these phrases.

The Dutch negotiator does not respond to this display of trouble with a display of empathy. He responds to the content of the argument which he counters by stating that China is subject to a huge inflation. Following excerpt (10), he goes on to argue that this means that both prices and wages in China are increasing and that a 20% price increase is not so problematic. He concludes this argument as follows:

excerpt (11)

```
548   D:    But all right. So (.) HERE I would like to:
549         (1.1) ASK you if you understand the
550         mechanics, (.) and the reason why (.) it is
551         normal that you e:r:r must consider, of can
552         consider (1.6) an higher price (.) in US
553         dollars,
554   C:    >y [ea<
555   D:       [than you were accustomed to. Even
556         thou:gh e:r thatuh y: we try every year to
557         decrease our PRIces. But this time we w
558         have to increase them. Just only (.) prices
559         in dollars. In guilders, we kee:p the price
560         (.) going down. (.) I want you to be sure
561         that/ that we are doing that.
562         (1.3)
563         We give you a ́d/ an d/ decrease in our
564         quotation in guilders, (0.8) but (.) due to
565         the dollar's (.) exchange rate, you will get
566         an increase°.
567   C:    .hh ye:s: (.) but you see::::. .hh as I
568         explained to you (.) ((using hand gesture))
569         although you: keep thi: .hh US dollar at
570         the same level <as you offered previously,>
```

571		(.) but in Chinese (.) COst (.) they are
572		just the same. (.) So f/f/f/for your side,
573		>maybe you see< you/ you/ you/ .hh you
574		think you have lostuh a lot. (.) But in my
575		cost (.) we have/
576		(0.9)
577		the i/ it still keep the same same cost.
578		(1.1)
579		If you change (.) your offer (.) in
580		guilders, that means (.) our import cost
581		(.) will be increased >°by twenty
582		percent°°<.
583	D:	Ye:s,
584	C:	Yeah. So in that case, we can continue (.)
585		our business (.) with you. (.) That'suh
586		point.
587	D:	>All right.<
588		(1.3)
589		But I try to explain you that (0.9) because
590		you have a high inflation (1.0) certainly
591		in the: (.) big cities in China,
592	C:	°yeah°
593	D:	I've seen it in Shanghai, I (hu) only to
594		have to take a taxi (.) (but you seen) a
595		hotel price,
596	C:	Yeah
597	D:	prices are jus:/ you getting sky hi:igh,
598	C:	((nodding))
599	D:	it means that the public in China, your
600		customers, are expecting ook an increase of
601		your (.) saling price.
602		So you have a possibility (.) to recuperate
603		(.) <pa:rt of: your increased cost price>.
604		(4.6) ((doors banging))
605		I think dit is butu::h (.) uh definitely an
606		issue (.) that (.) we have to be sure that
607		we both understand.
608	C:	Well, mister Verweel, I/ I/ I can give you:
609		my calculation. I (.) for example °you see°
610		((using hand gesture)) if you offer us (.)
611		in Rem/ in US dollar two months ago,
612		(0.9)
613	D:	Ye:s?
614	C:	hundred dollars (.) equal RMB (1.8) 822.

In this excerpt it becomes clear that the two negotiators themselves are aware of possible non-alignment. They explicitly wonder whether the other understands (e.g. "ask you if you understand" (549); "we have to be sure that we both understand" (606-607)), or observe that they are not succeeding in their explanations ("as I explained to you" (567-568); "I try to explain [to] you" (589)). But non-alignment also shows in the responses they give each other: the Chinese negotiator does not take up the topic of inflation but repeats his argument of devaluation rates (567-582), and, just as we saw in excerpt (9), the Dutch negotiator responds by saying that he tries to explain and then repeats his inflation argument. Excerpt (11) is concluded by the Chinese negotiator who again initiates a repetition of his argument, this time (following this excerpt) with a calculation of the Renminbi equivalent of a 20% price increase.

The conclusion of the discussion is presented in excerpt (12). In this excerpt the non-alignment of the two participants shows in the lack of synchronicity between them. We see pauses at turn transition points (671; 697) and simultaneous starts (672-673; 700-701) showing that the participants frequently fail to recognise the nature of each other's discursive actions, and are therefore unable to predict turn endings and relevant next actions (cf. Erickson & Shultz 1982).

excerpt (12)

663	D:	but >you always< A::LWAYS get (.) an an
664		inflamation (.) in your all products. (.)
665		Which are make locally. That's the DANGER
666		of yeah just of the inflation.
667		But
668		(2.1)
669		we have been talking about (0.8) to an
670		increase of prices
671		(1.4)
672	C:	well, [anyhow, you see
673	D:	[of twenty percent and you say it
674		gives me problems.
675	C:	Ehr:: (.) I understan::du::h (0.6) uh
676		you::r difficulty what you are facing
677		(0.9)
678		but I >hope< you understand (.) >what< thi:
679		difficulty we are °facing now°°.

680		So (0.8) u:h at <u>this</u> (.) difficultuh <u>stage</u>
681		(.) we must (.) <support with each other>
682		(.) anuh
683	D:	°Yeah°
684	C:	we should have a mutual understanding (.)
685		to <u>smoo</u>thly (.) to over (zi) (.) difficult
686		(.) period (.) so let's (ef<u>fe</u>ct) (.) the
687		<u>fu</u>ture so that we can continue our business
688		relationship (.) anuh develop further for
689		our future business.
690		(1.5)
691		So I: (.) ><u>hope</u>< (.) <hope you <u>do</u> not look
692		for> the: single/ the profit for the single
693		transaction.
694		(0.9)
695		I hope you will look forward for <u>long</u>-term
696		intrest.
697		(2.0)
698	D:	I fully agree [with you, mister Li°
699	C:	[Yeah yeah yeah°˙((nodding))
700	D:	[(° °)
701	C:	[I UNderstand <you are facing
702		difficulties°>.

After the Dutch negotiator has once more attempted to convince his Chinese partner with the inflation argument, the Chinese negotiator changes his strategy in the way we also saw in the currency discussion. Note in the first place the similarities in the way he phrases his utterance: both in excerpt (7) and in excerpt (12) the Chinese negotiator refers to difficulties and makes a request for mutual support and understanding, after which he concludes by making a request (both times introduced with "I hope") to consider a more long-term interest.

Not only can we see similarities in the ways Mr. Li twice phrases this request, there is also a strong parallel with respect to sequential placement. Both requests are placed as the conclusion of an exchange of arguments in which both negotiators repeat their arguments without coming any closer to each other. In the second discussion the two participants even overtly display their awareness of not-understanding.

A third parallel lies in the fact that in both cases it is the Chinese negotiator who makes the request and thereby intervenes in the dead end street of repeated arguments.

2.2.3. *'Support' and the alignment of interaction*

In the preceding section we have discussed two occasions where the Chinese negotiator refers to support and understanding in an attempt to bring a close to a discussion in which the two participants have been proceeding along non-aligned tracks. This sequential placement of the request for support seems to be peculiar to some uses of that request. On further occasions it is used in clear attempts by the Chinese negotiator to focus the discussion on the issue of price.

Preceding excerpt (13), the Dutch negotiator has made two offers to make up for the price increase: he has offered to make special designs for the Chinese customers, and he has offered a promotion brochure to help sell the products.

excerpt (13)

829	C:	Yes we can do, we can accept it as as an,
830		as an, as an advertising material,=
831	D:	=Exactly.=
832	C:	=to to the Chinese [consumers.
833	D:	[Yes, I am trying to
834		help your company to
835		[sell,
836	C:	[ye:s, but you see, at this moment, the
837		most important we need your your favourable
838		offer for these (.) one thousand pieces
839		foz/ for these three products. (.) Thatzi
840		essentials.
841		(1.0)
842	D:	YES=
843	C:	=So: we we .hh e:r we we need your your
844		support (.) in offering us (.) a favourable
845		(.) pri:ce. For this (.) substantial order.
846		(2.4)
847	D:	Well I mentioned t before I thought we
848		agre:ed,
849	C:	>yea<
850	D:	that e:r our prices (.) e:r has been
851		decreased in guilders, and that we: offer
852		it (.) for the price of H.

The Dutch negotiator shows he believes they have reached agreement on the selling price (H) (847-848). We cannot discuss this misunderstanding at length here, except for the aspect that prior to this excerpt the Dutch negotiator twice makes his understanding of the agreement known to the Chinese negotiator (792: "So we are on price H"; 819-822: "we have agreed on the price of H"). In other words, when the Chinese negotiator responds to the offer of the brochure in excerpt (13), he is potentially aware of the existing misunderstanding.

It seems then that the request for support is used on these occasions as a strong means to align the discussion after this has been observably non-aligned. In the discussion on currency we saw the two negotiators following different argumentative tracks, repeating their arguments without getting closer to overt (dis)agreement until the Chinese negotiator made the request for support. In the discussion on dollar fluctuation and inflation we saw the same phenomenon. Moreover, in that discussion the participants overtly displayed their awareness of failing comprehension. And also the request in excerpt (13) concludes a sequence in which for the Chinese negotiator the existence of a misunderstanding was potentially apparent. In this conclusion the Chinese negotiator attempts to resolve the misunderstanding and to align the two participants in a discussion of the price issue.

However, he is not successful in his attempt. Following excerpt (13), the Dutch negotiator responds "I think we have not understood each other" (865-866) and then repeats his arguments without aligning to the Chinese request to discuss only the price issue. This results in a repeated request by the Chinese to discuss the price, again supported by a request for support (933-935):

excerpt (14)

```
919    C:      So let's (.) firstu:h settle (.) for our
920            order.
921            (2.4)
922            for one  thousa[nd pieces.
923    D:                     [ye:s
924            (1.2)
925    C:      And for the new design, we have to: (.) to
926            do some advertisement (.) a:nu::h (.)
927            introduce (.) >to the new design to the to/
928            to thi:/ .hh to the consumers, (.)
929            attracting (.) their interests. At that
930            time (.) you will refer to the (.) order
931            (.) °of the new design°°.
```

932		(1.0)
933		So at <u>this</u> moment, mister <u>V</u>erweel, I would
934		like to: (.) to: to (.) to to have your
935		sup<u>port</u> (.) in your offering for the one
936		thousand pieces °for this three products°°.
937		(0.8)
938	D:	Yes
939	C:	°yeah°
940	D:	I explain to you that e::r I made already
941		(0.6) a <u>de</u>crease in our quotation in
942		guilders, (.) ntherefore you get my full
943		suppo:ort, (.) and <u>therefore</u> I said (.) I'm
944		going to take as company Campac, I'm going
945		to take e::r the losses (.) that e:r we are
946		suffering (.) from an external factor which
947		is (.) the decrease of the US dollar.

It is also clear that the Dutch negotiator has recognised that the use of support has a special impact: he adopts it in his reply (943). At the same time, however, his use of the word does not reveal whether he understood the meaning this word has for the Chinese: it is used as a phrase interjected between an argument and its conclusion. It seems to be a verbal repetition, displaying recognition of a special import of the word rather than recognition of its exact meaning.

Further evidence for the Chinese' use of the request for support as an alignment device comes from the last sequence in which the Chinese negotiator uses this request. This sequence immediately follows the excerpts discussed just now and also show the Chinese negotiator's attempts to focus the discussion on the price issue. In contrast, the Dutch negotiator makes several attempts to introduce other topics, each time receiving as a response the Chinese' request to focus on the price issue. His last plea (excerpt (15)) is phrased as a warning that other suppliers offer better prices, accompanied by a request for support (1199-1200):

excerpt (15)

1199	C:	so <u>we</u> are <u>still</u> e:r looking forward (.) for
1200		your suppo:rt (.) and th continue (.) ou:r
1201		(.) cooperation.
1202		(1.6)
1203		So if you (.) insist (.) your offer, (.) it

```
1204            force me (.) to: look for the other
1205            supply°. This isuh not my desire.
1206            (1.4)
1207   D:       Right, [but <WHAT is the difference that
1208   C:            [So:
1209   D:       you are getting from (.) those other
1210            suppliers?>
```

Again the Chinese negotiator's sequential placement of the request for support is interesting. As in the examples discussed above, the request seems to mark an ultimate attempt of the Chinese negotiator to convince the Dutch. This is also clear from the argument that a continuation of the cooperation between the two companies depends on a better price offer by the Dutch.

3.   'Support' as a cultural key word

In the preceding section we have analysed a negotiation session on the use the Chinese negotiator makes of the word 'support'. We have seen basically two different uses. The first was the use in an introductory phase of the interaction (excerpts (1) and (2)). Here it was used in a request for help or support in order to give face to the other. We saw that this request is part of a standardised sequence in Chinese discourse in which the other acknowledges the respect displayed in this request.

The second use is also most commonly found in a request for support, and once in an argument stating that the two companies have mutually supported each other in the past (excerpt (7), 383-385). The Chinese negotiator employs this use of the word as a last means to repair repeatedly experienced non-alignment and/or disagreement between the two participants.

We have also shown that the Dutch negotiator is uncertain about the responses expected from him following the references to 'support'. In the introductory phase the Dutch negotiator interprets the request as a display of Chinese distrust. In a later part of the negotiation session, the Dutch negotiator shows he recognises that the term 'support' has a special meaning for the Chinese negotiator, although he does not share this meaning with him.

Above, we already discussed the sequence in the introductory phase as a specific Chinese sequence in which the request for support was used to display respect for the other. This sequence is part of a more general Chinese practice of placing great value in personal relationships, displayed in discourse by making reference to these relationship. The Chinese term for this practice is *Guanxi*. Due to the clear Chinese distinction between ingroup and outgroup members (Huang 1988), ingroup members as bound by the *Guanxi* relationship are obliged to help members of their group, while outgroup members are allowed to act free of obligation. *Guanxi* and the "Guanxi distance" one has with one another (Wen 1988) is one of the basic cultural principles guiding Chinese behaviour.

> By allowing *Guanxi* to influence difference responses, the Chinese feel particularly comfortable with, are at the same time burdened with, obligations toward people of their own ingroup, since mutual support and help is most likely to occur when one is perceived as an ingroup member. (Chang & Holt 1991:257)

The fact that in the data presented above the Chinese recurrently appeals to the Dutch for support and understanding can therefore be seen as evidence that he perceives the Dutch partner as one special sort of ingroup member, possibly because of the good relationship between the two companies in the past six years. At the same time the Chinese appeals for support are the means by which the Chinese constructs the Dutch negotiator as an ingroup member in the there-and-then negotiation activity.

Pye (1992) has also observed this phenomenon in the context of negotiation:

> In their own distinct cultural fashion the Chinese attempt to create emotional ties with their negotiating partners. To some degree they seemed to be asking in a guarded and indirect fashion for help and protection. They would seek security by creating a dependency relationship that would at the same time oblige the powerful to treat them with consideration and not allow them to be hurt. (1992:98)

The clear distinction between ingroup and outgroup is that ingroup members focus upon caring for each other and helping each other in times of need and outgroup members focus upon the rules of equity, disregarding human feeling (Huang 1988). Also Pye concludes that the Chinese seem to transform the inherently adversary character of negotiations into a sheltering relationship (1992:71). In our analysis above we not only saw this phenomenon in the references the Chinese makes to (mutual) support, but also in the emotions he displays in excerpt (9), prosodically and verbally by repeating "that's the trouble".

From this cultural perspective we can observe that the failure of the Dutch negotiator to respond to the emotion displays and to the requests for support rather corresponds to Chinese behaviour towards outgroup members. In other words, from a Chinese point of view, the Dutch negotiator addresses the Chinese as an outgroup member rather than as an ingroup member.

At the same time we should also observe that the Chinese treatment of the Dutch partner as an ingroup member is not free of obligations for the latter. Whereas the request for support in the introductory phase (excerpts (1) and (2)) has primarily an interpersonal meaning, the latter requests are much more instrumental in getting the other to make concessions. These requests are not directed at establishing or defining an interpersonal relationship, but rather refer to that relationship in order to make the other comply to the obligations that belong to that relationship. The Chinese negotiator uses the requests for support as an ultimate means for resolving a situation of disagreement and non-alignment: he urges the Dutch negotiator to comply to his obligations as an ingroup member by aligning to certain discourse topics, or by conceding to a Chinese proposal (e.g. to use dollars).

Our analysis in the preceding section showed the Chinese negotiator to use the word 'support' in specific discourse contexts. These contexts allowed us to conclude that support is requested or claimed as a last means for repairing non-alignment and disagreement. In this section we have complemented our analysis with information from studies on Chinese thinking and practice to the effect that we can now understand why in Chinese discourse the requested or claimed 'support' can be used in such a way.

This combination of discourse analysis and studies of Chinese culture has allowed us to characterise the Chinese negotiator's use of the word 'support' as particular of Chinese culture. This is why we have called 'support' a 'cultural keyword': it is used with a meaning that is specific to its use in the Chinese cultural context. At the same time is has become clear that the *Guanxi* meaning of the word 'support' is not a feature of that word but rather a feature of the cultural practice in which the word is used. The practice and the meaning of the word are mutually dependent. It is not only the practice which lends meaning to the word, but it is also the word which gives meaning to the requests in which it is used.

Notes

1. We wish to thank Susanne Günthner and Susanne Niemeier for their helpful comments on an earlier version of this paper, and Charles Campbell for his help in producing correct English.

2. It is remarkable that our data show the Chinese using acknowledgement tokens extremely frequently and the Dutch using hardly any whereas research of Chinese-German interaction showed the opposite (Günthner 1993 a and b).

3. This structuring of information in the Chinese argumentation is in agreement with the end-focus information principle of the Chinese language (He 1992). The most important information, the appeal for support, is reserved for the end focus.

Appendix:

Transcription conventions

/	repair
( )	not understood
(walks)	good guess
(1.0)	pause of 1 second
(.)	pause of less than 0.5 second
((laughs))	naming a verbal activity
.	sentence-final falling intonation
,	non-sentence-final-rising intonation
?	sentence-final rising intonation
!	an animated tone, not necessarily an exclamation
<u>ask</u>	stressed
°now°	softly spoken
°let me know°°	volume diminishes towards end of utterance
NOW	loudly spoken
co:st	lengthened sound
<your part>	pronounced at slower speed than surrounding talk
>let me know<	pronounced at higher speed than surrounding talk
=	latching of contiguous utterances, with no interval or overlap
$	passages spoken in 'smile voice'
[ ]	overlapping talk
↓↑	marked falling and rising shifts in intonation

References

Brown, Penelope and Stephen C. Levinson. 1987. _Politeness: Some Universals in Language Usage._ Cambridge: Cambridge University Press.

Chang, Hui-Ching and G. Richard Holt. 1991. "More than relationship: Chinese interaction and the principle of Kuan-Hsi". _Communication Quarterly_, 39: 251-271.

Chang, Hui-Ching and G. Richard Holt. 1994. "A Chinese perspective on face as interrelational concern". In: Ting-Toomey, Stella (ed.), _The Challenge of Facework: Cross-Cultural and Interpersonal Issues._ Albany: State University of New York Press.

Chen, Rong. 1993. "Responding to compliments: A contrastive study of politeness strategies between American English and Chinese speakers". _Journal of Pragmatics_ 20: 49-75.

Erickson, Frederick and Jeffrey Shultz. 1982. _The Counselor as Gatekeeper. Social Interaction in Interviews._ New York: Academic Press.

Gu, Yueguo. 1990. "Politeness phenomena in modern Chinese". _Journal of Pragmatics_ 14: 237-257.

Gumperz, John. 1982. _Discourse Strategies._ Cambridge: Cambridge University Press.

Gumperz, John. 1992. "Contextualization revisited". In: Peter Auer and Aldo di Luzio (eds.), _The Contextualization of Language._ Amsterdam: John Benjamins, pp. 39-53.

Gumperz, John J. and Stephen C. Levinson (eds.). 1996. _Rethinking Linguistic Relativity._ Cambridge: Cambridge University Press.

Günthner, Susanne. 1993a. "German-Chinese interactions differences in contextualization conventions and resulting miscommunication". _Pragmatics_ 3, no.3: 283-304.

Günthner, Susanne. 1993b. _Diskursstrategien in der interkulturellen Kommunikation. Analysen deutsch-chinesischer Gespräche._ Tübingen: Niemeyer.

He, Young. 1992. _Aspects of Discourse Structure in Mandarin Chinese._ Ph.D. thesis, Columbia University.

Heritage, John and Rod Watson. 1979. "Formulations as conversational objects". In: G. Psathas (ed.) _Everyday Language: Studies in Ethnomethodology._ New York: Irvington, pp. 132-162.

Huang, K. -k. 1988. "The human feeling of the Chinese" [in Chinese]. In: K. -s Yang (ed.), _The Thinking and Behavior of the Chinese._ Taipei: Yuan-liou Publishing Company, pp. 45-58.

Kelley, H. H. 1966. "A classroom study of the dilemmas in interpersonal negotiations". In: Archibald, K. (ed.), _Strategic Interaction and Conflict._ Berkeley, California: Institute of International Studies, University of California.

Koole, Tom and Jan D. ten Thije. 1994. _The Construction of Intercultural Discourse: Team Discussion of Educational Advisers._ Amsterdam-Atlanta, GA: Editions Rodopi B.V.

Pye, Lucian W. 1982. _Chinese Commercial Negotiating Style._ Cambridge: Oelgeschlager, Gunn & Hain, Publishers, Inc.

Pye, Lucian W. 1992. _Chinese Negotiating Style: Commercial Approaches and Cultural Principles._ Westport: Quorum Books.

Sacks, Harvey, Emanuel Schegloff, and Gail Jefferson. 1974. "A simplest systematics for the organization of turn-taking for conversation". _Language_ 50: 696-735.

Schegloff, Emanuel and Harvey Sacks. 1974. "Opening up closings". In: R. Turner (ed.) *Ethnomethodology: Selected Readings*. Harmondsworth: Penguin.

Searle, John R. 1969. *Speech Acts*. Cambridge: Cambridge University Press.

Song Mei, Lee-Wong. 1993. *Requesting in Putonghua*. Ph.D. thesis, Department of Linguistics, Monash University, Australia.

Stokes, Randall and John P. Hewitt. 1976. "Aligning actions". *American Sociological Review* 41, 838-839.

Wen, C. -i. 1988. "The Kuan-hsi of the Chinese" [in Chinese]. In: K. -s. Yang (ed.), *The Thinking and Behavior of the Chinese*. Taipei: Yuan-liou Publishing Company, pp. 30-44.

Wierzbicka, Anna. 1991. *Cross-cultural Pragmatics*. Berlin: Mouton de Gruyter.

'Harmonious cooperation' in an English - German intercultural business negotiation

Ralf Pörings

University of Giessen, Germany

0. Introduction

The speech event *negotiating* is characterized by cooperation as well as by competition. Ulijn & Strother (1995:250) give the following definition:

> Negotiation is a process in which two or more entities discuss common and (apparently) different interests and objectives in order to reach an agreement or a compromise (contract) in mutual dependence because they see benefits in doing so.

Negotiation includes competitive elements: the aims of the negotiators might seem fundamentally different. Nevertheless, it also demands cooperative behaviour on the subject level in the sense that both are mutually dependent in that neither of them can reach their aims on their own (Wagner & Petersen 1991:271). Negotiation models and guides (Fisher & Ury 1991; Mastenbroek 1989; also Ulijn & Strother 1995 in a chapter on international business negotiation) advise negotiators to adopt a problem-solving approach (PSA) in which the differing interests are seen as a mutual problem that needs to be solved. The whole negotiation process is regarded as an effort on both sides to come to a mutual solution (agreement) rather than to bargain over positions closely tied to the persons involved in the negotiation. This approach is reflected by maxims such as "separate the people from the problem" (Fisher & Ury 1991), "be hard on the problem, soft on the people", "play the ball, not the man" (Mastenbroek 1989:36). In separating the subject level from the relationship or interpersonal level the partly conflicting interests should be negotiated in a cooperative rather than in a distributive fashion. The interpersonal relationship should not be affected too much by the negotiation. PSA should allow for a "smooth, harmonious" interaction.

It is not clear, however, what these concepts mean when they are used in the context of intercultural negotiations. Therefore it is necessary to take a closer look at how they can be defined in order to gain useful criteria for the description and interpretation of verbal interaction.

1. Cooperation

Argyle — from a sociological perspective — defines cooperation as "acting together in a coordinated way at work, leisure or in social relationships, in the pursuit of shared goals, the enjoyment of the joint activity, or simply further-ing the relationship" (1991:15). This definition includes the subject level as well as the interpersonal one. Other than in negotiations, however, it assumes that the goals of both interactants are identical. But even on the very basic level of cooperation in communication, this is not necessarily the case. Keller (1987) distinguishes two aspects of cooperation: a) cooperation in communi-cation, in order to reach aims that are interdependent; and b) communication as cooperation, i.e. the general aspects of relating to the other's utterance, reacting to it, creating cooperative slots, and filling them with actions. Here, aims are interdependent but not identical. It is this second aspect of communi-cation **as** cooperation that this paper focuses on. Cooperation as a prerequisite of communication, however, can be employed for both cooperative and competetive efforts **in** communication (Keller 1987:12-13).

Cooperation as a basic aspect of communication is closely tied to the 'atmosphere' of the communication situation: if a partner does not fill in cooperative slots with adequate verbal actions, if he does not respond or does not listen, etc., or rather if the interlocutor has the feeling that he does not do so, these aspects will influence the relationship between interlocutors.

In a harmonious communication situation, partners have the feeling that they cooperate. Harmony in this sense certainly means the absence of conflict on the interpersonal level. According to the PSA model in negotiation guides, the negotiation interaction can be harmonious even if there are differing and potentially conflicting interests. However, even if the possibly conflictive aspects are regarded as problems on the subject level that can be solved in a mutual endeavour, this separation alone does not necessarily guarantee harmonious cooperation on the interactional level. In fact, differing assumptions about what constitutes a good atmosphere, a 'smooth interaction' may lead to evaluations of the partner's actions that impede the efforts to solve the problem on the subject level.

2. Harmony in intra- and intercultural communication

Arndt & Janney (1987) present a model of communication in which behaviour is planned on the basis of hypotheses about the situation. These hypotheses about the situation are again formed on the basis of more general hypotheses about interaction shared by members of a specific culture. In order to signal their evaluation of the situation as well as of the other's behaviour they have access to specific strategies of tact to maintain a mutual affective basis.

In an intracultural interaction it might seem relatively clear to participants what is needed — or what is to be avoided — in order to keep up an atmosphere of harmonious cooperation. Here, both partners share similar general assumptions and, as a result, expectations about what kind of interactional behaviour of the other can be judged as cooperative and when, as a consequence of this judgement, the whole interaction is felt to be harmonious. On the basis of these general cultural assumptions, partners continuously interpret the observed behaviour of the other and plan their own behaviour on the basis of assumptions about the partner that are continuously formed in the situation: hypotheses about what he is like, whether he is cooperative, likeable, and so on. If these situational hypotheses cannot be confirmed by observed behaviour they will be remodelled. The more convergent the situational assumptions of both partners, the more they have the feeling to understand each other and to cooperate (Janney & Arndt 1992). According to Argyle (1991), cooperation leads to positive affect.

In an intercultural communication situation — such as an intercultural business negotiation — it might be more difficult to achieve a common interpersonal basis for a conflict-free interaction than in intracultural interaction. Communication partners with different cultural backgrounds may have differing cultural assumptions about what kind of behaviour harmonious interaction entails. On the basis of their respective general cultural assumptions, they interpret each others' behaviour, and the observed behaviour may lead to differing hypotheses about the situation. As a result of the differing expectations as to what kind of behaviour can be interpreted within a positive reference frame, some behaviour of the partner may not be explicable and, if recurring, it might eventually only be explicable within a negative reference frame as not cooperative and as that kind of behaviour only an opponent will show (Janney & Arndt 1992).

3. The concept of *harmony* in pragmatics

When referring to the affective level of communication in pragmatics, harmony is a frequently used label. It seems, however, that pragmatic studies all too often simply trust that the Anglo-American everyday meaning of this concept can be applied as if it were a universal. Wierzbicka (1991) challenges this view and spells out harmony concepts from various cultures in a semantic metalanguage.

What is judged as cooperative interactional behaviour in one culture may be seen as not cooperative in another. It is therefore necessary to take a closer look at what cooperative interaction includes in a given culture (cf. Wierzbicka 1991). Then these observations can be stated in a way that allows for comparison in order to find similarities as well as different understandings that might lead to distortion of the interaction. However, scripts can only be compared if they share the same underlying dimensions and if these are made explicit. In order to be able to look for what might be same or different in the discourse behaviour of interactants with a different cultural background one needs to identify the aspects of behaviour that are the constituents of the cultural scripts. Although Wierzbicka (1991) does not explicitly state what these dimensions are, her explications of harmony in 'Anglo', Polish and Japanese cultures show the following dimensions:

- a relation between I and YOU
- a tendency either TO SAY or NOT TO SAY THINGS
- an evaluation of affect (FEEL GOOD/BAD ABOUT THIS)

Wierzbicka's explications are based on studies by researchers in the field of pragmatics and on introspection. If pragmatic analyses should yield explications of cultural scripts such as *indirectness* or *harmony*, however, this poses one big question: how can the underlying dimensions of the scripts under investigation be operationalized?

3.1. Harmony and facework

The facework that can be observed in an interaction is an indicator to the claimed identities of the interactants (Cupach & Imahori 1993). The interaction strategies they use indicate what constitutes a face-threatening act — what aspect of the face is threatened by this act — and also what kind of behaviour constitutes such an enormous face threat that it has to be avoided. Within their framework of politeness theory Brown & Levinson (1987) define two aspects of face:

> a) "negative face: the basic claim to territories, personal preserves, rights, non-distraction — to freedom of interaction and freedom of imposition" and b) "positive face: the positive consistent self-image or 'personality' (crucially including the desire that this self-image be appreciated and approved of) claimed by interactants".

Ting-Toomey (1988) elaborates on Brown & Levinson's framework, adding a dimension of self-direction vs. other-direction of strategies. Behaviour in interaction is influenced by these needs (association-dissociation) and concerns (self-other).

For an analysis of politeness strategies the following three dimensions (Ting-Toomey 1988:230) are at the centre of interest when investigating the concept of harmony:

> 1. Face Concern
> Orientation: is facework self-directed/other directed?
> 2. Face Need
> Is there a stronger need for autonomy or for association?
> 3. Mode
> Consequence for action: directness (say/not say), affect (positive/negative), judgement of behaviour (feel good/bad)

The following analysis will focus on some aspects of interaction that relate to face. Though these aspects can be interpreted within the facework framework (cf. Penman 1994), a detailed analysis of the face-strategies used by participants is clearly beyond the scope of this article.

3.2. Harmony and conflict

Ting-Toomey (1993) defines conflict as "an identity bound concept, in which the faces or the 'situated identities' of the conflict interactants are called into question." Based on this definition, harmony shall be defined as the absence of conflict on the interpersonal level: a verbal interaction is felt to be harmonious when both partners succeed, by the use of certain communication strategies, in satisfying their own face wants as well as those of their partner. Expectations as to what is face-threatening in a specific situation may vary from culture to culture. As Brown & Levinson point out:

> Every observer in a foreign land knows that societies [...] differ in terms of what might be called 'ethos', the affective quality of interaction characteristic of members in a society [...] 'ethos' refers specifically to interactional quality. In some societies interactional 'ethos' is generally warm, friendly; in others stiff, formal, deferential. (1987:243)

As a foreign observer's judgement this judgment might be sufficient — with respect to his own cultural and personal expectations and his assumptions about when the climate of the interaction can be judged as warm and friendly vs. stiff and formal, polite or rude.

For a linguistic description of what makes a harmonious, cooperative interaction in a given culture, though, the observer should try to define what he is actually observing. Furthermore, he should try to operationalise the constructs he employs when interpreting the observed behaviour. Last but not least, he should try to state his interpretations in a way that avoids culture-bound concepts such as *friendly* or *formal* in order to avoid ethnocentric tendencies as far as possible (cf. Wierzbicka 1991).

3.3. *Harmony in verbal interaction*

In this paper, harmony is defined as a cultural assumption concerning the relationship of interactants. It encompasses a) how the partners see themselves in relation to the other and, following from this image of self and other, b) what can be said to the other, and c) how it can be said (viewpoint).

The fact that interactional harmony is a concept guiding verbal interaction poses a problem: concepts are of course not directly observable; only a specific behaviour of an interactant and his partner's reaction following this behaviour can be observed and then interpreted: what is the function of this behaviour and why did this kind of behaviour occur (cf. Wagner & Petersen 1991). In the present paper, the following aspects will be at the centre of the analysis:

a) how do interactants orient their utterances when talking to the other (perspective I - YOU - WE) = orientation

b) how do they state their relation to the facts (disclosures, mitigators) = subjective vs. 'objective' viewpoint

c) how do speakers relate their utterances to what the prior speaker has said (turn-taking) = coordination

4. Explication of interpretations in a semantic metalanguage

This paper aims at pointing out some linguistic aspects of verbal interaction that are related to the concept of harmony and that allow for an explication with regard to the three underlying dimensions of the concept. Attempts to interpret the analysed features in order to explicate an interactional script are based on just one German-English intercultural negotiation simulation. As a consequence one should be careful not to overgeneralize the resulting explications as general cultural scripts. Nevertheless, inherent in these explications are of course features of the cultural scripts of English and German concepts of interaction.

The aspects of discourse I will take into consideration here, namely speech acts (acknowledgement, disclosure, edification as defined by Stiles 1992), mitigators, and turn-taking (Sacks, Schegloff & Jefferson 1974) are in some way or other related to the participants' concept of their identity in the negotiation situation (commonly called *face*). Their frequent use across situations reflects what kind of behaviour is regarded as common and acceptable; it gives hints to the global assumptions of interaction.

The meaning of discourse features that interactants employ can be explicated in a semantic metalanguage as proposed by Wierzbicka (1991). This metalanguage consists of a number of basic semantic building blocks that Wierzbicka and her associates identified in a wide range of cultures (see Goddard & Wierzbicka 1994). The metalanguage includes

Table 1. Semantic building blocks

[substantives]	I, YOU, SOMEONE, SOMETHING, PEOPLE
[determiners, quantifiers]	THIS, THE SAME, OTHER, ONE, TWO, MANY, (MUCH), ALL
[mental predicates]	KNOW, WANT, THINK, FEEL, SAY
[actions, events]	DO, HAPPEN
[evaluative]	GOOD, BAD

[descriptors]	BIG, SMALL
[intensifier]	VERY
[meta-predicates]	CAN, IF, BECAUSE, NO (NEGATION), LIKE (HOW)
[time and place]	WHEN, WHERE, AFTER (BEFORE), UNDER (ABOVE)
[taxonomy, partonomy]	KIND OF, PART OF

In contrast to highly abstract, culturally-laden concepts of pragmatics such as *politeness* and *directness* these semantic building blocks are easily understandable. If the results of analysis and interpretation are stated in a semantic metalanguage, the explications allow for a discussion of details of the cultural scripts as well as for comparison. However, it cannot be discussed here whether these building blocks are of universal status and therefore "culture-free" (Wierzbicka 1991, 1994). For the present purpose they are simply considered a powerful tool to explicate interpretations of interactional behaviour in an intersubjectively understandable way.

5.   Analysis and interpretation of the 'Agent Case'

5.1. *Brief description of the simulation*

A German producer and an English sales agent are negotiating about representation, commission on sales, and the conditions of payment of the agent. The conflicting issue is the commission for the English agent who claims 15%, whereas the German considers 5% a fair share. The Agent Case is a videotaped negotiation simulation of about 35 minutes.

5.2. *Coordination (turn taking): waiting for a possible* transition relevance point *(TRP) or just stepping in?*

5.2.1. *The English agent: waiting for a possible TRP*
The English negotiator's predominant strategy for turn-taking is to self-select at a TRP (after falling intonation or pauses) - 83% of all. There is only a 6.5% use of interruption, not all of them are successful in that the other keeps his turn. There are no overlaps when the Englishman attempts to get the floor. This behaviour is very much in line with the turn-taking behaviour that Coulthard (1985:61) states for English culture:

...any participant may self-select at the end of any sentence. Thus a speaker is vulnerable at every sentence completion whether he selects next speaker action or not, and even if he gets past one sentence completion he is equally vulnerable at the end of the next sentence.

Coulthard mentions "simply breaking in" as a possible option, but also includes the possible effects such a behaviour may have on the interlocutor: "A non-speaker who wishes to speak, but is unable to find a suitable entry spot has the option of simply breaking in, though this is frequently heard of as rudeness" (1985:65). Argyle's observations are similar: "At Oxford we found that interruptions in the middle of phrases are definitely disapproved of, those at the ends of clauses less so, while those at the ends of sentences are acceptable" (1991:179). A predominant English concept of interaction is first to let the other finish his contribution. Wierzbicka (1991:80) explicates the cultural script for turn-taking in Anglo-American culture as follows:

SOMEONE IS SAYING SOMETHING NOW
I CAN'T SAY SOMETHING AT THE SAME TIME
I CAN SAY SOMETHING AFTER THIS.

What the next speaker says after this has to be related to what the other has said during his last turn. As the English negotiator does not interrupt the statements of the German to state his view and as just stepping in is perceived as rudeness, what he wants to say cannot immediately be linked to what the other has just said. The Englishman's strategy is to add his own view using *yes-but* strategies. The first part of such an utterance acknowledges what the other has said, sometimes followed by *well* as a hesitation marker in the function of a face threat mitigator:

(1) G: I feel rather fine and eh (1,2) rather eager to see what's coming out from out negotiation.
     E: Mhm, yes, I see. I see you came here via the Netherlands [...]
         (the German wants to get down to business whereas the English negotiator acknowledges and goes on with preliminary talk) (AC3/4)

(2) G: sorry to say that eh but it/I guess it's better to say to this point very clearly, it's outside of my fingertip feeling.
     E: Mhm, yes, but the figure to you sounds reasonable, so let's say twelve percent. Would that be a reasonable figure for you? (AC224-226)

(3) G: [talking about a business accountant in his company who set the commission]...eh we inside our company are very proud to have just this specialist eh with us, and shareholders are lucky, too.

> E: Mhm..yes, I appreciate that. Yes, but ehm (1.3) well let's say at this
>   point that it would be a commission of twelve percent. (AC231/4)

This strategy can be explicated as follows:

I SAY: I HEARD WHAT YOU JUST SAID	(acknowledgement: *mhm*)
AND NOW I KNOW WHY YOU SAY SO	(token agreement: *yes, I see*)
NOW I WANT TO SAY SOMETHING ELSE	(*well*)
I SAY WHAT I THINK.	(*but*)

5.2.2   *The German negotiator: just stepping in*

Quite in contrast to the Englishman's turn taking behaviour, the German negotiator takes his turn to a large extent using interruptions (33%) and overlap (19%). More than half of these overlaps (63%) occur after a question by the English negotiator. It can be concluded that they are not intended to be disruptive but cooperative. The turn-taking behaviour of the German negotiator with a large proportion of overlap and interruption can be explicated as follows:

> YOU SAID SOMETHING NOW
> I WANT TO SAY WHAT I THINK ABOUT THIS
> I WANT TO SAY IT NOW.

A look at the incidences of overlap and interruptions show that they are obviously not aiming at disruption but at immediately showing a high level of interest in the other's statement. Questions as a strategy of other select (Jefferson et al. 1974) are often followed by overlap that way showing readiness to comply with the request for information:

(4)   E: I hope your trip to London (1.7) went o [kay?
       G: [No problem with
              the traffic and no problem with accomodation. (AC1)

(5)   E: ehhm perhaps if you could just outline again (1.4s) what kind of
              relationship you ex [pe...
       G: ·   [we want to see, yes. To eh start fair and
              frankly, we didn't have... (AC121)

(6)   E: But what would [that mean?]
       G: [It's ehh three times means ehh our
              experience is to round about five per cent. (AC151/2)

(7)   E: yes, and then, we would then expand the [agreement...
       G: [then expand and
              we/you and eh we will have more informations and...(123/4)

There is no obvious conflict because of these predominant turn-taking strategies, but there are some passages in the interaction where the Englishman
encounters difficulties getting the floor in order to state his point of view — as
in the following example:

(10)   G: (It's rather a good) eh ehh idea to say eh (1,9) eh (1,7) up to
            our experience eh an agent like you ehhm is paid fairly with
            ehh seven to eight per [cent and eh
       E: [mhm well, if I could[**just** dare to
            interrupt you there and begin   these por/oh]
       G: [**just** in
            with   just in in   my   ]
       E: sorry. Please
            carry on.
       G: ehh just to repeat eh
       E: mhm mhm …
       G: permission paid if ehh...
       (AC178-81)

Prior to this passage the German has already held his turn for several
minutes. He states his insistence on a low commission of five percent as a
general procedure in his company. In line 178 the English negotiator tries
unsuccessfully to take his turn, at a transition relevance point indicated by
falling intonation of the German and after the utterance incompletor *and*.
Though the Englishman has been listening for some time now and really needs
to defend his claim of a 15% commission he does not succeed. Instead, he
initiates a repair introduced by *oh, sorry — please carry on* and immediately
acknowledges the German's speech.

This passage also shows a technique frequently used by the English
agent: he signals his intention to take his turn with repeated acknowledgements (*mhm, yeah, yes*) which is followed by *well* if the following utterance
includes a topic shift or stands in opposition to the prior utterance of the other
(cf. Schiffrin 1987:121). The German does not employ this strategy at all.

5.3. Appealing to cooperative action: *I think we should* vs. *what needs to be done*

5.3.1. The English agent: *I think we should...*
In the Englishman's appeals to some kind of cooperative action or when he
presumes knowledge of the other's experience, he always starts from his own

perspective. There is an overwhelming number of utterances that start with *I think* and then refer to the other person. According to Blum-Kulka et al. (1989) a speaker uses subjectivisers to "explicitly express his or her subject opinion vis-à-vis the state of affairs referred to in the proposition, thus lowering the assertive force of his request". It is a negative politeness strategy (hedge) the function of which is to show respect for the other's autonomy. It is the most frequently occuring politeness strategy in the Englishman's speech (25% of all strategies — 43% of all negative politeness strategies). Explicated in the semantic metalanguage, its meaning can be described as follows:

> I WANT YOU TO KNOW:
> I NOW SAY WHAT I THINK
> YOU DON'T HAVE TO THINK/SAY THE SAME
> BECAUSE I KNOW:
> YOU CAN THINK/SAY WHAT YOU WANT.

In research on negotiation behaviour and outcome, hedges and subjectivisers are obviously considered to play an important role: in an analysis of various linguistic structures in relation to seller's profit and buyer's satisfaction (using the Kelley-Game-simulation: American participants) Neu & Graham (1994:138) found that sellers used presumptive "you" more frequently, thus defining the other's reality for the buyer — but a more frequent use of presumptive "you" also preceded lower seller's profit. Hedges (*I guess, I think, sort of blue*), repairs, exclusive "we" and simultaneous talk all preceded lower buyer satisfaction. This might be regarded as evidence that interactional harmony does influence problem solving on the subject level of the negotiation. Nevertheless, nothing is said about when and why these features are employed by interactants.

5.3.2. *The German negotiator: What needs to be done...*
The German negotiatior's interaction behaviour in that respect is quite different. His requests for cooperative action either appeal to an inclusive "we" position (*let's say, let's exchange our ideas*) or they do not explicitly state that his utterances reflect his personal viewpoint:

> (9)   G: We eh feel, it would be a good agreement to come along with eh the payment of commission at that time/at that day...(AC168)

> (10)   G: In mentioning/let's say in discussing this eh permisson, it's the way of payment which must to/be clarified. (AC162)

In contrast to his English counterpart, his use of presumptive *you* is not mitigated by subjectivizers, such as *I think*:

(11) G: This may bring an additional reputation for you and your private company. (AC41)

(12) G: You will have to wait for a round about (..) two years. (AC110)

(13) G: Yeah, of course, with a very good fortune for you in this eh favoured way of doing this.. (AC240)

(14) G: And it would be of help to you especially after, may I say, beg your pardon, only five years of experience (AC166/7)

An analysis of the speech acts used by the interactants following the Taxonomy of Verbal Response Modes (Stiles 1992) coding form and intent showed that the German uses a high proportion of acts with disclosure intent, i.e. speech acts revealing thoughts, feelings, perceptions, or intentions of the speaker. However, about 25% of the German's utterances with disclosure intents are realized through edification form, i.e. not through an utterance form that indicates a subjective perspective on things but with one sharing a common or objective frame of reference, indicated by a declarative sentence in the third person using *he, she, it* or a noun. Consistent with this observation is the German negotiator's use of negative politeness strategies. The predominant strategies are those of impersonalising (avoidance of the pronouns *I* and *you*) and of nominalisation. The German does not explicitly relate a disclosure intent to his own perspective on things but states his point of view to a large extent as if it were factual information, the way things are. Stated in the semantic metalanguage:

I WANT YOU TO KNOW:
THIS IS THE WAY THINGS ARE
I THINK THIS IS TRUE.

5.4. *Speaking frankly and openly*

In the German's speech there are also expressions that obviously stem from the need to emphasize that he says very directly and openly what he thinks, providing factual information that the other should know. To 'be fair by being frank and open' is considered positive as it gives the other the chance to get to know the German's situation:

(15)   G: To start fair and frankly — we didn't have an agent outside Germany so far. (AC22)

(16)   G: It's I think fair by me to let you know that we are in close contact to an incurring office (AC173)

(17)   G: I feel free to say that our experience in having agents is [ ] to the Continent only (AC27)

This claim to openness also occurs when stating disagreement:

(18)   G: But frankly speaking — I do <u>not</u> see [...] that you can rely on a commission of twelve percent. (AC215)

(19)   G: It's outside of my eh — sorry to say that — eh but it/I guess it's better to say at this point very clearly: it's outside of my fingertip feeling. (G:225)

This attitude can be explicated as follows:

> I WANT YOU TO KNOW WHAT I THINK ·
> BECAUSE WE THEN BOTH KNOW
> WHERE WE THINK THE SAME/WHERE WE DON'T THINK THE SAME
> I THINK IT'S GOOD TO SAY WHAT I THINK.

6.   Conclusion

Summing up what has been stated so far for the English and the German negotiatior the following scripts can be presented:

Table 2. Coordination, orientation, and claim to subjectivity

English negotiator	German negotiator
turn-taking (coordination)	
YOU ARE SAYING SOMETHING NOW	YOU SAID SOMETHING NOW
I CAN'T SAY SOMETHING AT THE SAME TIME	I WANT TO SAY WHAT I THINK ABOUT IT
I CAN SAY SOMETHING AFTER THIS	I WANT TO SAY IT NOW
relating to other's prior utterance (orientation)	
IF I WANT TO SAY SOMETHING AFTER THIS I SAY: I HEARD WHAT YOU JUST SAID AND I NOW KNOW WHY YOU SAID IT I NOW WANT TO SAY SOMETHING ELSE/WHAT I THINK	I WANT YOU TO KNOW WHAT I THINK ABOUT WHAT YOU SAID NOW BECAUSE WE THEN BOTH KNOW WHERE WE THINK THE SAME I THINK IT IS GOOD TO SAY IT.

claim to subjectivity/objectivity	
WHEN I SAY THIS I WANT YOU TO KNOW: I SAY NOW WHAT I THINK YOU DON'T HAVE TO THINK THE SAME	I WANT YOU TO KNOW: THIS IS THE WAY THINGS ARE I THINK THIS IS TRUE BECAUSE OF THIS YOU SHOULD THINK THE SAME

The English negotiator waits until the other has finished his turn. Then he takes his turn and states his own point of view (I CAN SAY SOMETHING AFTER THIS). The German negotiator realizes what the other has just said, then he wants to step in and state what he thinks about it — there is a need to comment on the other's statement immediately. Interruptions and overlaps are often cooperative — it is important that both partners know what the respective other thinks and wants in order to find some kind of common ground to start from (WE THEN BOTH KNOW WHERE WE THINK THE SAME). The English negotiator acknowledges the other's speech (I HEARD WHAT YOU JUST SAID) and thereby signals that he has understood (I NOW KNOW WHY YOU SAID IT). Then he either comments on the other's statement or just adds to it what he thinks about the situation (I NOW WANT TO SAY WHAT I THINK/SOMETHING ELSE). He explicitly states that he knows that the other might not be of the same opinion (YOU DON'T HAVE TO THINK THE SAME). Quite in contrast to this behaviour the German negotiator takes a stand and wants to convince the other of his point of view or to be convinced by better arguments — at the time of speaking he claims that his point of view is right and thus can and should be shared by the other.

References

Argyle, Michael. 1991. *Cooperation. The Basis of Sociability*. London/New York: Routledge.

Arndt, Horst and Richard W. Janney. 1987. *InterGrammar: Toward an Integrative Model of Verbal, Prosodic and Kinesic Choices in Speech*. Berlin: Mouton de Gruyter.

Blum-Kulka, Shoshana, Juliane House and Gabriele Kasper (eds.). 1989. *Crosscultural Pragmatics: Requests and Apologies*. Norwood, N.J.:Ablex.

Brown, Penelope and Steven C. Levinson. 1987. *Politeness. Some Universals in Language Usage*. Cambridge: Cambridge University Press.

Coulthard, Malcolm. 1985. *An Introduction to Discourse Analysis*. New York: Longman.

Cupach, William R. and T. Todd Imahori. 1993. "Identity management theory: communication competence in intercultural episodes and relationships" In: Richard L. Wiseman and Jolene Koester (eds.), *Intercultural Communication Competence*. Newbury Park: Sage, pp. 112-131.

Fisher, Roger and William Ury. 1991. *Getting to Yes*. New York: Penguin.

Goddard, Cliff and Anna Wierzbicka. 1994. *Semantic and Lexical Universals. Theory and Empirical Findings*. Amsterdam/Philadelphia: John Benjamins.

Janney, Richard W. and Horst Arndt. 1992. "Intracultural tact versus intercultural tact". In: Richard J. Watts, Sachiko Ide and Konrad Ehlich (eds.). *Politeness in Language*. Berlin: Mouton de Gruyter, pp. 21-41.

Janney, Richard W. and Horst Arndt. 1994. "Interpersonal dimensions of intercultural communication". In: Heiner Pürschel et al. (eds.). *Intercultural Communication*. Frankfurt/Main: Lang, pp. 33-44.

Keller, Rudi. 1987. "Kooperation und Eigennutz [Cooperation and self-interest]". In: Frank Liedtke and Rudi Keller (eds.), *Kooperation und Kommunikation*. Tübingen: Niemeyer, pp. 1-16.

Mastenbroek, Willem. 1989. *Negotiate*. London: Basil Blackwell.

Neu, Joyce and John Graham. 1994. "A new methodological approach to the study of interpersonal influence tactics: a 'test drive' of a behavioral scheme". *Journal of Business Research* 29: 131-144.

Penman, Robyn. 1994. "Facework in communication: conceptual and moral challenges". In: Stella Ting-Toomey (ed.). *The Challenge of Facework*. Albany: State University of New York Press, pp. 15-45.

Sacks, Harvey, Emanuel A. Schegloff and Gail Jefferson. 1974. "A simplest systematics for the organization of turn-taking for conversation". *Language* 50/1: 696-735.

Schiffrin, Deborah. 1987. *Discourse Markers*. Cambridge: Cambridge University Press.

Stiles, William B. 1992. *Describing Talk. A Taxonomy of Verbal Response Modes*. Newbury Park: Sage.

Ting-Toomey, Stella. 1993. "Communicative resourcefulness. An identity negotiation perspective". In: R. Wiseman and Jolene Koester (eds.), *Intercultural Communication Competence*, Newbury Park: Sage, pp. 72-111.

Ulijn, Jan M. and Judith Strother. 1995. *Communicating in Business and Technology*. Frankfurt/Main: Peter Lang.

Wagner, Johannes and Uwe Petersen. 1991. "Zur Definition von Verhandeln unter besonderer Berücksichtigung von Geschäftsverhandlungen [Towards a definiton of negotiating with special focus on business negotiations]". In: Bernd-Dietrich Müller (ed.), *Wirtschaft und Sprache*. München: Iudicium Verlag, pp. 261-276.

Wierzbicka, Anna. 1991. *Cross-Cultural Pragmatics. The Semantics of Human Interaction*. Berlin: Mouton de Gruyter.

Wierzbicka, Anna. 1994. " 'Cultural scripts': A new approach to the study of cross-cultural communication". In: Heiner Pürschel et al. (eds.). *Intercultural Communication*. Frankfurt/Main: Lang, pp. 67-87.

V. Training

Raising awareness in business communication training

Lut Baten & Mia Ingels
University of Leuven, Belgium

1. Background and needs

In 1994, a new course on Business English for commercial engineers (advanced level) was organized at the KULeuven, Belgium. This was the final step in the implementation of a new three year curriculum for the foreign languages offered in the faculty of economics. Faculty, staff, and students were consulted as to their needs, expectations, and frustrations. As "end-users" they were also represented at the planning meetings. In short, the final course had to fulfill a double role: on the one hand provide for skills that future business people need for meeting and negotiating, by lack of any mother tongue class, and provide for the necessary mastery of English for functioning autonomously in the field. Companies in Belgium take it for granted that business graduates have a very good command of at least two foreign languages. Languages are a selection criterion of application procedures. Students very well realize that they will find themselves soon enough in actual business situations in which they have to negotiate in English with (non-) native speakers of English. Hence, they have high expectations as to the stepstones for assisting their communication in English.

As the curriculum was gradually implemented, the students had been made acquainted in the first two years of the program with task based approach, autonomy, group work, and simulations.

This method deviated from the functional approach that was still apparent in most materials available in the market. Materials for learning how to negotiate were developed for business students, focusing on functions such as "challenge and counter propose" and on the idioms and phrases that can be recognized. With our students but also with the teachers there was a need for more solid ground. In fact, ESP (=English for special purposes) practitioners knew little about far advanced interaction patterns used in negotiation, not even in their mothertongue. What was lacking was the link between theory on negotiation and discourse which was researched in linguistics and the practical training for foreign language acquisition. Methodologically speaking, as curriculum developers for this target group, we realized we could not merely transmit the linguistic theory. But on the other hand, we also knew that we had to refrain from involving students in mere language games or small situation activities, as there was the urge to use the high input of the advanced learners. Being university students, their authentic business experience was still low, but their general communication skills and their motivation were high, clearly surpassing the functional approach. So the challenge was not to teach a descriptive course on discourse, but to provide for a pragmatic and custom-tailored input, ready for processing by the learners in an authentic learning environment. In our faculty, where most teaching was and still is in the form of lectures, the concept of this course called "Interaction in a business context" was innovative and challenging to both students and teachers, who started to call themselves trainers.

2.   Concept of the course

When they began developing the course, the teacher-trainers realized that a stable common ground was necessary for the didactic approach and for the way language was dealt with. For the course to be an autonomous one, it was obvious that students needed to acquire the skills to observe the language used, control their own language, and be aware of what is going on during the interaction in order to optimally function in a successful negotiation. "Language" did not only mean the language of business, but also the cultural conventions of meetings/negotiations in an intercultural setting and the controllable systems in non-verbal communication. The question was: how could awareness be raised and strategies be built for establishing this autonomous self-steered behavior?

   In an article on the state of the art of Business English, St John (1996) states that a mere reliance on the materials that sprout from the writer's intuition, or "informed understanding", of business communication is not sufficient. She argues that there is a definite need, first, to understand more of the generic features of different events such as meetings; second, to identify common features of effective communications and, finally, to understand the role of cultural influences and the ways in which language and business strategies interact. In what follows we will describe which principles we adhered to in the creation of materials that aimed, first, to develop awareness of the stages in the negotiation process; second, to present language; third, to promote listening to others; fourth, to promote an understanding of cultural differences; and fifth, to include units on relationship building, questioning, options, and bargaining.

2.1. *Role of teacher-trainers*

The course was innovative because the responsibility and initiative were totally in the hands of the students. As a result, the topic of the first meetings was the course itself: the participation in the course, the whole set-up, the organization of the different projects, negotiations on accepting the projects of the different groups, and the role other groups had to play. In this learner-centered configuration the teacher no longer functioned as an omnipotent source of wisdom who bulks out encyclopedic knowledge for students to study but was rather a coach, a coordinator whose subject-matter knowledge was limited but who tried to steer the learners into a particular direction, helping them to create optimum conditions for the learning process to take place and ultimately helping students with learning how to learn. In small groups, preparatory and evaluative meetings were held with the teacher-trainer, who sustained the process rather than controlled it. Regular written reporting was required as it is the case in real projects as well.

2.2. *Roles of students*

2.2.1. *The role of the initiators*
The initiator subgroup had to set the goal for the simulation, select and prepare the language material to create a case study which was the basis for the class interaction. Hence, the core information was thoroughly prepared for and shared by initiators and participants. Both groups sat around the table communicating and solving the problem (inner circle). The subject of the

simulation did not require the students to play a role. They had to act and react from different points of view, separating their own personalities from the functions they had to take in, still remaining true to their principles (i.e. in the meeting between representatives of a chemical plant and neighborhood dwellers on noise and air pollution, a decision making on whether to invest in a project of not etc.). In this set-up the input is authentic, the teacher control is minimal and allows students to apply metacognitive, cognitive, and social strategies.

2.2.2. *The role of the participants*
As will be clear from the description of the initiator role, the participant role was also an active communication role but the preparation of the activity did not require this group to prepare the "case".

2.2.3. *The role of the prompters*
Prompters sat in the second circle behind the performers and assisted the doers by pointing to strategic errors, argumentative weaknesses (remarks passed on on small notes via the chairperson), reoccurring linguistic errors (passed on the speaker him/herself). Their function also entailed editing minutes (meeting) and reports (negotiation). In this semi-active semi-observant role we primarily aimed at stimulating the students' metacognitive awareness in that they had to correct and redirect other learners' strategies where necessary.

2.2.4. *The role of the evaluators*
Evaluators sat in the outer circle observing and taking notes about the interaction process concentrating on erratic tactical moves, communicative fluency, (in)appropriate use of strategies by the performers etc. Together with the teacher this group provided feedback to the people in the inner circle. In a number of occasions, the meeting took a break after half an hour, with a brief discussion among prompters, evaluators, and teacher. This was reported to the interlocutors prior to the continuation of the meeting, leaving the decisions up to the persons in charge. On the whole this improved the atmosphere of constructing a process — and resulted in a more positive evaluation at the end as the hardest errors were taken into consideration during the second half. The evaluators wrote up their remarks in a report submitted to the teacher and to the performers.

Again, in this role students were forced to reflect about the interaction process, identify the strategies used and evaluate the success or failure of strategies. Metacognitive awareness raising was the major aim.

3.   A cognitive approach

The approach we opted for was rooted within the more recent educational goal of setting up programs which train learners to acquire procedural knowledge rather than declarative knowledge to pave the way for them to the world beyond education. Because we wanted to direct the learning process beyond task execution by training students' language processing and language learning strategies (Oostdam & Rijlaarsdam 1995) and business interaction skills, we adopted a cognitive approach to learning in a predominantly learner-centered curriculum. This approach is intertwined with a three-step, spiral-like procedure: first illustrate (= a good model), then induce (= induction for effective learning by the learner), and finally interact (= the outcome). Having reached step 3, another step 1 might be needed to deepen the learning. We aimed at raising awareness, building strategies, and assisting in learning language for negotiation.[1]

3.1. *Raising critical self-awareness and awareness of the processes of interaction*

Raising critical self-awareness and awareness of the processes of interaction that take place in meetings and negotiations leads us to the meta-cognitive knowledge of the learner: i.e. the awareness of finding yourself in a particular cognitive condition (e.g., feeling the power of winning a deal, evaluating your success as a chairperson trying to maintain control over undisciplined participants). In our task-based approach, we put the learner himself in charge in the framework of the above mentioned stages. As such, the students had to prepare, on paper, a complete meeting. In the meantime audio- and video-taped models of negotiations were studied in class as well as different outputs in writing (how to draft a memo, an agenda, minutes of a meeting, a report). Each student in a group of four worked out a simulation which was discussed with the teacher and among themselves. One of these preparations could, but did not have to, function as the basis for a meeting/negotiation at a more formal level of the actual interaction. In this portfolio approach to learning, it is the learner who invests: if a weak simulation was presented, the job would have to be repeated as the other ones would not accept it.

Then the simulated interactions with the other groups took place, in which each group took turns as to the responsibilities: every group was responsible for the organization and completion of a meeting/negotiation (a simulation completely constructed by the group in charge with members of other groups participating). As such the learners see themselves functioning as initiators of a meeting (with a chairperson, a minutes taker, financial/personnel managers, representatives, etc.), being well prepared before the meeting takes place. These students also participate in the meetings prepared by other groups: as active participants to the meeting (with a prepared agenda and dossier, but reacting from their own knowledge, and with less crucial functions) and at other occasions as evaluators and prompters of task performances of other learners-initiators.

Let us analyze the learning impact. All the groups of one class assume all the tasks at different moments in time. Over time, a meta-learning effect is apparent: students learn how to better steer each other. As initiators they actively prepare the processes going on. They have to foresee which directions the meeting can take and be prepared for different outcomes. They preside over the meeting and take final responsibility. In the role of participants they perceive the processes. They have prepared themselves for a meeting called by other persons, thus the outcome of the meeting is not acted, as in a role-play, but is realized on the spot with participants acting on their own behalf. The evaluation of attitude during the meeting is also based on their own common sense. Here the prompters play an important role as they are alert to the process and verbalize their insight in order to help steer the communication. To that end, all meetings have a break in which prompters confer with evaluators and teacher to decide whether the members of the meeting have to be called in for inbetween coaching or steering. On a number of occasions, this intervention helped a lot. As evaluators they reflect on the communication that took place and draw their conclusions which they communicate to the others. These students also focused on the linguistic aspects of general and specific English and on the verbalization of interactions (e.g. how to ask for the floor, interfere, etc.). The problem of evaluation is not the teacher's but their own.

3.2. *Strategies*

"Few studies have examined how strategies for productive language can be trained" (O'Malley & Chamot 1990:152). Learning strategies are defined as steps taken by the learner to aid the acquisition, storage, and retrieval of information. Strategies can be formulated as mottos. The student can store the motto in memory and link situations with it and thus build a procedural knowledge base he can put to use in different situations.[2]

Our course set-up intended to train students to come to grips not only with mere language learning strategies and language processing strategies but also with extra-linguistic and behavioral strategies used by professionals. In this respect, the task setting clearly went beyond a language learning task; it was an interaction task requiring the training of interaction skills which most students still needed to acquire in the mother tongue as well. We also aimed at the so-called compensation strategies or communication strategies which may serve both as negotiation tools and tactics and as language learning strategies.[3]

Metacommunicative expressions do not add new propositional information but are preceding or following bits of information and say something about the participants' communicative activities (Neumann 1994). Examples of metas are idiomatic phrases to take turns, to refer to what was said earlier, etc. It is here that, on the part of the teacher, consulting background was lacking as to discourse modeling (Van Rees 1994). Also extra-language skills and tools were discussed such as the presence of agendas, ultimatums, "good cop, bad cop" technique, timing, politeness strategies, etc.

3.3. *Language in view of communication strategies*

At these advanced levels of communication we considered that students would create the learning opportunities for themselves once they had been introduced to core conditions, strategies, and functions. They provided the content and the language input themselves. The language input which was provided by the teacher was restricted to the functional metacommunicative expressions typically used in negotiations, meetings, social talk (e.g. idiomatic expressions used to chair a meeting, to introduce a person, etc.). Again, from studies in discourse analysis, a better model could be provided to students as to recognize and use moves for

framing
> e.g. now then, right

transaction
> e.g. now then, right + question and answer sequence,
> by the way, to change the subject

boundary markers
> e.g. for openings (with the intonation pattern of a jump),
> for closures (with the intonation pattern of a drop)

topicalization
> start - grow - shift
> e.g. STILL + summary and/or general evaluation, indi-
> cating a clear shift to another topic.

The teacher-trainers are actually still in search of a strategy possibly resembling the reading strategies: in a text, connectors fulfil crucial roles as stepstones in the macro-structural organization of a text and hence assisting a lot in prediction, hypothesis-formation, skimming, and scanning. Are likely (didactic) stepstones recognizable in oral communication of meetings and negotiations?

In listening activities, the language awareness of how speakers mark topic shifts can be raised by means of activities focusing a point where speakers make summaries and evaluations and on markers and pitch changes. We can actually help participants in decision-making discussions by focusing on the discussion procedure. It is hard to objectively determine the quality of a decision, but we can see to what degree the discussion procedure permits and enables the systematic critical testing of ideas. Thus we can illustrate potential weaknesses and mistakes. To that end, Van Rees (1992) is setting up a method of analysis. By observing negotiations, she tries to chart which points of view the participants take and how they defend them. She also looks at how the participants respond to one another' contributions. Thus she traces the exact course of the discussion and the way in which the verbal behaviour of the participants determines it. It is studies like these that provide teachers with a tool to assist the learning process in its second stage, the stage of induction. These studies help practitioners to highlight to their students in what respects, at what points in the discourse, and in what ways participants make decisions or not.

4. Evaluation

As the learning process at hand involved a complex task addressing complex mental activities we would like to evaluate the students' and our input at the level of inappropriate or non-use of strategies as to
1. Preparation;
2. Communicative fluency or strategic competence (primarily a language learning task);
3. Business communication strategic management (essentially an interaction task).

4.1. *Preparation*

Students had to build an active knowledge base which they could rely on to find arguments to be used during the simulation. The words, the arguments, the reactions had to come on the spot. In the previous course in English, students had been trained in the prepared language of presentation, which is a mono-directional talk. But in meetings and negotiation the interaction is multifold. Hence the emphasis was on a very active preparation which is knowledge- and content-based. It was observed that the less efficient learners refused to see the full weight and importance of a thorough preparation. Therefore the requirement of a prior, individual, written preparation of a simulation was introduced, one of which could serve as the final one by group consensus.

4.2. *Communicative fluency*

On the second level we evaluate the students' language fluency which we would like to define as "the skill of expressing one's thoughts easily, both orally or verbally as well as {the skill of} easily storing text phrases in the memory" (Oóstdam & Rijlaarsdam 1995:23). In oral communication this means being able to retain someone's saying, interpret it, reformulate it, and use it intentionally (argumentative strength). This process is quite difficult and goes beyond a language learning task. It is an interaction task students need to address also in their mother tongue.

Weaker students do not seem to have applied cognitive strategies to process the input language material before the simulation. Good performers have summarized information, planned their part carefully, used mnemonic aids, etc. When we look at how these students actually performed, we notice that weaker students have sometimes insurmountable difficulties getting their message across: they formulate a limping message barely understood by listeners and are not able to reformulate to clarify their point; they just read out aloud what is written in front of them without paying attention to cooperative principles. In the worst case they just say nothing at all, missing the opportunity to train their skills.

A disturbing lack of active and passive vocabulary prevented them from varying the lexis in their interventions and more importantly from expressing nuances of meaning. This lack of vocabulary obviously irritated the other interlocutors who grew impatient and bored. In some occasions students blocked emotionally. The emotional involvement is high, so that students sometimes have emotional outbursts after class due to frustrations on the interactional level during language training sessions.

4.3. *Business communication strategic management*

As mentioned above, common sense activation plays a crucial role in the acquisition of professional negotiation strategies and tactics. Hence, language learning strategies are embedded in the requirements of how to conduct a good meeting/negotiation. At this level different types of skills have to be mastered, such as protocol (behavioral, social codes for social talk, opening and closing a meeting, introducing people...); the use of communication strategies to safeguard effective communication and/or to overcome word/argument finding difficulties; argumentative strength and finally cooperative/responsive skills. The latter include the willingness and ability to adapt flexibly to the natural course of the meeting/negotiation, readiness to listen to and interact with the other party, and skill to use protocol, communication, and argumentative strength for manipulative, strategic purposes.

Protocol strategies such as introducing, taking the floor, asking the floor still seem to belong to the declarative knowledge base of the weaker students who do observe the rules but fail to incorporate them flexibly in the interaction task. There is still this artificial flair in their behavior by which a novice differs from an expert. They do use metacommunication but still sound very unnatural and not convincing. Typical non-linguistic, behavioral protocol errors include a performer addressing only the chair or people talking at the same time. This observation implies that students need more practice before their declarative knowledge can become proceduralized. Let us discuss more aspects of this interaction such as communication strategies, argumentation, and cooperative/responsive skills.

4.3.1. *Communication strategies*
Concerning the use of metacommunication by the weaker students we noted that it was restricted to the core of functional expressions and once again these expressions were used artificially and not usually as tactical tools; also the intonation remained quite flat. The better students used these communication strategies frequently and functionally to safeguard effective communication. They also acknowledged their usefulness as pause fillers and gainers of processing time to build up intelligent argumentation, to think creatively on the spot, to think clearly under stress, to steer the interaction in the right direction, to remain critically alert. They compensated for gaps in their lexical knowledge by circumlocution. Another group of students would overuse the strategies, violating the economy principle (e.g. a speaker echoes another speaker, endlessly repeats the same strategy irrespective of conditions, etc.).

4.3.2. *Argumentation*
Some students show an inability to set up argumentation due to lack of preparation (for arguments, for metacommunication), but they also display an inability to support a claim by (reasonable) evidence, to think on the spot, to reason abstractly. Students suffocate in the swamp of concrete details, failing to see the course the interaction takes. If these students are not coached well enough, the negative influence on their confidence and self-image is detrimental and often leads to a premature end of the interaction. Conversely, students who think they can triumph by suddenly throwing in new facts are violating the rules of good argumentation, and are consequently discouraged even if their intervention was of an extraordinary high quality of English.

4.3.3. *Cooperative/responsive skills*
Students performing well at this stage flexibly adapted to the situation and conditions. They manipulated the arguments and the metacommunicative expressions with playful ease and were masters in convincing other participants. They also possessed the skills to listen carefully and patiently, so that their reactions were always to the point and sometimes witty.

5. Discussion and conclusion

With the simulations and the student comments in hindsight, we can conclude that the autonomous learning environment strongly appeals to the vast majority of our students because it is challenging, forcing students to largely organize their learning themselves, addressing the more mature and advanced faculties of the human mind. Still, the course organization may have to be fine-tuned in a number of respects.

The autonomous learning environment needs to be embedded in a strongly learner-controlled frame. Before embarking on the autonomous learning task, the educational goal and the function of the learning task need to be clearly and explicitly communicated to the learners not least to prevent false expectations and misconceptions from negatively influencing the learning process.

As was also convincingly argued by Lillie (1994), even at this advanced level there is the continued need for confidence-building guided exercises. This need was partly confirmed by the reactions of our students who wanted more extensive modeling of the strategies by the teacher and more guided practice of subgoals accompanied by feedback before the start of the autonomous learning activity.

Therefore, we would like to adhere to the three directions mentioned above: discourse analysis of unprepared spoken conversations, modeling of decision making, and metalanguage. Many students have developed the meta-cognitive awareness of the learning opportunity provided by evaluation and self-evaluation. With the students and St John (1996), we have to acknowledge that in order for the students to apply the business interaction strategies in a completely autonomous way, more needs to be understood of the generic features of meetings, of effective communications, and of the role of cultural influences. A better grip is necessary on the ways in which language and business strategies interact. With this in store, materials can be developed that very well serve the three stages of learning: illustration, induction, and interaction. This is not the task of the sole teacher anymore, but of a team of researchers and professional trainers and teachers.

It was observed that even students who were well prepared and used stategies like planning, monitoring, checking and evaluating, trying to regulate their learning optimally, still fell short in the complexity of the whole task. The reason is that they were involved in an interactive activity which requires skills they still need to acquire in their mother tongue as well. Hence they engage in an actual learning task while they function in the target language, and this proves to be difficult.

To help the students accomplish this task more successfully, we have to make students aware, furthermore, of the stepwise attainment of perfection with good modeling behind illustration, induction, and interaction. The recent developments in multi-media should allow course developers, together with a multi-disciplinary team, to provide for accessible and well-directed materials in which authentic business communication can be explored as part of the illustration and induction. Merely showing a video recording of a good negotiation is a start, but falls short at the further levels of induction and interaction. More can be done to help build strategies.

It cannot be stressed enough — both to the language learner and to the negotiator — that success on the highest level can only build on efficient control of the levels of preparation and communicative quality. The better the learner is in control of the requirements at these two lower levels, the more processing time and opportunity he will have left during the interaction to control the variables defining the level of performance. This control is enhanced by good materials. As this succession of tasks also seems to hold for the professional negotiator, the aim of this course was not only to train the students to become permanent language learners but also future professional negotiators, chairmen, business interactants. Here some work still needs to be done in bridging the separated fields of theory and practice.

Notes

1. A complete description of the course objectives and the cognitive approach of awareness raising, can be found in Baten & Ingels 1995.

2. By means of the four tasks (initiating, participating, prompting, and evaluating of task performances) in different interactive forms, the learners in our course gain insight in how the interaction goes on from different angles.

3. In order to build in different cultural contexts, foreign (Erasmus) students were invited to join the meetings. These occasions were very highly valued by the students, primarily because of the real sense of authentic communication.

References

Baten, Lut and Mia Ingels (to appear). "Business interaction learning strategies: a course assessment". _Proceedings of the European LSP Conference_, Vienna 1995.

Bialystock, Ellen. 1991. "Achieving proficiency in a second language: a processing description". In: R. Phillipson (ed.). _Foreign/Second Language Pedagogy Research._ Clevedon (UK.): Multilingual Matters Ltd., pp. 63-78.

Economy, Paul. 1994. _Business Negotiating Basics._ New York: Irwin Professional Publishing.

Ingels, Mia. 1991. "Communicative fluency practice via project-centered autonomous work, culminating in a formal presentation". In: Serge Verlinde (ed.). _Proceedings of the Symposium on Differentiation in LSP, Learning and Teaching_, Leuven: ILT, pp. 201-206.

Karrass, C.L. 1992. _The Negotiating Game._ New York: Harper Collins Publishers.

Lillie, Elisabeth M. 1994. "Language for business: postgraduate students and effective language learning". In: Magnar Brekke and Ingrid Neumann (eds.). _Applications and Implications of Current LSP Research,_ Vol I. Bergen: John Grieg AS, pp. 278-286.

Neumann, Ingrid. 1994. "Metacommunicative expressions in intercultural negotiations". In: Magnar Brekke and Ingrid Neumann (eds.). _Applications and Implications of Current LSP Research_, Vol I. Bergen: John Grieg AS, pp. 141-150.

Nunan, David. 1988. _The Learner-Centered Curriculum._ Cambridge: Cambridge University Press.

O'Malley, John M. and A. Uhl Chamot. 1990. _Learning Strategies in Second Language Acquisition._ Cambridge: Cambridge University Press.

Oostdam, Ron and Gert Rijlaarsdam. 1995. _Towards Strategic Language Learning._ Amsterdam: Amsterdam University Press.

Oxford, Rebecca and D. Crookall. 1989. "Research on language learning strategies: methods, findings and instructional issues". In: D.P. Benseler (ed.). _The Modern Language Journal_ Vol 73. Madison: University of Wisconsin Press, pp. 404-419.

St John, Maggie Jo. 1996. "Where are we in Business ESP?" _ESP_, Vol 15, n°1, 1-18.

Van Rees, Agnes. 1992. _The Use of Language in Conversation. An Introduction to Research in Conversation._ Adam: sicsat.

Van Rees, Agnes. 1994. "Analysing and evaluating small-group decision-making discussions". In: Luc Van Waes, Ed Woudstra and Paul van den Hoven. _Functional Communication Quality._ USL & C Utrecht Studies in Language and Communication. Amsterdam: Rodopi, pp. 149-162.

Wilkinson, Robert. 1994. "Repetition, rephrasing and reconstructing in international business: enhancing understanding and confidence in the other tongue". In: Magnar Brekke and Ingrid Neumann (eds.). _Applications and Implications of Current LSP Research,_ Vol I. Bergen: John Grieg AS, pp. 151-162.

The experience of sameness in differences

A course in international business writing

J. Piet Verckens, Teun De Rycker and Ken Davis

Handelshogeschool Antwerp (Belgium) / Indiana University (USA)

0. Introduction

To prepare our students for a life in an ever-smaller world, a world with increasing possibilities of fast communicative action and reaction, but also a world of many cultures, languages, and regional communities, business communication instructors must offer them real-life experience in the essence of living in such a world. This experience has to move beyond the simulation games which we find in many courses (see e.g. Gibbs 1988, Harcourt 1988, Jameson 1993, Martin & Chaney 1992, O'Rourke 1993, Ranney & McNeilly 1996, Sterkel 1988, and Victor 1988) and handbooks in interpersonal and/or cross-cultural communication (see e.g. Samovar & Porter 1995 or Cushner & Brislin 1996). We designed our own course in international business writing (CIBW). The first year Ulla Connor (as a visiting professor from Indiana University and Purdue University at Indianapolis, IUPUI) and Meg Phillips coached Finnish students at Åbo Akademi, Turku; while Ken Davis was the instructor at IUPUI, Indiana USA; and Teun de Rycker and J. Piet Verckens were instructors at the Handelshogeschool Antwerpen, Belgium.

The CIBW is based on three pillars: a theoretical pillar, a practical field-research pillar, and an experiential pillar. The theoretical component is made up of the study of a major textbook on the subject of cross-cultural communication. During the first year we made use of Victor (1992) but this year we changed to the more up-to-date publication of Varner & Beamer (1995). This theoretical basis functions as a framework within which the results of the field research can be compared.

The field-research component makes students look *beyond the wall of the educational institution* to find out what goes on in the real world of business with regard to cross-cultural communication. The students, using a questionnaire, are asked to interview a manager who has to communicate internationally in order to perform his/her tasks. The results are used to critically reflect on the general theories, methods, and statements and particular anecdotes that our source books present.

Finally, the experiential component is a business game that consists of four steps in which the U.S., Belgian, and Finnish participants have to produce written documents that are actually sent to each other and that are reacted to in the course of the game. This part of the CIBW is based on the AIP-project, which we presented at the L.A.U.D.-Symposium in 1992 (see Davis, De Rycker & Verckens 1994).

The main objective of the CIBW is to give our students the opportunity to become acquainted with *sameness in differences*. As members of a specific culture, but living in the global village, students should have the opportunity to experience, in reality, what it means to communicate and (simulate to) do business with people who are different in certain respects but who nonetheless are obviously alike in several basic ways.

Important assets of the CIBW include the opportunity to

1. **actually communicate** in writing with people from different cultures;
2. **actually compete** in a cross-cultural environment and thereby experience real anxiety and uncertainty; and
3. **practise** a foreign language in a normal-functional context that urges participants to do more than simply try to be correct or please the instructor.

In what follows, we will present the specifics of the course, its advantages for advanced students of economics and business, and the pedagogical and scientific basis on which it is founded. Preliminary tests and evaluation questionnaires suggest that students need and appreciate this unparallelled course as an almost compulsory initiation into the specifics of *sameness in differences*.

1. The specifics of the CIBW

A random check of the relevant literature gave us an insight into the specifics of a course in international/intercultural business communication (see also Davis & Verckens 1997 for an annotated version of major books). Martin & Chaney (1992) produced an extended list of topics to be dealt with in a collegiate course in intercultural business communication. They distilled from a triple Delphi panel (international business persons, intercultural communication educators, and members of the Academy of International Business) nine essential content areas to be covered in the ideal course:

Table 1. Essential Content Areas

1. universal systems
2. contrasting cultural values
3. verbal and nonverbal patterns
4. language
5. communication strategies
6. negotiation process
7. country specific information
8. laws and
9. culture shock

Source: Martin & Chaney 1992

Gatenby & McLaren (1993) present another picture of what a course in intercultural/international/cross-cultural communication should deal with and how it should try to reach its goals. The scholars questioned the members of the (international) Association for Business Communication as regards their teaching of international topics:

Table 2. Topics Addressed

1. language and translation pitfalls
2. cultural variables
3. variations in written communication
4. negotiations in international settings
5. nonverbal communication differences
6. training for overseas assignments
7. other = international trade practice, foreign trade correspondence, professional expressions, variations in oral communications, linguistic evidence of cultural variations, multiculturalism, social psychology of cross-cultural relations, and skill development

Source: Gatenby & McLaren 1993:13

Their fourth conclusion is worth repeating here:

> Teachers in both groups (i.e. U.S. ABC members and members beyond the U.S.) primarily used lectures on international communication. However, teachers beyond the United States were more likely also to use exercises, case studies, and films. (Gatenby & McLaren 1993:10)

As early as 1988 the Teaching Methodology & Concepts Committee of the Association for Business Communication already neatly spelled out what a course in intercultural communication would have to aim at and how the objectives of such a course could be reached. The teaching unit they suggested is reproduced below.

Table 3. Teaching Unit

    I.   Objectives of the Unit
           Students will be able to:
    A.   Explain the increasing importance of intercultural communication
    B.   Understand the dynamics of the intercultural process
    C.   Understand how cultural factors affect one's thoughts, feelings, values, and perceptions
    D.   Appreciate the validity of various viewpoints of people from different cultures
    E.   Understand the numerous problems involved in intercultural communication
    F.   Act effectively in intercultural encounters

    II.   Classroom activities
    B.   Self-Instructional Guide
    C.   Role Playing: Intercultural Awareness and Stereotyping
    D.   Intercultural Cases
    E.   Critical Incidents

    III. Summary

Source: Gibbs et al. 1988:4

The committee stressed the fact that

> Intercultural communication is facilitated when participants demonstrate the qualities of patience, tolerance, objectivity, empathy and respect. Although these qualities are important in all communication, they are critical in intercultural exchanges. (Gibbs et al. 1988:3)

One could easily question the possibility of actually showing these qualities to be present in classroom activities in which self-instructional guides, role playing, intercultural cases, and critical incidents (see also Cushner & Brislin

1996) are the only building blocks. However, both role playing and simulation games have been the major educational tool with which courses of intercultural, international, or cross-cultural work (see Harcourt 1988, Sterkel 1988, Victor 1988, Jameson 1993, and O'Rourke 1993).

The CIBW is no different in this respect. Compared to the general content areas and methods put forward in the literature, however, the CIBW is also explicitly meant to present students with a simultaneity of experiences, activities, and methods. This simultaneity is built into a normal-functional teaching environment (see Ten Brinke 1976:107ff.) in which the main activity is (written) communication (in a foreign language for two of the three partici-

Table 4. CIBW Business Game

	A Company (Publishing)	**B Company (Recruiting)**	**C Company (Training)**
Phase 1	Organize and name company; write job description	Organize and name company; write sales letter	Organize and name company; write sales letter
Deadline 1	Job description to foreign B Companies	Sales letter to foreign C Companies	Sales letter to foreign A Companies
Phase 2	define training needs; write request for proposals	as individual students, apply for foreign jobs	define recruitment needs; write request for proposal
Deadline 2	request for proposal to foreign C Companies	application letters and resumes to foreign A Companies	request for proposal to foreign B Companies
Phase 3	screen job applications, write responses	help local A Company with screening; write proposal	plan training for foreign A Companies; write proposals
Deadline 3	rejection letters and interview invitations to students in foreign B Companies	proposals to foreign C Companies	proposals to foreign A Companies
Phase 4	decide among training proposals	{outside simulation} critique foreign application letters and resumes	decide among recruitment consulting proposals
Deadline 4	acceptance/rejection letters to foreign C Companies	{outside simulation} critiques to students in foreign A Companies	acceptance/rejection letters to foreign B Companies

pants). The topics with which the CIBW deals are verbal patterns (and nonverbal patterns if we see lay-out and other mechanics of correspondence as nonverbal phenomena), language (especially for the two groups in which English is a foreign language), (written) communication strategies, and culture "shock" (when students find out that what they thought and expected does not really turn out to be correct). The writing tasks fit into a business game that takes the form above.

The most important characteristic of this four-phase simulation is its authenticity (also one of the major characteristics of the AIP-project; see Davis, De Rycker & Verckens 1994:243ff.). Authenticity in our view is not just a quality of the product, but also and foremost a feature of the process. More specifically, the writing environment is a multiplication of the following basic exchange structure (reproduced from Davis, De Rycker & Verckens 1994:251ff.) :

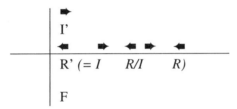

Figure 1. Basic exchange structure

The educational environment is represented by the vertical line in italics. The authenticity of the business game (as a process) is represented on the horizontal line. The game starts in three locations (Belgium, Finland, and the United States) at the same time. The introduction of the business game *I'*, by the teachers, sets off the actual international chains of activity. As a reaction (*R'*) the students form three groups (the three companies A (= in publishing), B (= in recruiting), and C (= in training) and start their writing assignments (see above). As such nine groups (or more, dependent on the amount of students enrolled) begin and go through the Initiation moves, the Response/Initiation moves, and Response moves that make up the authenticity of the game. At the end the instructors only have to finalize this part of the course by producing the necessary components of feedback such as the case-study report and the final (student) critique and evaluation.

However, the CIBW does not only aim at authenticity, it also makes the participants aware of their audience, more than they would normally be in "everyday" educational writing tasks. Having to respond to actual letters and proposals, and having to evaluate letters with a view to taking important business decisions is an extraordinary situation for most students. Thus, they experience the very strange feelings of having their homework responded to at overseas educational institutions by peers whom they do not really know.

The Belgian students are asked to write to the U.S. and Finnish companies following the outlined scenario. They are not explicitly told to write two (or more) different letters, depending on their audience being U.S. or Finnish, but after the first letter has been sent off and the first reply has been received, the question is asked and the problem of *adapting to the audience* is raised during an open discussion in class. We will return to these discussions in part three of this article.

Students should adapt to their audiences. They can do so in such specific messages. The reason why they should do this, and how they should tackle this task, and why they should do it this way are issues answered by means of the results of the field-research part of the CIBW. Students are sent into the field to interview a business person who is faced with cross-cultural communication as part of his or her everyday job. The questionnaire used in the field research deals with general and specific cultural issues. These issues could be the reason why, in actual (written) encounters, business persons write different messages than they would produce if the audience consisted of members of their cultural community. The issues have been taken from Hofstede (1991), Samovar & Porter (1995), Trompenaars (1993), and Victor (1992). The validity of these topics is confirmed by studies such as Gibbs et al. (1988), Martin & Chaney (1992), Gatenby & McLaren (1993), and Hugenberg, LaCivita & Lubanovic (1996). The issues of the questionnaire are reproduced below.

Table 5. Questionnaire set up

principles	(written) business communication: the time spent on it (dis)advantages of writing for international communication "you" communicate with whom, on what, by which channel, in what context, how often
process	strategies used to become a better communicator
particulars	differences in communicating with different cultures & results of these differences: individualism vs. collectivism gender & age, differences, anxiety/change & time experience

With the results that students bring from the real world of business they can critically read general textbooks, such as Victor (1992) or Varner & Beamer (1995), in an effort to see what can actually be accepted as valid generalizations, models, and theories. Since the students have to present a case-study report that is sent to the participating students in the two other countries, they obtain a wealth of information that they can use to try to answer the questions on audience adaptation.

In this way the CIBW gives students the possibility of actually communicating with people from their own culture (the business person they interview) and with members from different cultures (the students at Åbo Akademi, Turku Finland; and Indiana University and Purdue University at Indianapolis USA). Moreover, the participants of the three companies (A-, B-, and C-) actually competed with each other in a cross-cultural environment, thereby experiencing anxiety and uncertainty.

2. Advantages of the CIBW

Most university students enter the real world of business with little or no knowledge of what goes on in that part of the world (see Smeltzer 1996). Their education has kept them "far from the madding crowd" in the realms of theories and models of idealized situations and activities. Having to write an application letter is for most of these students the first written assignment on which a future decision rests that goes beyond the linguistic, stylistic, and other feedback given by the teacher or instructor.

In the CIBW, students have to write four different documents within the period of eight weeks to two groups of students at foreign institutions of higher education. These documents are reacted to by peers. These reactions determine the further development of the simulation. If a group of students reacts by not responding to a sales letter or job advertisement, none of the instructors will intervene. Thus, anxiety as to how the others will react (such as is typical of the real world outside) is built into the simulation game.

The CIBW also asks students to contact a local business person, to ask him/her to react to and reflect on particular topics dealing with cross-cultural communication in real life. Both the asking and the listening, and later on reporting on it, are actions undertaken by youngsters that bring about some kind of anxiety, which later on turns into deep satisfaction at seeing a job well done. The fact that the report is presented in writing to peers in the other institution, and in writing and in an oral presentation to peers in the home institution, gives participating students the added value of being able to practice oral and written communication in normal-functional class situations (see also O'Rourke 1993).

Finally, the CIBW brings students to the point where they start questioning themselves, the others, and especially the stereotypes with which they live. That this advantage does not turn out well for all participants will be illustrated in the following part.

3. The CIBW and stereotyping

From the beginning (see Gibbs et al. 1988) intercultural/international or cross-cultural (business) communication courses have dealt with stereotyping and how to live with it. However, many U.S. textbooks and studies, though they claim to be unprejudiced, show some "imperialistic" trait as to how to respond to cultures' do's and don'ts (see Carroll 1987, Frederick 1993, Gudykunst 1994, Samovar & Porter 1995, Varner & Beamer 1995; and for an entirely different — European — point of view Billig 1987, and Potter & Wetherell 1987). Therefore it is important to try to come to terms with this problematic intercultural and cross-cultural phenomenon.

The participating students of the CIBW are on the one hand citizens from the European countries Belgium (Flanders) and Finland, and on the other hand from the USA (Indiana). Since Finland joined the European Union they have become more closely tied to Belgium and Brussels, the capital of the E.U., but the Finns carry with them a history of oppression from the Swedes and from Russia (which will show in the way they see themselves). Belgians on the other hand are a mixture of northern (germanic) and southern (romanic) characteristics (see Hofstede 1991, Trompenaars 1993:8, and Mole 1995: 111ff. and 121ff., amongst others).

To bring up the "stereotype" issue, without however drawing the attention of the participants to it, the introductory session in Belgium and Finland starts with an informal round of questions:

1. What do you think U.S.students/ Finns think about Belgium (Flemings, Walloons?)
2. Characteristics: indicate how much you expect to detect a characteristic in U.S. students, Finns, Belgians (Flemings, Walloons)?
3. Have you ever met a U.S.student/Finn? Where? What were your impressions.

Question 2 is based on Dirven & Pütz (1994).

The same questions are used in the final session to see how impressions have changed as a result of the eight-week simulation. As an illustration last year's participants indicated the following characteristics:

Table 6. Pre-CIBW characteristics

FINNS see			BELGIANS see		
U.S. students AS:	BELGIANS	THEMSELVES	U.S. students AS:	FINNS	THEMSELVES
talkative	international/	quiet	enthusiastic	cautious	ambitious
superficial	European	honest	materialistic	conservative	cautious
friendly	friendly	shy	talkative	methodical	materialistic
extrovert/	extrovert/	introvert	ambitious	modest	methodical
open	outgoing	intelligent	hospitable	punctual	reliable
patriotic	intelligent	positive	animal	good-	efficient
self-	well-	happy	loving	natured	modest
conscious	educated	proud	pleasure	realistic	realistic
humorous/	open-minded	hardworking	loving	democratic	
funny	humorous/	polite	sportsmanlike		NOT AT ALL:
conservative	funny	well-	vivid/lively	NOT AT ALL:	aggressive
polite	happy	educated	creative	aggressive	
materialistic		friendly	democratic	arrogant	
sociable		lonely	dominant		
ambitious		sporty	friendly		
		insecure	individualistic		
			sociable		
			self-confident		
			NOT AT ALL:		
			unprejudiced		
			cautious		
			realistic		

The characteristics ascribed to the three nations are of the stereotypical sort. As such they do not claim Belgians/Finns/U.S. students to be "...", but they give an impression of what these students at that particular time thought of themselves and the other participants. As we move from the top of the scheme to the bottom, we go from "highest score" (= foremost characteristic) to "lowest score" (= least prominent characteristic). It is interesting to note that Finns view

1. U.S. students as mixed (positive/negative characteristics) persons
2. Belgians as (very) positive
3. themselves as partly positive and partly negative (quiet, shy, lonely, insecure).

By contrast Belgians view

1. U.S. students as almost entirely positive (except for "dominant", "prejudiced", "not cautious", and "not realistic")
2. Finns as almost entirely positive (except for "conservative")
3. themselves as entirely positive.

Table 7. Pre-CIBW characteristics

FINNS see			BELGIANS see		
U.S. students AS:	BELGIANS	THEMSELVES	U.S. students AS:	FINNS	THEMSELVES
talkative	formal	quiet	self-confident	friendly	cautious
friendly	impolite/rude	polite	ambitious	democratic	conservative
sociable	friendly	well-educated	democratic	enthusiastic	democratic
open	quiet	friendly	enthusiastic	individualistic	hospitable
superficial	well-educated	reserved	vivid/lively	sociable	individual-
noisy(loud)	narrow-	honest	practical/	sportsmanlike	istic
active	minded	shy	handy	efficient	sociable
patriotic	stingy	nature	sociable		punctual
straight-	international	loving	sportsmanlike		friendly
forward	honest	stubborn			
happy	polite	patriotic	NOT AT ALL:		
explicit	undetailed	international	unprejudiced		
self-confident			modest		
narrow-minded					
over-detailed					

That students changed as a result of the CIBW can be seen by the way they view each other and themselves afterwards. Finns view

1. U.S. students as friendlier and more sociable than they expected, and less superficial, less patriotic, and less self-confident
2. Belgians as (very) different from what they expected: only two characteristics are present both in the pre- and post-CIBW evaluation: "friendly" and "well-educated". Because of delays in sending documents, and because of letters looking "too businesslike" the Finnish students drastically changed their opinion of the Belgian participants
3. themselves as more positive than before the seminar: they are more polite, more "well-educated", friendlier, but also less honest, and less shy. Moreover, the "lonely" and "insecure" characteristics have been traded for "reserved", "stubborn", "patriotic", and "international".

On the other hand, Belgians still view

1. U.S. students as almost entirely positive (except for "dominant", "prejudiced", and "not modest"). But U.S. students are (even) more dominant than before the seminar; on the other hand they are seen to be less ambitious, less enthusiastic
2. Finns as almost entirely positive, and they are not "conservative" any more
3. themselves as a mixture of positive and negative qualities: they are "conservative", less "social", and less "friendly", and not so "punctual".

4. Conclusion: Experiencing sameness in differences

The Course in International Business Writing is attractive to participating students for its extraordinary experiences. Students actually have the possibility of working within a microcosm that really reflects the macrocosm of international business. Even so, for the three groups there are differences.

The major difference that participating students experience is the language characteristic. Finns and Belgians speak and write English as a second (or third) language, whereas U.S. students have the advantage of speaking and writing English as their mother tongue. This difference is always mentioned as the foremost disadvantage for the Belgian students. However, this difference turns out to be a *sameness* when looked upon from a macro point of view: (U.S.) English (as claimed by Reinsch 1996) "will maintain its status as the world's business language".

A second difference that arises during the eight-week simulation game and in the reports of the case-study, is the cultural background of the participating students. The students are well aware of this cultural background. This is clear when we look at the (stereotypical) way that students portray themselves and the foreign participants before and after the CIBW. This attitude also lays at the basis of the Belgian complaint about the use of language(s). It finally appears when we study the case-study reports the students have to prepare for each other (see Verckens 1995 for a detailed discussion).

However, the CIBW provides the possibility of experiencing *sameness*. All participants start with the basic experiences of anxiety and uncertainty — two typical characteristics of any business situation. They know that they start a chain of written communication, but they do not know if the chain will not be broken, and if not, how the chain will be formed, i.e., how the others will respond to their initiating moves.

Thus, all students learn (as part of their audience awareness) to grow "patience, tolerance, objectivity, empathy, and respect" for themselves and for their foreign peers. They experience this sameness in a normal-functional context of an authentic process of writing. This experience, as one of the Belgian students suggested, is of such importance that it should be a compulsory part of any education in which young people are being prepared for the world business, trade, and commerce.

References

Billig, Michael. 1987. *Arguing and Thinking. A Rhetorical Approach to Social Psychology* (European monographs in social psychology). Cambridge/Paris: Cambridge University Press/Editions de la Maison des Sciences de l'Homme.

Carroll, Raymonde. 1987. *Évidences Invisibles. Américains et Français au quotidien.* Paris: Éditions du Seuil.

Cushner, Kenneth and Richard W. Brislin. 1996. *Intercultural Interactions. A Practical Guide* (2nd ed.) (Cross-Cultural Research and Methodology, Vol. 9). Thousand Oaks: Sage.

Davis, Kenneth, Teun De Rycker and J. Piet Verckens. 1994. "'Dear personnel manager': some ELT/ESP aspects of developing cross-cultural awareness through interactive writing". In: Heiner Purschel (ed.), pp. 233-260.

Davis, Kenneth, and J. Piet Verckens. 1997. *International Business Communication.* S.l.: Association of Professional Communication Consultants.

Dirven, René and Martin Pütz. 1994. "Intercultural communication". In: Heiner Purschel (ed.), pp. 1-32.

Frederick, Howard H. 1993. *Global Communication & International Relations*. Belmont CA: Wadsworth.

Gatenby, Bev and Margaret C. McLaren. 1993. "Teaching international topics in the business communication course: a survey of ABC members beyond the United States". *The Bulletin of the Association for Business Communication*, Vol. LVI, No. 4: 10-15.

Gibbs, Meada et al. 1988. "How to teach intercultural concepts in a basic business communication class". *The Bulletin of the Association for Business Communication*, Vol. LI, No. 3: 2-7.

Gudykunst, William B. 1994. *Bridging Differences. Effective Intergroup Communication* (2nd Ed.) (Interpersonal commtexts 3). Thousand Oaks: Sage.

Harcourt, Jules. 1988. "A new cross-cultural communication course: communication in the international business environment". *The Bulletin of the Association for Business Communication*, Vol. LI, No. 3: 11-13.

Hofstede, Geert. 1991. *Allemaal andersdenkenden. Omgaan met cultuurverschillen* (Translated from *Cultures and Organizations. Software of the Mind*). Amsterdam: Uitgeverij Contact.

Hugenberg, Lawrence W., Renée M. LaCivita and Andra M. Lubanovic. 1996. "International business and training: preparing for the global economy". *The Journal of Business Communication*, Vol. 33, No. 2: 205-222.

Jameson, Daphne A. 1993. "Using a simulation to teach intercultural communication in business communication courses". *The Bulletin of the Association for Business Communication*, Vol. LVI, No. 1: 3-11.

Martin, Jeanette S. and Lillian H. Chaney. 1992. "Determination of content for a collegiate course in intercultural business communication by three Delphi panels". *The Journal of Business Communication*, Vol. 29, No. 3: 267-283.

Mole, John. 1995. *Mind your Manners. Managing business across cultures in Europe* (new edition). London: Nicholas Brealey Publishing.

O'Rourke, James S. IV. 1993. "Intercultural business communication: building a course from the ground up". *The Bulletin of the Association for Business Communication*. Vol. LVI, No. 4: 22-27.

Potter, Jonathan and Margaret Wetherell. 1987. *Discourse and Social Psychology. Beyond Attitudes and Behaviour*. London: Sage Publications.

Pürschel, Heiner (ed.). 1994. *Intercultural Communication*. Frankfurt am Main: Peter Lang Verlag.

Ranney, Frances J. and Kevin M. McNeilly. 1996. "International business writing projects: learning content through process". *The Business Communication Quarterly*, Vol. 59, No. 1: 9-26.

Reinsch, N. Lamar Jr. 1996. "Business communication: present, past, and future". *Management Communication Quarterly*, Vol. 10, No. 1: 27-49.

Samovar, Larry A. and Richard E. Porter. 1995. *Communication Between Cultures* (2nd ed.). Belmont: Wadsworth.

Smeltzer, Larry R. 1996. "Communication within the manager's context". *Management Communication Quarterly*, Vol. 10, No. 1: 5-26.

Sterkel, Karen S. 1988. "Integrating intercultural communication in the communication class". *The Bulletin of the Association for Business Communication*, Vol. LI; No. 3: 14-16.

Ten Brinke, Steven. 1976. *The Complete Mother-tongue Curriculum*. Groningen: Wolters-Noordhoff Longman.

Trompenaars, Fons. 1993. *Riding the Waves of Culture*. London: Nicholas Brealey.

Varner, Iris and Linda Beamer. 1995. *Intercultural Communication in the Workplace*. Chicago: Irwin.

Verckens, J. Piet. 1995. "An international course in international business writing: case studies". Paper presented at the 14th International Annual Conference on Languages and Communication for World Business and the Professions, Eastern Michigan University.

Victor, David A. 1988. "Cross-cultural influences on business communication: applications for teaching and practice". *The Bulletin of the Association for Business Communication*, Vol. LI, No. 3: 8-13.

Victor, David A. 1992. *International Business Communication*. New York: Harper Collins.

Name Index

Subject Index